The Trouble with
Black Boys

The Trouble with Black Boys

And Other Reflections on Race, Equity, and the Future of Public Education

Pedro A. Noguera

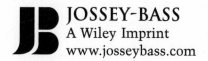
JOSSEY-BASS
A Wiley Imprint
www.josseybass.com

Published by Jossey-Bass
A Wiley Imprint
989 Market Street, San Francisco, CA 94103-1741—www.josseybass.com

Jossey-Bass books and products are available through most bookstores. To contact Jossey-Bass directly call our Customer Care Department within the U.S. at 800-956-7739, outside the U.S. at 317-572-3986, or fax 317-572-4002.

Jossey-Bass also publishes its books in a variety of electronic formats. Some content that appears in print may not be available in electronic books.

Credits are on page 323.

Library of Congress Cataloging-in-Publication Data

Noguera, Pedro.
   The trouble with Black boys : and other reflections on race, equity, and the future of public education / Pedro A. Noguera.—1st ed.
      p. cm.
   Includes bibliographical references and indexes.
   ISBN 978-0-7879-8874-6 (cloth)
      1. Educational equalization—United States. 2. Academic achievement—Social aspects—United States. 3. Minorities—Education—United States. I. Title.
   LC213.2.N64 2008
   371.829073—dc22
                                                                          2007049671

Printed in the United States of America
FIRST EDITION
HB Printing   10 9 8 7 6 5 4 3 2 1

Contents

This book is dedicated to the memory of Patricia Rocio Vattuone, my wife of twenty-five years, who passed away on April 7, 2006. In addition to being the mother of our four children—Joaquin, Amaya, Antonio, and Naima—she was my confidante, my counselor, my comrade in struggle, and my best friend. She was known by others as a tireless fighter for peace and justice, an artist and a musician, a gardener and a building contractor, a student, a mother, and a daughter. Born in Lima, Peru, and raised by a single parent in the projects of San Francisco, Patricia went on to graduate with honors from the University of California at Berkeley and to earn a master's degree in public policy at the Kennedy School of Government at Harvard University. For all children and parents who are struggling to use education as a means to overcome obstacles and to make the world more just and humane, Patricia is an example from whom we can learn and be inspired.

The Author

Pedro A. Noguera is a professor in the Steinhardt School of Education at New York University, the executive director of the Metropolitan Center for Urban Education, and the codirector of the Institute for the Study of Globalization and Education in Metropolitan Settings (IGEMS).

An urban sociologist, Noguera has focused his scholarship and research on the ways in which schools are influenced by social and economic conditions in the urban environment. He has served as an advisor to and engaged in collaborative research with several large urban school districts throughout the United States. He has also done research on issues related to education and economic and social development in the Caribbean, Latin America, and countries in other areas.

From 2000 to 2003, Noguera served as the Judith K. Dimon Professor of Communities and Schools at the Harvard Graduate School of Education. From 1990 to 2000, he was a professor in social and cultural studies at the Graduate School of Education and the director of the Institute for the Study of Social Change at the University of California, Berkeley.

He has published over 150 research articles, monographs, and research reports on topics such as urban school reform, conditions that promote student achievement, youth violence, the potential impact of school choice and vouchers on urban public schools, and race and ethnic relations in American society. His work has appeared in major research journals, and much of it is available online at inmotionmagazine.com. He is the author of *The Imperatives of Power: Political Change and the Social Basis of Regime Support in Grenada* (1997) and *City Schools and the American Dream* (2003), winner of the *ForeWord Magazine* Gold Award, and he is the coeditor of *Beyond Resistance: Youth Activism and Community Change* (with Shawn Ginwright and Julio Camarota, 2006). His most recent book is *Unfinished Business: Closing the Achievement Gap in Our Nation's Schools* (with Jean Yonemura Wing, 2006).

Noguera has served as a member of the U.S. Public Health Service Centers for Disease Control Taskforce on Youth Violence, the chair of the Committee on Ethics in Research and Human Rights for the American Educational Research Association, and a member of numerous advisory boards to local and national education and youth organizations. He was a K–12 classroom teacher for several years and continues to teach part-time in high schools. From 1986 to 1988, he served as the executive assistant to the mayor of Berkeley, California, and from 1990 to 1994, he was an elected member and the president of the Berkeley School Board. From 2005 to 2006, he served as the president of the Caribbean Studies Association and was a member of the Commission on the Whole Child (Association of Supervision and Curriculum Development).

In 1995 he received an award from the Wellness Foundation for his research on youth violence, in 1997 he was the recipient of the University of California's Distinguished Teaching Award, in 2001 he received an honorary doctorate from the University of San Francisco and the Centennial Medal from Philadelphia University for his work in the field of education, and in 2005 he received the Eugene Carothers Award and the Whitney Young Award from the National Urban League, both for leadership in the field of education. Noguera is the father of four children and resides in New York City.

Introduction

Black males in American society are in trouble. With respect to health, education, employment, income, and overall well-being, all of the most reliable data consistently indicate that Black males constitute a segment of the population that is distinguished by hardships, disadvantages, and vulnerability (Littles, Bowers, and Gilmer, 2007).

Although they comprise a relatively small portion of the American population (less than 6 percent), Black males occupy a large space within the American psyche and imagination. Throughout much of American history, Black males have served as the ultimate "other." In literature and film, they have been depicted as villains, con men, and feebleminded buffoons. Indeed, the image of the Black man has sometimes been used to symbolize the very embodiment of violence (Apel, 2004). Most often, Black men have been regarded as individuals who should be feared because of their uncontrolled and unrefined masculinity. And their very presence, particularly when they are encountered in groups, has been regarded as a menace to innocents (particularly white women) and a potential danger to the social order. They are a threat that must be policed, controlled, and contained (Baker, 1998).

Today the popular images of Black males are less extreme but no less distorted. Black males are omnipresent in the media, but in a departure from the past, they are as often idolized as heroes because of their accomplishments in sports and popular music as they are scorned for their misdeeds, both real and imagined. These newer images of Black males may appear to be more positive than the ones from the past, but they have not supplanted the more traditional negative characterizations; rather, the two cohabit the same social and psychological space. For every story devoted to the feats of a Black sports hero, there are others where Black men are decried as irresponsible fathers, drug dealers, and sexual predators. As cultural theorist Homi Bhabha (1994) has written in reference to other subordinate groups, societies frequently conjure up phobias and fetishes toward marginalized groups and individuals. In the United States, the stereotypes and images associated with Black males have the effect of magnifying the attention and scrutiny directed toward them in ways that result in their being both vilified and valorized and that make living an ordinary life a tremendous challenge.

It is ironic that the lead character of Ralph Ellison's *Invisible Man* is a Black man, one who is so marginal and irrelevant that he is literally unseen. Today Black males are anything but invisible or unseen. In fact, they are so prominently positioned as celebrities and criminals that hardly a day passes when one is not the subject of news in the media. Be it the latest golf tournament victory of Tiger Woods, an act of violence perpetrated by a criminal, or the latest song by Jay-Z, Kanye West, or 50 Cent, the visibility of Black males far exceeds their actual numbers in American society. For Black males, adulation and scorn are often two sides of the same coin, and as we have seen in the cases of O. J. Simpson, Michael Vick, and Michael Jackson, even those who seem to be loved and adored can easily and quickly fall from grace and find themselves hated and despised.

The dichotomous nature of the lens through which Black males are perceived poses a tremendous problem for ordinary men and boys. The vast majority of Black men are not star athletes or glamorous entertainers; neither are they hoodlums or gangsters. Yet the images and stereotypes of Black males that permeate American society compel all Black men and boys to contend with character-izations and images that are propagated in the media and with the perceptions that lurk within imaginations. Black males who are everyday fathers, sons, factory workers, college students, profession-als, and craftsmen often find that they must prove their trustworthi-ness and convince others that they are not individuals who should be feared. Unlike men and women from other racial and ethnic groups, Black males are rarely seen as individuals in possession of a full range of attributes and flaws, strengths and weaknesses. The stereotypes that shape the American images of Black males are so stark and extreme that even the most ordinary and unexceptional Black males find they are forced to contend with the fantasies and fears that others hold toward them.

It is important to point out that in certain contexts—predominantly White schools and colleges, for example—Black males occasionally encounter stereotypes that might be construed as positive. Among some classmates and instructors, there may be an assumption that Black males are inherently gifted athletes, good dancers, and natu-rally "cool." In settings where Black males are regarded as novelties rather than threats, they may experience attention that may not be totally negative, especially if they are star athletes. Yet a closer examination of the assumptions operative in such contexts reveals how often they negate attributes such as honesty, integrity, and intellectual ability and serve to limit and constrain the develop-ment of a well-rounded personality. Moreover, as my colleague Ron Mincy, a six-foot-four professor of economics at Columbia Uni-versity, pointed out, having others assume you can play basketball is not a compliment when you are being considered for a job as a professor or being reviewed for tenure.

Still, no matter how annoying assumptions about one's athletic ability might be, the negative stereotypes associated with Black males are a far more onerous burden. How many Black men have been stopped for no justifiable reason by police officers because they are said to fit the description of a suspect or because their mere presence in a public setting evokes fear and suspicion? According to a recently released study by the Rand Corporation, a statistical analysis of police stops in New York City carried out between 2004 and 2006 found that Black men were stopped, frisked, and detained by police at a rate that is 50 percent greater than their representation in the residential census (Ridgeway, 2007). The stress and humiliation of such experiences undoubtedly take a toll on psychological well-being and serve as a reminder to Black men that they will never be judged as individuals.

For Black men, police harassment is by no means limited to New York City. How many Black men have seen strangers cross the street as they walk toward them? How common is it for Black men to be subjected to additional scrutiny by a security guard, to be asked to produce extra proof that they have the funds in their account to cover a check, or been asked to produce additional identification to make a credit card purchase? My friend and colleague Antwi Akom, a professor at San Francisco State University, was beaten and arrested by campus police when he entered his office at night (with his key) to retrieve a book while his two young daughters waited for him in their car. Major offenses like this one, as well as minor indignities, or what psychologist Chester Pierce (1995) referred to as micro-aggressions, are so common and pervasive that for many parents, preparing their Black sons for the likelihood of an interrogation by the police has become an increasingly regular part of socialization to manhood.

Lani Guinier, the acclaimed Harvard Law School professor, points out that even she, an upper-middle-class intellectual, cannot shield her son from the threats that Black males experience. As a result, she feels compelled to prepare him for the trials and tribulations he may face living in American society. In describing her quandary over how to educate her son about race and racism in the United States, she writes "that a failure to acknowledge difference is a failure to prepare him for a world in which his differences may matter—a world in which when he walks down the street, white cops may stop him or other Black males may resent him, in both cases because of a potentially deadly combination of racism and machismo" (Guinier and Torres, 2002, p. 3). Like many other parents, Guinier laments the need to burden her son with an awareness that he may be subjected to harassment and hostility, not because of something he has done but simply because of the reactions that his race and gender evoke. She resents the need to prepare him because she understands that by engaging in this form of socialization, she is in effect "reinforcing hierarchy, not resisting it" (p. 3).

Sadly, part of what Guinier and other parents must prepare their Black sons for is the prospect, and even the probability, that the group he is most likely to experience conflict and hostility with is not the police or the Ku Klux Klan but other Black males. For reasons that can never be fully explained, Black males kill and harm one another at a rate that far exceeds any other segment of the American population (Bell and Jenkins, 1990; Earls, 1994). The alarming homicide rates among young Black males is one of the major factors that has led to Black males being the only segment of the U.S. population with a declining life expectancy (Earls, 1994). Gangs, drug dealing, and the availability of guns are certainly contributing factors, but there is more going on related to the phenomenon of violence among and between Black males that defies easy explanation.

I once found myself in the middle of a heated argument that nearly erupted into violence between Black men over nothing more than a basketball game. At the time, I was a professor at Harvard University, living in Cambridge, Massachusetts, and as was my custom, I went to play basketball at a court where men my age (roughly between thirty and forty-five) played ball on Saturday mornings. Most of the men playing were employed, some like me as professionals, and most were husbands and fathers with children. This was a typical pickup game of street ball—an informal form of recreation with no uniforms or referees. Teams are chosen just before the start of the game, and nothing is at stake: no one is getting paid, it really does not matter who wins or loses, and there are no spectators present to impress other than the men waiting to play next. One morning during a game that was becoming particularly intense, two players who had been engaged in friendly banter over who was the better player began arguing over how closely and aggressively they were guarding each other. Finally one player took a hard fall to the ground after a flagrant foul by the other player, and the two men began posturing as if they were about to fight. After cursing, yelling, and exchanging threats with each other for several minutes, a few other men joined the fray, some attempting to make peace so that we could get on with the game, while others egged on the two as though they hoped a fight between the two men might actually erupt. As the threats and arguing escalated, one man announced that he was going to his car to get his gun, at which point several of the other men and I left the court with great haste.

On my drive home, I asked myself why grown men with so much to lose—families, jobs, reputations—would threaten to kill each other over a basketball game. Although no one was actually killed that morning, the fact that threats of death were exchanged over something so trivial suggested something profound was going on. As I thought about it, I realized that the incident made no sense by considering only what was happening on the court, so I thought about the lives of these Black men beyond the court: the pressures they experience in their jobs, the scrutiny they endure in many contexts and situations, the burden so many bear to prove their competence and worthiness, and the mask of aggression that many Black men feel compelled to don as a method of warding off threats on the streets. I then understood that this fight over basketball was emblematic of a much larger phenomenon. Several researchers have found that the pressures that Black men and boys experience exact a toll on their (our)[1] psychological and emotional well-being. How they respond to these pressures is undoubtedly a factor that contributes to the high rate of interpersonal violence between and among Black males. It is also the reason that it is so important that the challenges confronting Black males not be framed in ways that characterize them as helpless victims.

Trouble Begins at School

Sadly, the pressures, stereotypes, and patterns of failure that Black males experience often begin in school. I say *sadly* because we might hope, and even expect, that school would be a place where Black males are nurtured and supported, where they receive encouragement to excel and guidance on how to achieve their goals and dreams. Yet for many Black males, the opposite is true. Throughout the United States, Black males are more likely than any other group in American society to be punished (typically through some form of exclusion), labeled, and categorized for special education (often without an apparent disability), and to experience academic failure (Schott Foundation, 2004). The existence of such patterns does not mean that Black male students are innocent victims of unfair treatment, but it does raise the possibility that in schools throughout the United States, the failure of Black males is so pervasive that it appears to be the norm and so does not raise alarms.

School discipline patterns are just one of several troubling indicators commonly associated with Black males. When the full picture of educational performance among Black males is analyzed, the results are even more disturbing. On every indicator associated with progress and achievement—enrollment in honors courses, Advanced Placement, and gifted programs—Black males are vastly underrepresented, and in every category associated with failure and distress—discipline referrals, dropout rates, grade retention—Black males are overrepresented (Schott Foundation, 2004). In what is perhaps the most ominous and obvious sign of distress, for the past several years, there have been more Black males between the ages eighteen and twenty-four in prison than in college (Littles et al., 2007). Such patterns of failure and hardship are so pronounced and entrenched that they end up shaping adult outcomes and have broad and far-reaching implications for the status of Black men and Black people in American society.[2]

What is perhaps even more troubling than the numbers, which are themselves overwhelming and disturbing, is the weakness of the response to these problems. In many schools in the United States, educators have grown so accustomed to seeing Black male students drop out, fail, and get punished that their plight is barely regarded as a cause for alarm. In fact, it could be argued that the problems confronting Black males are so pervasive and commonplace that they have been normalized. Like other social problems that have been normalized—attitudes toward the homeless, or society's tolerance for the large number of people who lack access to adequate health care—a sense of complacency characterizes how many Americans think about the failure of Black males. Because the educational problems afflicting Black males have been normalized, the barrage of dismal statistics barely registers a sense of outrage or concern, with the notable exception of many Black communities. Were the problems confronting Black males regarded as an "American" problem, meaning an issue like cancer or global warming that must be taken on by the entire society in order to be addressed, the plight of Black males would be a subject that policymakers and research centers would embrace in an effort to find ways to reduce and ameliorate the hardships.

Although there have been calls for urgent action of this kind, it is hard to argue that recognition of the need to address this pressing problem is widespread. This is why the mass incarceration of Black males (Black males comprise approximately 50 percent of the adult male prison) has elicited few calls for action to reverse these trends (Belk, 2006). Black males are ten times more likely to be incarcerated than any other segment of the U.S. population, but little public concern is expressed about the impact this problem has on Black families or Black men themselves. Although the majority of men behind bars are there for nonviolent crimes and although a substantial number of those we incarcerate are poor, uneducated, and mentally disabled, very little public concern has registered over the injustices of the criminal justice system. Today there are few serious calls for alternatives to incarceration even for the aged or the drug addicted, and surprisingly little focus on what might be done to educate and rehabilitate those who are warehoused in our nation's prisons.

In public schools, the normalization of failure on the part of Black males is equally pervasive. This is undoubtedly because many educators have grown accustomed to the idea that a large percentage of the Black male students they serve will fail, get into trouble, and drop out of school. Such complacency is present not only in large urban school systems, where it could be argued that failure for many different kinds of students (boys and girls of various races) has long been accepted, but in more affluent suburban schools as well.

Not long ago I was leading a workshop on the achievement gap for principals in an affluent school district. I presented a set of strategies that I suggested could be used to address lagging achievement among certain groups of students. At the end of the presentation, I encouraged the principals to do more to address the blatant ways in which students were denied learning opportunities through what I described as structural indifference. During the discussion that followed, one of the principals posed what I felt was a fairly provocative question. He explained that he had recently been hired by the district and was still becoming familiar with his school. One of the things about the school that he did not understand was why he consistently observed a large group of Black males loitering in the hallways after the bell had rung. He had made efforts to encourage them to get to class on time, yet he felt they were deliberately taking their time and that teachers and administrators at the school seemed to ignore their lingering. Disturbed by their apparent intransigence and curious about where they might be going, he decided to follow them to their destination. After chatting casually about the importance of being in class on time, he was surprised to find that all of the young men in this group were descending to the basement of the school. When I asked why they were going to the basement, he explained that the special education classes were located there. With a note of sarcasm in his voice, he asked, "Do you think that maybe they're embarrassed to be seen heading into the basement? Do you think it might be a good idea to take those classes out of the basement?"

In schools across the country, it is surprising that more educators are not calling for Black males and other students who are denied educational opportunities to be removed from basements, detention centers, and classrooms where they are not learning. They should object not merely to the ways in which some students are physically marginalized in educational settings, but to the ways in which they have been psychologically and socially isolated as well. A large body of research has shown that when students are labeled and sorted into groups on the basis of their academic ability or behavior (that is, as troublemakers or underachievers), the behaviors that were ostensibly targeted for treatment are often reinforced instead of being ameliorated (Oakes, 1985). This is because such practices almost always lead to lowered expectations on the part of the adults assigned to teach them. Even more insidious, those who are labeled often internalize the labels assigned to them. As a result, instead of providing a setting where problematic behaviors can be modified, the sorting practices many schools use reinforce the very behaviors they were intended to correct (Obidah, 1995).

How is it possible that schools would adopt practices designed to help students that end up having the opposite effect? Much of the answer to this question lies in the assumptions and expectations that many educators hold toward Black males and other students they have grown accustomed to seeing struggle and fail in school. What is needed to reverse these trends is more than a new program or policy. There must instead be a complete interrogation of the thinking that has allowed such practices to operate without challenge. The assumptions held toward Black males that allow them to be regarded largely as a problem, pathologize their needs, and deny them the opportunity to learn must be thoroughly discussed, debated, and challenged. It is important for educators to understand that the practices that result in the marginalization of Black boys in school mirror the attitudes and beliefs that rationalize the marginalization of Black men in society at large. In too many cases, educators do not question the assumptions they hold, and as a result, those who are charged with teaching, advising, and mentoring Black males too often inadvertently adopt attitudes and postures that are unsupportive and even hostile toward the boys they serve.

The Trouble with Black Boys

The trouble with Black boys is that too often they are assumed to be at risk because they are too aggressive, too loud, too violent, too dumb, too hard to control, too streetwise, and too focused on sports. Such assumptions and projections have the effect of fostering the very behaviors and attitudes we find problematic and objectionable. The trouble with Black boys is that most never have a chance to be thought of as potentially smart and talented or to demonstrate talents in science, music, or literature. The trouble with Black boys is that too often they are placed in schools where their needs for nurturing, support, and loving discipline are not met. Instead, they are labeled, shunned, and treated in ways that create and reinforce an inevitable cycle of failure.

I was reminded of just how unsupportive some educators can be toward Black male students when I was visiting an elementary school in the San Francisco Bay Area. After the assistant principal gave me a tour and proudly pointed out the new library and computer facilities, he shook his head with disgust as he noticed a little boy waiting for him outside his office. Seeing the boy, he turned to me and declared, "You know, there's a prison cell in San Quentin waiting for that boy." I responded with shock: "Really!

How do you know?" He explained that the boy's father and brother were in prison and then prophesied, "I can tell from the way that he behaves that he's headed to prison too." I then looked at him and asked, "Well, given what you know about this boy and his circumstances at home, what is the school doing to keep him out of prison?" The assistant principal reacted to my question with incredulity. He explained that the boy was frequently in trouble and that what he was about to do was to place the boy, only eight years old, on an extended and indefinite suspension. Due to his misbehavior in school, he was going to be sent home, where he would be under the supervision of his sick grandmother. His schoolwork was to be delivered to his house and collected at the end of each week until they felt he was ready to return to school. I asked the assistant principal if he thought this strategy would help this child, and he responded by saying he was more concerned about the "students who wanted to learn." He elaborated, "A child like this needs more attention than we can provide. I can't allow one kid to take up so much of my time that I end up ignoring the needs of others." Though he didn't admit it, that assistant principal was in effect washing his hands of this boy and allowing him to head on the path to prison, just as he had predicted.

What I find troubling about this incident is that the assistant principal never considered the possibility that the school or even the community might be able to do something to help this boy and thereby reduce the likelihood that he would one day end up in prison. Perhaps even more disturbing, the assistant principal was a Black man.

I do not make light of the difficulty in addressing the needs of troubled students. Children who come from homes without adequate supervision, guidance, and support pose a tremendous challenge to the educators charged with serving their academic needs. I also do not take the position that schools should be expected to solve these problems by themselves. Charged with the task of educating disadvantaged and neglected children, many educators find themselves overwhelmed by their needs, many of which have little to do with academic learning, but are much more related to their health, unmet social needs, and emotional well-being. In cities, towns, trailer parks, and housing projects across the United States, there are growing numbers of children in such circumstances (Children's Defense Fund, 2006). If our society is to find ways to reduce the numbers who end up permanently unemployed, incarcerated, or prematurely dead, we must do more to address their needs, especially while they are young.

I fully acknowledge that Black males are not helpless victims in this situation. In fact, it is my contention that the only way we will begin to break the cycle of failure is if Black males are empowered and engaged in addressing these issues themselves. To not acknowledge that Black males have the capacity to make choices that will positively affect their lives—to study, work hard, not take drugs, or not abuse women, to support their children and raise their families in a responsible manner—is merely another way of inadvertently contributing to their marginalization and powerlessness. Certainly there are many factors that Black males do not control that have tremendous bearing on the quality of their lives: the quality of the school they attend, the kind of neighborhood they live in, whether there are jobs available or employers who will hire them, whether police officers will stop them without justification or judges will treat them fairly, or even if they will be born healthy and raised in loving, supportive families. Nonetheless, there are factors that they can and must exercise control over.

I made this point recently to a large group of incarcerated Black and Latino young men whom I was asked to address at New York City's Rikers Island, the largest penal facility in the world. Prior to my visit, I spent a great deal of time thinking about what I could possibly say that might serve as a source of inspiration to them. I knew the statistics: two-thirds would end up back in prison in two years or less, and I knew that despite their age, many of them had already experienced so much failure and rejection that in all likelihood, they had already given up on the prospect of living productive lives. Still, the challenge of saying something that might inspire even a few to recognize that they had the power to make different choices on how they wanted to live intrigued me, and I embraced the task.

Upon entering the prison and gradually making my way through a vast series of security checkpoints, I entered a large room where several hundred young men were seated. With guards posted all around and sullen, expressionless looks on the faces of most of the young men, I opened my lecture with a statement that I hoped would provoke and shake them out of the utter resignation that seemed to engulf them. "There is a conspiracy to keep you in prison," I charged, "and there are many people whose jobs and income depend on keeping you here." Seeing some of them sit up in their seats and sensing that I now had their attention, I went on. "There are policymakers planning to build more prisons right now, and whole towns in upstate New York that rely upon their prisons for jobs and economic development. There are corporations that run prisons for profit, taking advantage of the low wages prisoners receive for the work they do. Even the guards in this room, while they may not be part of the conspiracy, understand that their jobs depend on you." At that point, several of the guards looked at me with expressions of concern on their faces. I continued, "My question to you is this: Are you part of the conspiracy? These prisons can't stay filled unless you mess up again, unless you make bad choices, and do stupid things that will allow you to be put back into a place like this after you are released. The statistics show that most of you will be back in prison in less than two years after you've been released. So I want to know: Are you part of the conspiracy to keep Black and Latino men in prison?"

My tactic worked. My charge that they might be part of a conspiracy to keep them in prison drew them out of their stupor and resignation and spurred a lively discussion and debate about personal responsibility.

I believe that we must engage Black men and boys in debates about personal responsibility, preferably before they enter prison. I agree with Bill Cosby and Alvin Poussaint, authors of the new book poignantly titled *Come On People,* that parents must take more responsibility in raising their children. However, I completely disagree with their approach. I see very little evidence that condemning parents for doing a poor job in raising their children will improve the situation. Unlike Cosby and Poussaint, I also believe that our society—its schools, churches, private businesses and corporations, and local government—must do more to address the ways in which Black boys and men are set up for failure. What would happen if instead of sending the eight-year-old boy home, the assistant principal had engaged him in a discussion about his behavior in the classroom and tried to get him to understand how he was affecting others? What would have happened if the assistant principal had initiated a conversation with his students about why their classroom was in the basement and, after agreeing to work with them to get it removed, challenged them to take their education seriously and encouraged them to enter the classroom on time regardless of where the room was located?

The Miner's Canary: The Need for Equity in an Inequitable Society

Lani Guinier and Gerald Torres implore us to view those who are racially marginalized like the miner's canary: vulnerable populations whose hardships alert us to the dangers confronting our society. They write:

> Those who are racially marginalized are like the miner's canary: their distress is the first sign of danger that threatens us all. It is easy enough to think that when we sacrifice this canary, the only harm done is to communities of color. Yet others ignore problems that converge around

racial minorities at their own peril, for these problems
are symptoms warning us that we are all at risk. . . . The
miner's canary metaphor helps us to understand why and
how race continues to be salient. Racialized communities signal problems with the ways we have structured
power and privilege. These pathologies are not located
in the canary [pp. 11, 12].

Black boys are the miner's canary in our nation's schools, but
they are not the only vulnerable group. In some schools, immigrant
students, particularly those who are undocumented, are the most
vulnerable. Their right to an education, while recognized by the
courts,[3] is under attack from militias, television pundits, politicians,
and others who are waging a war against the undocumented. But
even those they call "illegal immigrants" are vital to this nation's
economy because they come to this country to work in jobs that
most Americans refuse to accept. Yet they are increasingly being
hunted down like fugitives and relegated to lives at the margins
and in the shadows of society. Today undocumented students who
study hard and apply themselves must face the fact that for most,
their diligence will more likely lead not to college but to the same
low-wage, dirty jobs their parents hold.[4]

Poor Whites in trailer parks, rust belt towns, and rural areas
across the country also find themselves among the vulnerable and
disadvantaged. Too often those who champion civil rights ignore
the fact that while race sometimes acts as a protective buffer
against the hardships associated with poverty in the United States,
it does not work this way all of the time. There are poor Whites in
rural Maine, Arkansas, and West Virginia whose chances of going
to college are no better than that of Blacks in the inner city. Unlike
the visibility and attention frequently directed toward poor Blacks (a
mixed blessing at best), poor Whites are almost invisible in America,
and few policy initiatives are aimed at addressing their plight. For
poor White students, the pursuit of equity in education could also
serve as a means to counter the pernicious effects of poverty.

Despite its many flaws and shortcomings, public education remains the "one best system" (Tyack, 1974); it is the only system that turns no child away, regardless of race, status, language, or need. For this reason, public schools are perhaps the only institution that is positioned to play a role in addressing the effects of poverty and social marginalization and furthering the goal of equity. Christopher Jencks (1972) reminds us that equity is not the same as equal opportunity. When practiced in the context of education, equity is focused on outcomes and results and is rooted in the recognition that because children have different needs and come from different circumstances, we cannot treat them all the same.

This book articulates the need for equity in public education and calls attention to the many factors that undermine and thwart efforts to make it an attainable goal. Although I do not claim to have spelled out a complete agenda for pursuing equity in our nation's public schools, I do hope that readers will identify strategies and approaches that they can apply to achieve similar goals. My hope is that after reading this book, you will feel a bit like I hoped those young men at Rikers might feel: more empowered to recognize that each of us can play a role in furthering equity through education and less inclined to accept the status quo.

Despite all of the ways in which recent educational reforms may have taken the soul out of education—overemphasizing testing and underemphasizing learning, treating teachers like technicians rather than creative professionals, humiliating schools that serve poor children rather than providing them with the support and resources that they need—the fact remains that through education, we have the potential and power to open minds, tap the imagination, cultivate skills, and inspire the innate ability in all human beings to dream and create. This is what makes education such a special endeavor, and this is why public schools remain our most valuable resource.

Black boys are merely one of several canaries in the mines of our schools. Our challenge as educators, parents, policymakers, and activists is to find ways not merely to save Black boys and others who are at risk but to create conditions so that saving is no longer necessary. How we respond to our schools and those who are not now well served there is more than merely a call to do good. What happens in our nation's schools is truly a matter of self-preservation, for whether we can use education to transform lives and expand opportunities will ultimately determine what kind of society we live in.

Part I

The Student Experience

1

Joaquin's Dilemma

Understanding the Link Between Racial Identity and School-Related Behaviors

When I am asked to speak or write about the relationship between racial identity and academic performance, I often tell the story of my elder son, Joaquin. Joaquin did extremely well throughout most of his early schooling. He was an excellent athlete (participating in soccer, basketball, and wrestling), played piano and percussion, and did very well in his classes. My wife and I never heard any complaints about him. In fact, we heard nothing but praise about his behavior from teachers, who referred to him as "courteous," "respectful," and "a leader among his peers." Then suddenly, in the tenth grade, Joaquin's grades took a nosedive. He failed math and science, and for the first time he started getting into trouble at school. At home he was often angry and irritable for no particular reason.

My wife and I were left asking ourselves, "What's going on with our son? What's behind this sudden change in behavior?" Despite my disappointment and growing frustration, I tried not to allow his behavior to drive us apart. I started spending more time with him, and I started listening more intently to what he had to tell me about school and his friends. As I did, several things became very clear to me. One was that all of the friends he had grown up with in our neighborhood in South Berkeley (one of the poorest areas of the city) were dropping out of school. These were mostly Black, working-class kids who didn't have a lot of support at home or at school and were experiencing academic failure. Even though

Joaquin came from a middle-class home with two supportive parents, most of his reference group—that is, the students he was closest to and identified with—did not.

The other thing that was changing for Joaquin was his sense of how he had to present himself when he was out on the streets and in school. As he grew older, Joaquin felt the need to project the image of a tough and angry young Black man. He believed that in order to be respected, he had to carry himself in a manner that was intimidating and even menacing. To behave differently—too nice, gentle, kind, or sincere—meant that he would be vulnerable and preyed on. I learned that for Joaquin, part of his new persona also involved placing less value on academics and greater emphasis on being cool and hanging out with the right people.

By eleventh grade, Joaquin gradually started working out of these behaviors, and by twelfth grade, he seemed to snap out of his angry state. He became closer to his family, his grades improved, he rejoined the soccer team, he resumed playing piano, and he even started producing music. As I reflected on the two years of anger and self-destructiveness that he went through, I came to the conclusion that Joaquin was trying desperately to figure out what it meant to be a young Black man. As I reflect on that period, I realize that like many other Black male adolescents, Joaquin was trapped by stereotypes, and they were pulling him down. During this difficult period, it was very hard for me to help him through this process of identity formation. While he was in the midst of it, the only thing I could do was talk to him, listen to him, and try to let him know what it was like for me when I went through adolescence.

As a high school student, I had coped with the isolation that came from being one of the few students of color in my advanced classes by working extra hard to prove that I could do as well as or better than my White peers. However, outside the classroom, I also worked hard to prove to my less studious friends that I was cool or "down," as we would say. For me this meant playing basketball, hanging out, fighting when necessary, and acting like "one of the guys." I felt forced to adopt a split personality: I behaved one way in class, another way with my friends, and yet another way at home.

The Emerging Awareness of Race

Adolescence is typically a period when young people become more detached from their parents and attempt to establish an independent identity. For racial minorities, adolescence is also a period when young people begin to solidify their understanding of their racial identities. For many, understanding the significance of race means recognizing that membership within a racial category requires certain social and political commitments. Adolescence is often a difficult and painful period for many young people. And for young people struggling to figure out the meaning and significance of their racial identities, the experience can be even more difficult.

Awareness of race and the significance of racial difference often begins in early childhood. We know from psychological research that the development of racial identity is very context dependent, especially in the early years. Children who attend racially diverse schools or reside in racially diverse communities are much more likely to become aware of race at an earlier age than children in more homogeneous settings.[1] In the latter context, race is often not a defining issue or a primary basis for identity formation. When children see their race as the norm, they are less likely to perceive characteristics associated with it (for example, physical appearance) as markers of inferiority.

In contrast, children who grow up in more integrated settings become aware of physical differences fairly early. Interacting with children from other racial and ethnic backgrounds in a society that has historically treated race as a means of distinguishing groups and individuals often forces young people to develop racial identities early. However, prior to adolescence, they do not usually understand the political and social significance associated with differences in appearance. For young children, being a person with different skin color may be no more significant than being thin or heavy, tall or short. Differences in skin color, hair texture, and facial features are simply seen as being among the many differences that all children have. In environments where racist and ethnocentric behavior is common, children may learn fairly early that racist speech is hurtful.[2] They may know that calling someone a nigger is worse than calling that person stupid, but they may not necessarily understand the meaning of such words or know why their use inflicts hurt on others.

In 1999 I was conducting research with colleagues at an elementary school in East Oakland. We were interested in understanding how the practice of separating children on the basis of language differences affected their social relationships and perceptions of students from other groups. As is true in many other parts of California, East Oakland was experiencing a major demographic change as large numbers of Mexican and Central American immigrants were moving into communities that had previously been predominantly African American. As is often the case, schools in East Oakland serve as the place where children from these groups encounter one another, and at several of the high schools there had been a significant increase in interracial conflict.[3]

In the elementary school where we did our research, we found that most of the Black and Latino students had very little interaction with each other. Although they attended the same school, the students had been placed in separate classes, ostensibly for the purpose of serving their language needs. From our interviews with students, we learned that even very young children viewed peers from the other racial group with suspicion and animosity, although they could not explain why. Interestingly, when we asked the students why they thought they had been placed in separate classrooms, most thought it was to prevent them from fighting. We also found that the younger Mexican students (between ages five and eight) saw themselves as White, and the Black students also referred to the Mexican students as White. However, as the children entered early adolescence (age nine or ten), the Mexican youth began to realize that they were not considered White outside this setting, and they began to understand for the first time that being Mexican meant something very different from being White.

Depending on the context, it is not uncommon for minority children to express a desire to reject group membership based on skin color, especially during early adolescence. As they start to realize that in this society to be Black or Brown means to be seen as "less than"—whether it be less smart, less capable, or less attractive—they often express a desire to be associated with the dominant and more powerful group. This tendency was evident among some of the younger Mexican students in our study. However, as they grew older, the political reality of life in East Oakland served to reinforce their understanding that they were definitely not White. As one student told us, "White kids go to nice schools with swimming pools and grass, not a ghetto school like we go to."

In adolescence, awareness of race and its implications for individual identity become even more salient. For many young men and women of color, racial identity development is affected by some of the same factors that influence individual identity development in general. According to Erikson and other theorists of child development, as children enter adolescence, they become extremely conscious of their peers and seek out acceptance from their reference group.[4] As they become increasingly aware of themselves as social beings, their perception of self tends to be highly dependent on acceptance and affirmation by others. For some adolescents, identification with and attachment to peer groups sometimes takes on so much importance that it can override other attachments, to family, parents, and teachers.

For adolescents in racially integrated schools, racial and ethnic identity also frequently take on new significance with respect to friendship groups and dating. It is not uncommon in integrated settings for preadolescent children to interact and form friendships easily across racial boundaries—if their parents or other adults allow them to do so.[5] However, as young people enter adolescence, such transgressions of racial boundaries can become more problematic. As they become increasingly aware of the significance associated with group differences, they generally become more concerned with how their peers will react to their participation in interracial relationships, and they may begin to self-segregate. As they get older, young people also become more aware of the politics associated with race. They become more cognizant of racial hierarchies and prejudice, even if they cannot articulate the political significance of race. They can feel its significance, but they often cannot explain what it all means.

Between 2000 and 2003, I worked closely with fifteen racially integrated school districts in the Minority Student Achievement Network (MSAN). At the racially integrated high schools in MSAN, students often become much more aware that racial group membership comes with certain political commitments and social expectations. In these schools, high-achieving students of color (like my son Joaquin) are sometimes unwilling to enroll in Advanced Placement courses or engage in activities that have traditionally been associated with White students because they fear becoming estranged from their friends. If they appear to engage in behavior that violates racial norms, they may be seen as rejecting membership in their racial group and run the risk of being regarded as a race traitor. For this reason, I have urged the districts in MSAN not to rely on the initiative of students to break down racial barriers but to put the onus on school leaders to take steps that will make this border crossing easier and more likely.[6]

Theories of the Identity-Achievement Connection

For educators, understanding the process through which young people come to see themselves as belonging to particular racial categories is important because it has tremendous bearing on the so-called achievement gap. Throughout the United States, schools are characterized by increasing racial segregation[7] and widespread racial disparities in academic achievement.[8] Blatant inequities in funding, quality, and organization are also characteristic of the American educational system. Despite overwhelming evidence of a strong correlation between race and academic performance, there is considerable confusion among researchers about how and why such a correlation exists.

The scholars whose work has had the greatest influence on these issues are John Ogbu and Signithia Fordham, both of whom have argued that Black students from all socioeconomic backgrounds develop "oppositional identities" that lead them to view schooling as a form of forced assimilation to White cultural values.[9] Ogbu and Fordham argue that Black students and other "nonvoluntary minorities" (such as Chicanos, Puerto Ricans, Native Americans, and others whose groups have been dominated by White European culture) come to equate academic success with "acting White." For these researchers, such perceptions lead to the devaluation of academic pursuits and the adoption of self-defeating behaviors that inhibit possibilities for academic success. In this framework, the few students who aspire to achieve academically must pay a heavy price for success. Black students who perform at high levels may be ostracized by their peers as traitors and "sellouts" and may be forced to choose between maintaining ties with their peers or achieving success in school.[10] This would explain why middle-class minority students like my son Joaquin would underperform academically despite their social and economic advantages.

My own research challenges Ogbu and Fordham's "acting-white" thesis. While carrying out research among high school students in northern California, I discovered that some high-achieving minority students are ostracized by their peers, but others (like me) learn how to succeed in both worlds by adopting multiple identities. Still others actively and deliberately challenge racial stereotypes and seek to redefine their racial identities by showing that it is possible to do well in school and be proud of who they are.

Claude Steele's work on the effects of racial stereotypes on academic performance helps to provide a compelling explanation for the identity-achievement paradox. Through his research on student attitudes toward testing, Steele (twin brother of the more conservative Shelby) has shown that students are highly susceptible to prevailing stereotypes related to intellectual ability.[11] According to Steele, when "stereotype threat" are operative, they lower the confidence of vulnerable students and negatively affect their performance on standardized tests. Steele writes, "Ironically, their susceptibility to this threat derives not from internal doubts about their ability but from their identification with the domain and the resulting concern they have about being stereotyped in it."[12] According to Steele, the debilitating effects of stereotypes can extend beyond particular episodes of testing and can have an effect on overall academic performance.

Race in the School Context

Stereotypes and Expectations

As Steele's research illustrates, in the United States, we have very deeply embedded stereotypes that connect racial identity to academic ability, and children become aware of these stereotypes as they grow up in the school context. Simply put, there are often strong assumptions made in schools that if you're White, you'll do better in school than if you're Black; or if you're Asian, you'll do better at school than if you're Latino. These kinds of stereotypes affect both teachers' expectations of students and students' expectations of themselves.

One of the groups most affected by these stereotypes is Asian Americans. There is a perception in many schools that Asians are "naturally" academically gifted, especially in math. This stereotype is based on the following notions: (1) that Asians are inherently smart (either for genetic or cultural reasons), (2) that they have a strong work ethic, (3) that they are passive and deferential toward authority, and (4) that unlike other minorities, they don't complain about discrimination. These perceptions make up what is often called the "model minority" stereotype.[13]

One of my former students, Julian Ledesma, now a researcher in the Office of the President of the University of California, has been doing research on the model minority stereotype at a high school in Oakland, California. He started his work by interviewing various teachers and students about who they believed were "the smartest kids." In nearly every case, those he asked reported that the Asians were the "smartest" students. Even Asian students who were doing poorly in school reported that Asians were the smartest. The surprising thing about their responses to this question is that the average grade point average for Asians at the school was 1.8.

One reason for the gross misconception at this school is that Asians were overrepresented in the honors courses and among students with the highest ranks in their class. Yet these successful students were not representative of Asians as a whole at the school. Overall, Asian students were dropping out in high numbers and not doing very well academically. The school where Julian did his research also had a considerable gang problem among Asians. Yet because the stereotype is so powerful, students and teachers at the school were more likely to regard the majority of Asian students as the exceptions, and the smaller numbers who were successful as the norm.

The stereotypical images we hold toward groups are powerful in influencing what people see and expect of students. Unless educators consciously try to undermine and work against these kinds of stereotypes, they often act on them unconsciously. Our assumptions related to race are so deeply entrenched that it is virtually impossible for us not to hold them unless we take conscious and deliberate action.

Sorting Practices and "Normal" Racial Separation

Beyond these stereotypes, there are also the sorting practices that go on in schools that send important messages to students about the meaning of racial categories. For example, in many schools, the remedial classes are disproportionately Black and Brown, and students often draw conclusions about the relationship between race and academic ability based on these patterns. They might say to themselves, "Well, I guess the kids in these 'slow' classes are less smart than those other kids who are in the honors classes." They also notice that the students who are most likely to be punished, suspended, and expelled also are more likely to be the darker students.

In addition to reinforcing stereotypes, grouping practices, which teachers and administrators say are not based on race but on ability or behavior, often have the effect of reinforcing racial separation. Unless the adults in a school are conscious of how this separation influences their own perceptions and that of students, over time this separation may be regarded as normal. For example, Black students may assume that because there are no Black students in advanced or honors courses they cannot excel academically. Of course, Black students can distinguish themselves in sports because there are numerous examples of Black individuals who do. Similarly, White students may assume that they should not seek academic assistance from tutorial programs, especially if those programs primarily serve Black or Brown students. When the norms associated with race take on a static and determining quality, they can be very difficult to undermine. Students who receive a lot of support and encouragement at home may be more likely to cross over and work against these separations. But as my wife and I found for a time with Joaquin, middle-class African American parents who try to encourage their kids to excel in school often find this can't be done because the peer pressures against crossing these boundaries are too great.

The racial separation we see in schools might also be seen as an element of the "hidden curriculum," an unspoken set of rules that "teaches" certain students what they can and cannot do because of who they are. There are aspects of this hidden curriculum that are not being taught by the adults. It may well be that students are the ones teaching it to each other. No adult goes onto the playground and says, "I don't want the boys and girls to play together." The girls and boys do that themselves, and it's a rare child who crosses over. Why? Because those who violate gender norms are often ostracized by their peers. The girls who play with the boys become known as the tomboys, and the boys who play with the girls become known as the sissies. Although the children are sanctioning each other without instruction from adults, they are also engaging in behavior that has been learned from adults—not explicitly, but implicitly. Adults can reinforce narrow gender roles by promoting certain activities such as physical sports for boys and other things such as dance for girls.

With respect to race, children receive messages all the time about beauty standards. Who are the favored students, and what are their characteristics? Who are the people who get into trouble a lot, and what are their characteristics? Much of the time preferential (or nonpreferential) treatment is very much related to race.

In many schools, there may not be many explicit messages about race, but students receive implicit messages about race all the time that informs what they think it means to be a member of a particular racial group. When they see Black students overrepresented on the basketball team but underrepresented in Advanced Placement courses, or Latino students overrepresented among those who've gotten into trouble but underrepresented among those receiving awards, they get a clear sense about the meaning of race. The hidden curriculum related to race presents racial patterns as normal and effectively reinforces racial stereotypes. When it is operative, it can completely undermine efforts to raise student achievement because students may believe that altering racial patterns simply is not possible.

Too often, educators assume because of the choices Black students make about who to socialize with, which classes to take, and so forth that they are anti-intellectual.[14] However, the vast majority of Black students I meet express a strong desire to do well in school.

The younger students don't arrive at school with an anti-intellectual orientation. To the degree that such an orientation develops, it develops in school and from their seeing these patterns and racial hierarchies as permanent. Because a great deal of this behavior plays out in schools, educators can do something about it.

What Can Educators Do?

Understanding and debunking racial stereotypes, breaking down racial separations, and challenging the hidden curriculum are challenges not just for teachers but for principals, administrators, and entire school communities. In addition, there are a number of things educators can do to support their students' positive racial identity development.

First, educators can make sure that students are not segregating themselves—sitting in racially defined groups in the classroom. For teachers, this can be as simple as mixing students and assigning them seats. Or if work groups are created, students can be assigned to groups in ways that ensure that students of different backgrounds have an opportunity to work together. This approach to race mixing is often far more effective than holding an abstract conversation about tolerance or diversity. By working together, students are more likely to form friendships naturally, and as students gain familiarity with one another, they may be more willing to break racial norms. If teachers let students choose, they will more than likely choose those whom they perceive to be "their own kind."

Second, educators can encourage students to pursue things that are not traditionally associated with members of their group. If students of color are encouraged by adults to join the debating team or the science club, play music in the band, or enroll in advanced courses, it will be possible for greater numbers to challenge racial norms. Extracurricular activities in particular can serve a very important role in this regard and give young people a chance to get to know each other in situations that are not racially loaded. As is true for work groups, in the course of playing soccer or writing for the newspaper, students can become friends. Research on extra-curricular activities has shown that sports, music, theater, and other activities can play an important role in building connections among young people and breaking down the very insidious links between racial identity and academic achievement.[15]

Third, teachers can find ways to incorporate information related to the history and culture of students into the curriculum. This is important in helping students understand what it means to be who they are, an essential aspect of the identity formation process for adolescents. Literature—novels and short stories—can be very effective in this regard because it can help students to identify and empathize with children who may be from different backgrounds. Field trips and out-of-class experiences that provide students with opportunities to learn about the experiences of others can also help in expanding their horizons.

Finally, an effective teacher who is able to inspire students by getting to know them can actually do a great deal to overcome antiacademic tendencies. They can do this by getting students to believe in themselves, by getting them to learn how to work hard and persist, and by getting them to dream, plan for the future, and set goals. Over and over again, when you talk to students who have been successful, they speak about the role that significant adults have played at various points in their lives.[16] They talk about how these adults helped them recognize their own potential and how they opened doors that they previously did not know existed.

I believe there are many young people who are crying out for supportive relationships with caring adults. Differences in race, gender, or sexual orientation need not limit a teacher's ability to make a connection with a young person. In my own work with students and schools, I have generally found kids to be the least prejudiced of all people. They tend to respond well to caring adults regardless of what they look like. However, they can also tell if the adults who work with them are sincere, and those acting out of guilt and faked concern can generally be detected.

Today most social scientists recognize race as a social rather than as a biological construct. It is seen as a political category created largely for the purpose of justifying exploitation and oppression.[17] For many adults and kids, especially those of mixed heritage, the categories often do not even correspond to who they think they are. Rather than being a source of strength, the acquisition of racial identities may be a tremendous burden.

For many years to come, race will undoubtedly continue to be a significant source of demarcation within the U.S. population. For many of us, it will continue to shape where we live, pray, go to school, and socialize. We cannot simply wish away the existence of race or racism, but we can take steps to lessen the ways in which the categories trap and confine us. Educators, who should be committed to helping young people realize their intellectual potential as they make their way toward adulthood, have a responsibility to help them find ways to expand identities related to race so that they can experience the fullest possibility of all that they may become.

2

The Trouble with Black Boys

The Impact of Social and Cultural Forces on the Academic Achievement of African American Males

A ll of the most important quality-of-life indicators suggest that African American males are in deep trouble. They lead the nation in homicides, as both victims and perpetrators,[1] and in what observers regard as an alarming trend, they now have the fastest-growing rate for suicide.[2] For the past several years, Black males have been contracting HIV and AIDS at a faster rate than any other segment of the population,[3] and their incarceration, conviction, and arrest rates have been at the top of the charts in most states for some time.[4] Even as babies, Black males have the highest probability of dying in the first year of life,[5] and as they grow older, they face the unfortunate reality of being the only group in the United States experiencing a decline in life expectancy.[6] In the labor market, they are the least likely to be hired and, in many cities, the most likely to be unemployed.[7]

Beset with such an ominous array of social and economic hardships, it is hardly surprising that the experience of Black males in education, with respect to attainment and most indicators of academic performance, also shows signs of trouble and distress. In many school districts throughout the United States, Black males are more likely than any other group to be suspended and expelled from school.[8] From 1973 to 1977, there was a steady increase in African American enrollment in college. However, since 1977, there has been a sharp and continuous decline, especially among males.[9]

Black males are more likely to be classified as mentally retarded or suffering from a learning disability and placed in special education[10] and more likely to be absent from Advanced Placement and honors courses.[11] In contrast to most other groups where males commonly perform at higher levels in math and science-related courses, the reverse is true for Black males.[12] Even class privilege and the material benefits that accompany it fail to inoculate Black males from low academic performance. When compared to their White peers, middle-class African American males lag significantly behind in both grade point average and on standardized tests.[13]

It is not surprising that there is a connection between the educational performance of African American males and the hardships they endure within the larger society.[14] In fact, it would be more surprising if Black males were doing well academically in spite of the broad array of difficulties that confront them. Scholars and researchers commonly understand that environmental and cultural factors have a profound influence on human behavior, including academic performance.[15] What is less understood is how environmental and cultural forces influence the way in which Black males come to perceive schooling and how those perceptions influence their behavior and performance in school. There is considerable evidence that the ethnic and socioeconomic backgrounds of students have bearing on how students are perceived and treated by the adults who work with them within schools.[16] However, we know less about the specific nature of the perceptions and expectations that are held toward Black males and how these may in turn affect their performance within schools. More to the point, there is considerable confusion regarding why being Black and male causes this segment of the population to stand out in the most negative and alarming ways, in both school and the larger society.

This chapter is rooted in the notion that it is possible to educate all children, including Black males, at high levels. This idea is not an articulation of faith, but rather a conclusion drawn from a vast body of research on human development and from research on the learning styles of Black children.[17] Therefore, it is possible for schools to take actions that can reverse the patterns of low achievement among African American males.

The fact that some schools and programs manage to do so already is further evidence that there is a possibility of altering these trends. To the degree that we accept the idea that human beings have the capacity to resist submission to cultural patterns, demographic trends,[18] and environmental pressures and constraints, bringing greater clarity to the actions that can be taken by schools and community organizations to support the academic achievement of African American males could be the key to changing academic outcomes and altering the direction of negative trends for this segment of the population.[19]

This chapter explores the possibility that the academic performance of African American males can be improved by devising strategies that counter the effects of harmful environmental and cultural forces. Drawing on research from a variety of disciplines, the chapter begins with an analysis of the factors that place certain individuals (African American males) at greater risk than others. This is followed by an analysis of the ways in which environmental and cultural forces interact and influence academic outcomes and how these factors shape the relationship between identity, particularly related to race, gender, and school performance. Finally, strategies for countering harmful environmental and cultural influences, both the diffuse and the direct, are explored, with particular attention paid to recommendations for educators, parents, and youth service providers who seek to support young African American males.

The Nature of the "Risk"

The good news is that not all Black males are at risk. I was reminded of this fact on my way to work one morning. Before driving to San Francisco with a colleague, another Black male academic, we stopped to pick up a commuter so that we could make the trip across the Bay Bridge in the faster car pool lane during the middle of the rush hour. As it turned out, the first car pooler to approach our car was another Black male. As we drove across the bridge, we made small talk, going from basketball, to the merits of living in the Bay Area, until finally we approached the subject of our careers. The rider informed us that he managed a highly profitable telecommunications firm, and if his plans progressed as he hoped, he would be retiring on a very lucrative pension in Hawaii before the age of fifty. Contemplating his financial good fortune and that of my colleague and myself (although the two of us had no plans for early retirement), I posed the question, "What explains why we are we doing so well, and so many brothers like us are not?"

The answer was not obvious. All three of us were raised in working-class families, had grown up in tough neighborhoods, had close friends and family members who had been killed while they were young, and knew others who were serving time in prison. What made our lives, with our promising careers and growing families, so fortunate and so different? All three of us were raised by both of our parents, but further exploration revealed that none of us had regular contact with our fathers. We all attended public schools, but each of us felt that we had succeeded in spite of, and not because of, the schools we attended. With time running out as we approached our rider's stop, we threw out the possibility that the only thing that spared us the fate of so many of our brethren was luck—not getting caught for past indiscretions and not being in the wrong place at the wrong time.

Viewed in the context of the negative social patterns cited previously, the explanation for our apparent good luck does not seem mysterious. While it is true that many Black males are confronted with a vast array of risks, obstacles, and social pressures, the majority manages to navigate these with some degree of success. The good news is that most Black males are not in prison, do not commit suicide, and have not contracted HIV/AIDS. These facts do not negate the significance of the problems that confront

Black males, but they do help to keep the problems in perspective. Understanding how and why many Black males avoid the pitfalls and hardships that beset others may help us to devise ways to protect and provide support for more of them.

The effects of growing up in poverty, particularly for children raised in socially isolated, economically depressed urban areas, warrants greater concern, especially given that one out of every three Black children is raised in a poor household.[20] Here the evidence is clear that the risks faced by children, particularly African American males, in terms of health, welfare, and education, are substantially greater.[21] A recent longitudinal study on the development of children whose mothers used drugs (particularly crack cocaine) during pregnancy found that when compared to children residing in similar neighborhoods from similar socioeconomic backgrounds, the children in the sample showed no greater evidence of long-term negative effects. This is not because the incidence of physical and cognitive problems among the sample was not high, but because it was equally high for the control group. The stunned researchers, who fully expected to observe noticeable differences between the two groups, were compelled to conclude that the harmful effects of living within an impoverished inner-city environment outweighed the damage inflicted by early exposure to drugs.[22]

A vast body of research on children in poverty shows that impoverished conditions greatly increase the multiplier effect on risk variables (single-parent household, low birth weight, low educational attainment of parents, and others).[23] Poor children generally receive inferior services from schools and agencies that are located in the inner city, and poor children often have many unmet basic needs. This combination of risk factors makes it nearly impossible to establish cause-and-effect relationships among them. For example, research has shown that a disproportionate number of poor children suffer from various sight disorders.[24] Throughout the country, Black children are overrepresented in special education programs, and those most likely to be placed are overwhelmingly

Black, male, and poor.[25] However, the disabilities experienced by children are often related to poverty rather than a biological disorder. For example, because poor children often lack access to preventive health care, their untreated vision problems are inaccurately diagnosed as reading problems, and as a consequence, large numbers are placed in remedial and special education programs.[26]

The situation in special education mirrors a larger trend in education for African Americans generally, and males in particular. Rather than serving as a source of hope and opportunity, schools are sites where Black males are marginalized and stigmatized.[27] Consistently, schools that serve Black males fail to nurture, support, or protect them. In school, Black males are more likely to be labeled as behavior problems and less intelligent even while they are still very young.[28] Black males are also more likely to be punished with severity, even for minor offenses, for violating school rules,[29] often without regard for their welfare. They are more likely to be excluded from rigorous classes and prevented from accessing educational opportunities that might otherwise support and encourage them.[30]

However, changing academic outcomes and countering the risks experienced by Black males is not simply a matter of developing programs to provide support or bringing an end to unfair educational policies and practices. Black males often adopt behaviors that make them complicit in their own failure. It is not just that they are more likely to be punished or placed in remedial classes, it is also that they are more likely to act out in the classroom and to avoid challenging themselves academically. Recognizing that Black males are not merely passive victims but may also be active agents in their own failure means that interventions designed to help them must take this into account. Changing policies, creating new programs, and opening new opportunities will accomplish little if such efforts are not accompanied by strategies to actively engage Black males and their families in taking responsibility to improve their circumstances. Institutionally this may require programmatic interventions aimed at buffering and offsetting the various risks to which Black males are particularly vulnerable. However, to be effective, such initiatives must also involve efforts to counter and transform cultural patterns and what some have called the "oppositional identities" adopted by Black males that undermine the importance they attach to education.

As I will illustrate, one of the best ways to learn how this can be done is to study those schools and programs that have proven successful in accomplishing this goal. In addition, it is important for such work to be anchored in a theoretical understanding of how the pressures exerted on Black males in American society can be contested. Without such an intellectual underpinning, it is unlikely that new interventions and initiatives will succeed at countering the hazardous direction of trends for African American males.

Structural Versus Cultural Explanations

Epidemiologists and psychologists have identified a number of risk factors within the social environment that, when combined, are thought to have a multiplier effect on risk behavior. Lack of access to health care, adequate nutrition, and decent housing; growing up poor and in a single-parent household; being exposed to substance abuse at a young age; and living in a crime-ridden neighborhood are some of the variables most commonly cited.[31] Similarly, anthropologists and sociologists have documented ways in which certain cultural influences can lower the aspirations of Black males and contribute to the adoption of self-destructive behavior. John Ogbu has argued that community-based "folk theories," which suggest that because of the history of discrimination against Black people, even those who work hard will never reap rewards equivalent to Whites, can contribute to self-defeating behaviors.[32] There is also evidence that many Black males view sports or music as more promising routes to upward mobility than academic pursuits.[33] Finally, some researchers have found that for some African American students, doing well in school is perceived as a sign that one has "sold out" or opted to "act White" for the sake of individual gain.[34]

Despite their importance and relevance to academic performance, risk variables and cultural pressures cannot explain individual behavior. Confronted with a variety of obstacles and challenges, some Black males still find ways to survive, and in some cases to excel. Interestingly, we know much less about resilience, perseverance, and the coping strategies employed by individuals whose lives are surrounded by hardships than we know about those who succumb and become victims of their environment. Deepening our understanding of how individuals cope with, and respond to, their social and cultural environments is an important part of finding ways to assist Black males with living healthy and productive lives.

In the social sciences, explanations of human behavior, especially that of the poor, have been the subject of considerable debate. Most often the debate centers on those who favor structural explanations of behavior and those who prefer cultural explanations of behavior. Structuralists generally focus on political economy—the availability of jobs and economic opportunities, class structure, and social geography.[35] From this perspective, individuals are viewed as products of their environment, and changes in individual behavior are made possible by changes in the structure of opportunity. From this theoretical perspective, holding an individual responsible for his or her behavior makes little sense since behavior is shaped by forces beyond the control of any particular individual.

Drug abuse, crime, and dropping out of school are largely seen as social consequences of inequality. According to this view, the most effective way to reduce objectionable behavior is to reduce the degree and extent of inequality in society.

In contrast, culturalists downplay the significance of environmental factors and treat human behavior as a product of beliefs, values, norms, and socialization. Cultural explanations of behavior focus on the moral codes that operate within particular families, communities, or groups.[36] For example, the idea that poor people are trapped within a "culture of poverty," which has the effect of legitimizing criminal and immoral behavior, has dominated the culturalists' perspective of poverty.[37] For the culturalists, change in behavior can be brought about only through cultural change. Hence, providing more money to inner-city schools or busing inner-city children to affluent suburban schools will do little to improve their academic performance since their attitudes toward school are shaped by the culture brought from home and the neighborhood.[38] According to this view, culture provides the rationale and motivation for behavior, and cultural change cannot be brought about through changes in governmental policy or by expanding opportunities.

A growing number of researchers are trying to find ways to work between the two sides of the debate. Dissatisfied with the determinism of the structuralists, which renders individuals as passive objects of larger forces, and with the "blame-the-victim" perspective of the culturalists, which views individuals as hopelessly trapped within a particular social and cultural milieu,[39] some researchers have sought to synthesize important elements from both perspectives while simultaneously paying greater attention to the importance of individual choice and agency.[40] From this perspective, the importance of both structure and culture is acknowledged, but so too is the understanding that individuals have the capacity to act and make choices that cannot be explained through the reductionism inherent in either framework.[41] The choices made by individuals may be shaped by the available opportunities and by the norms present within the cultural milieu in which they are situated. However, culture is not static, and individual responses to their environment cannot be easily predicted. Both structural and cultural forces influence choices and actions, but neither has the power to act as the sole determinant of behavior because human beings also have the ability to produce cultural forms that can counter these pressures.[42]

This is not to suggest that because individuals have the capacity to counter these forces many will choose or be able to do so. The effects of poverty can be so debilitating that a child's life chances can literally be determined by a number of environmental (for example, the quality of prenatal care, housing, and food available to their mothers) and cultural factors that are simply beyond the control of an individual or even of concerted community action. It would be naive and a mistake to conclude that strength of character and the possibility of individual agency can enable one to avoid the perils present within the environment, or that it is easy for individuals to choose to act outside the cultural milieu in which they were raised. Even as we recognize that individuals make choices that influence the character of their lives, we must also recognize that the range of choices available is profoundly constrained and shaped by external forces. For this reason, efforts to counter behaviors that are viewed as injurious—whether it be dropping out of school, selling drugs, or engaging in violent behavior—must include efforts to comprehend the logic and motivations behind the behavior. Given the importance of agency and choice, the only way to change behavioral outcomes is to understand the cognitive processes that influence how individuals adapt, cope, and respond.

In a comprehensive study of teen pregnancy, Kristen Luker demonstrates the possibility for synthesizing the two perspectives— structural and cultural explanations of human behavior—that have traditionally been seen as irreconcilable. Teen pregnancy, which for years has been much more prevalent among poor minority girls than middle-class White girls, has traditionally been explained as either the product of welfare dependency and permissive sexual mores (the culturalists), or the unfortunate result of inadequate access to birth control and economic opportunities (the structuralists). Through detailed interviews with a diverse sample of teen mothers, Luker puts forward a different explanation that draws from both the cultural and the structural perspectives and acknowledges the role and importance of individual choice. She points out that while both middle-class and lower-class girls engage in premarital sex and sometimes become pregnant, middle-class girls are less likely to have babies during adolescence because they have a clear sense that it will harm their chance for future success. In contrast, when confronted with an unexpected pregnancy, poor girls are more likely to have babies because they do not perceive it as negatively affecting their future, since college and a good job are already perceived as being out of reach. In fact, many girls in this situation actually believe that having a baby during adolescence will help them to settle down since they will now be responsible for another life.[43]

Given the importance of individual "choice" to this particular behavior, any effort to reduce teen pregnancy that does not take into account the reasoning that guides decision making is unlikely to succeed. Similarly, efforts to improve the academic performance of African American males must begin by understanding the attitudes that influence how they perceive schooling and academic pursuits. To the extent that this does not happen, attempts to help Black males based primarily on the sensibilities of those who initiate them are unlikely to be effective and may be no more successful than campaigns that attempt to reduce drug use or violence by urging kids to "just say no."[44]

Investigations into the academic orientation of Black male students must focus on the ways in which the subjective and objective dimensions of identity related to race and gender are constructed within schools and how these influence academic performance. Although psychologists have generally conceived of identity construction as a natural feature of human development,[45] sociologists have long recognized that identities such as social roles are imposed on individuals through various socialization processes.[46] The processes and influences involved in the construction of Black male identity should be at the center of analyses of school performance since it is on the basis of their identities that Black males are presumed to be at risk, marginal, and endangered in school and throughout American society.[47]

Structural and cultural forces combine in complex ways to influence the formation of individual and collective identities, even as individuals may resist, actively or passively, the various processes involved in the molding of the self. The fact that individuals can resist, subvert, and react against the cultural and structural forces that shape social identities compels us to recognize that individual choice, or what many scholars refer to as agency, also plays a major role in the way identities are constructed and formed.[48] For this reason, research on identity must pay careful attention to the attitudes and styles of behavior that African American males adopt and produce in reaction to the social environment, and how these influence how they are seen and how they see themselves within the context of school. Writing on the general importance of identity to studies of schooling, Levinson, Foley, and Holland argue that "student identity formation within school is a kind of social practice and cultural production which both responds to, and simultaneously constitutes, movements, structures, and discourses beyond school."[49]

Students can be both unfairly victimized by the labeling and sorting processes that occur within school, in addition to being harmed by the attitudes and behavior they adopt in reaction to these processes. For this reason, it is important to understand the factors that may enable them to resist these pressures and respond positively to various forms of assistance that may be provided within school or in the communities where they reside. By linking a focus on identity construction to an analysis of cultural production, it is my hope that we can gain greater insight into how schools can be changed and how support programs can be designed to positively alter academic outcomes for African American males.

Identity and Academic Performance

It has long been recognized that schools are important sites of socialization. Schools are places where children learn how to follow instructions and obey rules, how to interact with others, and how to deal with authority.[50] Schools are important sites for gender role socialization,[51] and in most societies, they are primary sites for instruction about the values and norms associated with citizenship.[52]

For many children, schools are also places where they learn about the meaning of race. While this may occur through lesson plans adopted by teachers, it is even more likely that children learn about race through the hidden or informal curriculum[53] and through nonstructured school activities such as recess.[54] Even when teachers do not speak explicitly about race and racial issues with children, children become aware of physical differences related to race quite early.[55] However, children do not become aware of the significance attached to these physical differences until they start to understand the ideological dimensions of race and become cognizant of differential treatment that appears to be based on race.[56] Name-calling, including the use of racial epithets, serves as one way of establishing racial boundaries even when children do not fully understand the meaning of the words that are used.[57] Similarly, school practices that isolate and separate children on the basis of race and gender also send children important messages about the significance of race and racial differences.[58] Schools certainly are not the only places where children formulate views about race, but because schools are often sites where children are more likely to encounter persons of another race or ethnic group, they play a central role in influencing the character of race relations in communities and the larger society.[59]

As young people enter adolescence and develop a stronger sense of their individual identities,[60] the meaning and significance of race also change. Where it was once an ambiguous concept based largely on differences in physical appearance, language, and styles of behavior, race becomes a more rigid identity construct as children learn the historical, ideological, and cultural dimensions associated with racial group membership.[61] Even children who once played and interacted freely across racial lines when they were younger often experience a tightening of racial boundaries and racial identities as they get older and begin following patterns of interaction modeled by adults.[62] Peer groups play a powerful role in shaping identity because the desire to be accepted by one's peers and fit in with one's peers often becomes a paramount concern for most adolescents. Research has shown that in secondary school, peer groups assume a great influence over the orientation young people adopt toward achievement, [63] and they profoundly shape the way identities are constituted in school settings.[64] As adolescents become clearer about the nature of their racial and gender identities, they begin to play a more active role in maintaining and policing these identities. Peer groups are also likely to impose negative sanctions on those who violate what are perceived as established norms of behavior and attempt to construct identities that deviate significantly from prevailing conceptions of racial and gender identity.[65]

Despite the importance that several researchers have placed on the role of peer groups in the socialization process, peer groups are by no means the only forces that shape the social construction of identity within schools.[66] The structure and culture of school plays a major role in reinforcing and maintaining racial categories and the stereotypes associated with them. As schools sort children by perceived measures of their ability and as they single out certain children for discipline, implicit and explicit messages about racial and gender identities are conveyed. To the degree that White or Asian children are disproportionately placed in gifted and honors classes, the idea that such children are inherently smarter may be inadvertently reinforced.[67] Similarly, when African American and Latino children are overrepresented in remedial classes, special education programs, or on the lists for suspension or expulsion, the idea that these children are not as smart or as well behaved is also reinforced. Such messages are conveyed even when responsible adults attempt to be as fair as possible in their handling of sorting and disciplinary activities. Because the outcomes of such practices often closely resemble larger patterns of success and failure that correspond with racial differences in American society, they invariably have the effect of reinforcing existing attitudes and beliefs about the nature and significance of race.

For African American males, who are more likely than any other group to be subjected to negative forms of treatment in school, the message is clear: individuals of their race and gender may excel in sports, but not in math or history. The location of Black males within schools—in remedial classes or waiting for punishment outside the principal's office—and the roles they perform within school suggest that they are good at playing basketball or rapping, but debating, writing for the school newspaper, or participating in the science club is strictly out of bounds. Such activities are out of bounds not just because Black males may perceive them as being inconsistent with who they think they are, but also because there simply are not enough examples of individuals who manage to participate in such activities without compromising their sense of self. Even when a small number of Black males do engage in activities that violate established norms, their deviation from established patterns often places them under considerable scrutiny from their peers. who are likely to regard their transgression of group norms as a sign of "selling out."

Researchers like John Ogbu and Signithia Fordham have attributed the marginality of Black students to oppositional behavior.[68] They argue that Black students hold themselves back out of fear that they will be ostracized by their peers. Yet what these researchers do not acknowledge is the dynamic that occurs between Black students, males in particular, and the culture that is operative within schools. Black males may engage in behaviors that contribute to their underachievement and marginality, but they are also more likely to be channeled into marginal roles and to be discouraged from challenging themselves by adults who are supposed to help them. Finally, and most important, Ogbu and Fordham fail to take into account the fact that some Black students, including males, find ways to overcome the pressures exerted on them and manage to avoid choosing between their racial and gender identity and academic success. Even if few in number, there are students who manage to maintain their identities and achieve academically without being ostracized by their peers. Understanding how such students navigate this difficult terrain may be the key to figuring out how to support the achievement of larger numbers of Black students.

A recent experience at a high school in the Bay Area illustrates how the interplay of these two socializing forces—peer groups and school sorting practices—can play out for individual students. I was approached by a Black male student who needed assistance with a paper on *Huckleberry Finn* that he was writing for his eleventh-grade English class. After reading what he had written, I asked why he had not discussed the plight of Jim, the runaway slave who is one of the central characters of the novel. The student informed me that his teacher had instructed the class to focus on the plot and not to get into issues about race, since according to the teacher, that was not the main point of the story. He explained that two students in the class, both Black males, had objected to the use of the word *nigger* throughout the novel and had been told by the teacher that if they insisted on making it an issue, they would have to leave the course. Both of these students opted to leave the course even though it meant they would have to take another course that did not meet the college preparatory requirements. The student I was helping explained that since he needed the class, he would just "tell the teacher what he wanted to hear." After our meeting, I looked into the issue further and discovered that one student, a Black female, had chosen a third option: she stayed in the class but wrote a paper focused on race and racial injustice, even though she knew it might result in her being penalized by the teacher.

This example reveals a number of important lessons about the intersection of identity, school practices, and academic performance.

Confronted by organizational practices, which disproportionately place Black students in marginal roles and groupings, and pressure from peers, which may undermine the importance attached to academic achievement, it will take considerable confidence and courage for Black students to succeed. The four Black students in this English class were already removed from their Black peers by their placement in this honors course. In such a context, one seemed to adopt what Fordham has described as a "raceless" persona (the student I was assisting) to satisfy the demands of the teacher, but this is only one of many available options. Two others responded by choosing to leave for a lower-level class, where they would be reunited with their peers with their identities intact but with diminished academic prospects. The option exercised by the female student in the class is perhaps the most enlightening yet difficult to enact. She challenged her teacher's instructions, choosing to write about race and racism even though she knew she would be penalized for doing so. Yet she also had no intention of leaving the class despite the isolation she experienced to seek out the support of her peers.

This case reveals just some of the ways Black students may respond to the social pressures inherent in school experiences. Some actively resist succumbing to stereotypes or the pressure of peers, while others give in to these pressures in search of affirmation of their social identity. For those who seek to help Black students, and males in particular, the challenge is to find ways to support their resistance to negative stereotypes and school sorting practices and to make choosing failure a less likely option for them. The teacher described in the previous example may or may not have even realized how her actions in relation to the curriculum led her Black students to make choices that would profoundly influence their education. As I show in the following section, when educators are aware of the social and cultural pressures exerted on students, the need to choose between one's identity and academic success can be eliminated.

Learning from Students and the Schools That Serve Them Well

Fortunately, there is considerable evidence that the vast majority of Black students, including males, would like to do well in school.[69] In addition, there are schools where academic success for Black students is the norm and not the exception.[70] Both of these facts provide a basis for hope that achievement patterns can be reversed if there is a willingness to provide the resources and support to create the conditions that nurture academic success.

In my own research at high schools in northern California, I have obtained consistent evidence that most Black students value education and would like to succeed in school. In response to a survey about their experiences in school, nearly 90 percent of the Black male respondents ($N = 147$) responded "agree" or "strongly agree" to the questions, "I think education is important," and "I want to go to college." However, in response to the following questions: "I work hard to achieve good grades" and "My teachers treat me fairly," less than a quarter of the respondents—22 percent and 18 percent, respectively—responded affirmatively. An analysis of just these responses to the survey suggests a disturbing discrepancy between what students claim they feel about the importance of education, the effort they expend, and the support they receive from teachers.[71] Similar results were obtained from a survey of 537 seniors at an academic magnet high school. African American males were least likely to indicate that they agreed or strongly agreed with the statement, "My teachers support me and care about my success in their class" (Table 2.1).

Rosalind Mickelson's research has found similar discrepancies between expressed support for education and a commitment to hard work. Her research findings have led her to conclude that some Black students experience what she refers to as an "attitude-achievement paradox." For Mickelson, the reason for the discrepancy is that while many Black students say they value education,

Table 2.1.   Percentage of African American Males Responding to, "My Teachers Support Me and Care About My Success in Their Class" (N = 537)

	Black Male	Black Female	Asian Male	Asian Female	White Male	White Female
Strongly Agree	8%	12%	24%	36%	33%	44%
Agree	12	16	42	33	21	27
Disagree	38	45	16	15	18	11
Strongly Disagree	42	27	18	16	28	18

such an expression is little more than an "abstract" articulation of belief. However, when pressed to state whether they believe that education will actually lead to a better life for them, the Black students in Mickelson's study expressed the "concrete" belief that it would not. Mickelson concludes that the contradiction between abstract and concrete beliefs toward education explains why there is a discrepancy between the attitudes expressed by Black students and their academic outcomes.[72]

Although Mickelson's findings seem plausible, I think it is also important to consider how the experiences of Black students in schools, especially males, may result in a leveling of aspirations. If students do not believe that their teachers care about them and are actively concerned about their academic performance, the likelihood that they will succeed is greatly reduced. In the Metropolitan Life annual survey on teaching, 39 percent of students surveyed (N = 3,961) indicated that they trust their teachers "only a little or not at all." When the data from the survey were disaggregated by race and class, minority and poor students indicated significantly higher levels of distrust (47 percent of minorities and 53 percent of poor students stated that they trusted their teachers only a little or not at all).[73] Although it is still possible that some students will succeed even if they do not trust or feel supported by their teachers, research on teacher expectations suggests that these feelings have a powerful effect on student performance.[74] Moreover, there is research that suggests that the performance of African Americans, more so than other students, is influenced to a large degree by the social support and encouragement they receive from teachers.[75] To the extent this is true, and if the nature of interactions between many Black male students and their teachers tends to be negative, it is unlikely that it will be possible to elevate their achievement without changing the way in which they are treated by teachers, and the ways in which they respond to those who try to help them.

However, there are schools where African American male students do well and where high levels of achievement are common. For example, a recent analysis of the academic performance indicators (API) of public schools in California revealed that there are twenty-two schools in the state where Black students comprise 50 percent or more of the student population and have aggregate test scores of 750 or greater (1000 is the highest possible score).[76] Most significant, when the test score data for these schools were disaggregated on the basis of race and gender, there was no evidence of an achievement gap. Although schools like these are few in number, given there are over two thousand public schools in California, the fact they exist suggests that similar results should be possible elsewhere.

Researchers who have studied effective schools have found that such schools possess the following characteristics: (1) a clear sense of purpose, (2) core standards within a rigorous curriculum, (3) high expectations, (4) commitment to educate all students, (5) a safe and orderly learning environment, (6) strong partnerships with parents, and (7) a problem-solving attitude.[77] Although the criteria used to determine effectiveness rely almost exclusively on data from standardized tests and ignore other criteria, there is no disagreement that such schools consistently produce high levels of academic achievement among minority students. Researchers on effective schools for low-income African American students also cite the supportive relations that exist between teachers and students, and the ethos of caring and accountability that pervades such schools as other essential ingredients of their success.[78] Educational reformers and researchers must do more to figure out how to adopt strategies that have proven successful at schools where achievement is less likely. As Ron Edmonds, formerly one of the leading researchers on effective schools, has stated: "We already know more than enough to successfully educate all students."[79] The challenge before educators and policymakers is to find ways to build on existing models of success.

Unfortunately most African American children are not enrolled in effective schools that nurture and support them while simultaneously providing high-quality instruction. Even as pressure is exerted to improve the quality of public education so that the supply of good schools is increased, other strategies must be devised at the community level to provide Black children with support. There are long-standing traditions within Jewish and many Asian communities to provide children with religious and cultural instruction outside school. In several communities throughout the United States, Black parents are turning to churches and community organizations as one possible source of such support.[80] In northern California, organizations such as Simba and the Omega Boys Club (both are community-based mentoring programs) provide African American males with academic support and adult mentors outside school.[81] Organizations like these affirm the identities of Black males by providing them with knowledge and information about African and African American history and culture and by instilling a sense of social responsibility toward their families and communities.[82] Unfortunately these organizations are small and are largely unable to serve the vast numbers of young people in need. Moreover, it is unlikely that such organizations can completely counter the harmful effects of attendance in unsupportive and even hostile schools because they are designed to complement learning that is supposed to go on in school. Still, the model they provide demonstrates that it is possible to work outside schools to have a positive influence on the academic performance of African American youth. Given their relative success but small size, it would be advisable to find ways to replicate them elsewhere.

Drawing from the research on mentoring and student resilience that has identified strategies that are effective in supporting the academic achievement of African American students, community organizations and churches can attempt to compensate for the failings of schools. Through after-school and summer school programs, these groups can provide young people with access to positive role models and social support that can help buffer young people from the pressures within their schools and communities.[83] While such activities should not be seen as a substitute for making public schools more responsive to the communities that they serve, they do represent a tangible action that can be taken immediately to respond to the needs of Black youth, particularly males who often face the greatest perils.

Conclusion: The Need for Further Research

Although I have made reference to the cultural forms, attitudes, and styles of behavior African American males may adopt and produce, which can diminish the importance they attach to academic achievement, the emphasis of this chapter has been on the ways in which schools misserve and underserve this population of students. I believe that such an emphasis is appropriate because research on effective schools has shown that when optimal conditions for teaching and learning are provided, high levels of academic success for students, including African American males, can be achieved. Put differently, if we can find ways to increase the supply of effective schools, it may be possible to mitigate against some of the risks confronting Black males. This does not mean the question of how to influence the attitudes, behaviors, and stances of Black males toward school and education generally does not need to be addressed or that it does not require further investigation. To the extent that we recognize that all students are active participants in their own education and not passive objects whose behavior can be manipulated by adults and reform measures, then the importance of understanding how to influence behavior cannot be understated. It is my belief that learning how to influence their attitudes and behaviors must begin with an understanding of the ways in which structural and cultural forces shape their experiences in school and influence the construction of their identities. In this regard, it is especially important that future research be directed toward a greater understanding of youth culture and the processes related to cultural production.

Like popular culture, youth culture, and all the styles and symbols associated with it, is dynamic and constantly changing. This is particularly true for inner-city African American youth, whose speech, dress, music, and tastes often establish trends for young people across America. For many adults, this culture is also impenetrable and often incomprehensible. Yet despite the difficulty of understanding and interpreting youth culture, it is imperative that efforts to help Black youth be guided by ongoing attempts at understanding the cultural forms they produce and the ways in which they respond and adapt to their social and cultural environment. Without such an understanding, efforts to influence the attitudes and behaviors of African American males will most likely fail to capture their imaginations and be ignored.

I was reminded of the importance of understanding youth culture when I embarked on research on how the popular media influence the attitudes of young people toward violence. As part of this research, I attempted to study how young people react to violent imagery in films by watching segments of popular movies with groups of middle school students and discussing their interpretations and responses to the ways violence was depicted. Following a series of discussions focused on their moral and ethical judgments of the violence conveyed in the films, the students asked if we could watch the film *Menace to Society* as part of the research exercise. To my surprise, several of the students owned copies of the film, and many had seen the film so many times that they had memorized parts of the dialogue. The film, which tells the story of a young man growing up in South Central Los Angeles, is filled with graphic images of violence. After viewing it, I was certain that there might be some truth to the idea that violent films did condition young people to rationalize violent behavior as a legitimate and appropriate way for resolving conflicts and getting what they wanted. However, when discussing the film, it became clear that most were repulsed by the violence even though they were entertained by it, and rather than identifying with perpetrators of violence in the film, they identified most strongly with those characters who sought to avoid it.[84]

This experience, and others like it, made me realize how easy it is for adults to misinterpret and misunderstand the attitudes and behavior of young people. Generational differences, especially when compounded by differences in race and class, often make it difficult for adults to communicate effectively with youth. Many adults are aware of the chasm that separates them from young people, yet adults typically take actions intended to benefit young people without ever investigating whether the interventions meet the needs or concerns of youth. There is a need to consult with young people on how the structure and culture of schools contribute to low academic achievement, and to enlist their input when interventions to improve student performance are being designed and implemented.

In addition to research on youth culture, there is a pressing need for further research on how identities—especially related to the intersection of race, class, and gender—are constructed within schools and how these identities affect students' attitudes and dispositions toward school, learning, and life in general. Currently such an analysis is largely absent from the policies and measures that are pursued to reform schools and improve classroom practice. Consistently, the focus of reform is on what adults and schools should do to improve student achievement, while students are treated as passive subjects who can easily be molded to conform to our expectations. To devise a policy that will enable successes achieved in a particular program, classroom, or school to be replicated elsewhere, we must be equipped with an understanding of the process through which identities are shaped and formed within schools. There is also a need for further research on peer groups and their role in influencing the academic orientation of students. Much of what I know about the plight of African American males comes from my personal experience growing up as a Black male and raising two sons. I have an intuitive sense that the way we are socialized to enact our masculinity, especially during adolescence, is a major piece of the problem. Researchers such as Geneva Smitherman and others have argued that Black children, and males in particular, often behave in ways that are perceived as hostile and insubordinate by adults.[85] Others suggest that males generally, and Black males especially, have particularly fragile egos and are susceptible to treating even minor slights and transgressions as an affront to their dignity and sense of self-respect.[86] Such interpretations resonate with my own experience, but it is still not clear how such knowledge can be used to intervene effectively on behalf of African American males.

As a young man, I recall that I often felt a form of anger and hostility that I could not attribute to a particular incident or cause. As a teacher, I have observed similar forms of hostility among Black male students, and for the past three years, I witnessed my elder son exhibit the same kinds of attitudes and behavior. Undoubtedly some of this can be explained as a coping strategy: Black males learn at an early age that by presenting a tough exterior, it is easier to avoid threats or attacks.[87] It may also be true, and this is clearly speculation, that the various ways in which Black males are targeted and singled out for harsh treatment (at school or on the streets by hostile peers or by the police) elicit postures of aggression and ferocity toward the world.

Given the range and extent of the hardships that beset this segment of the population, there is no doubt that there are some legitimate reasons for young Black males to be angry. Yet it is also clear that this thinly veiled rage and readiness for conflict can be self-defeating and harmful to their well-being. One of the consequences of this hostility and anger may be that such attitudes and behaviors have a negative effect on their academic performance. Adults, especially women, may be less willing to assist a young male who appears angry or aggressive. A colleague of mine has argued that what some refer to as the "fourth-grade syndrome"—the tendency for the academic performance of Black males to take a decisive downward turn at the age of nine or ten—may be explained by the fact that this is the age when Black boys start to look like young men.[88] Ron Ferguson has found in his research in Shaker Heights, Ohio, that Black students were more likely than White students to cite "toughness" as a trait they admired in others.[89] If these researchers are correct and if the toughness admired by Black males evokes feelings of fear among some of their teachers, it is not surprising that trouble in school would be common. Gaining a clearer understanding of this phenomenon may be one important part of the process needed for altering academic trends among Black males.

Still, it would be a mistake to conclude that until we find ways to change the attitudes and behaviors of Black males, nothing can be done to improve their academic performance. There is no doubt that if schools were to become more nurturing and supportive, students would be more likely to perceive schools as a source of help and opportunity rather than an inhospitable place that one should seek to escape and actively avoid. Changing the culture and structure of schools such that African American male students come to regard them as sources of support for their aspirations and identities will undoubtedly be the most important step that can be taken to make high levels of academic achievement the norm rather than the exception.

3

And What Will Become of Children Like Miguel Fernández?/ Y Qué Pasará Con Jóvenes Como Miguel Fernández?

Education, Immigration, and the Future of Latinos in the United States

It is a common cliché to say that the youth are our future, but if this is the case for Latinos in the United States, then we have good reason to be worried. Latinos have the highest dropout rates and the lowest college attendance rates (Garcia 2001). On most measures of academic performance, we are overrepresented in the negative categories (for example, enrollment in special education and remedial programs and the number of students who are suspended or expelled) and underrepresented in the positive categories (honors and Advanced Placement courses, gifted and talented programs) (Meier and Stewart 1991). In higher education, we are not at the bottom of the achievement hierarchy, but since the advent of high-stakes testing in several states across the country, more and more Latino students are leaving high school without diplomas and are unable to matriculate in college (Haney 2003).

Miguel Fernández is one such student. Miguel is from the South Bronx, a community once described by a presidential candidate as a "hell hole" and by yet another as the poorest census tract in the United States (Kozol 1995). Despite these negative characterizations of his community, for Miguel the South Bronx is home. He doesn't think much about the fact that his neighborhood has some of the highest rates for asthma, teen pregnancy, or juvenile homicide in the nation or, for that matter, the highest unemployment rates in the city (Gonzalez 2004). The litter on the streets, the deteriorated and dilapidated buildings, or the long walk he must take to the subway to get to and from school doesn't bother him either. For Miguel, the South Bronx is where his *abuelita*, his *familia*, his many, many *primos* all live, as does his *novia* Sonja and Wilson, his best friend. In fact, Miguel has a sense of pride about being from the Bronx, and he'll be the first to tell you that it is home to Jennifer Lopez, the world-famous New York Yankees, and a long list of notable Latinos.

Although I was born in Manhattan and raised in Brooklyn, I have a connection to the South Bronx too. Unlike Miguel, my thoughts of the South Bronx aren't so pleasant. When I think of the South Bronx, the image that comes most quickly to my mind is one of violence and danger. I remember when the South Bronx was burning in the 1970s as a result of fires set by arsonists working for absentee landlords who would rather burn down beat-up old buildings and collect insurance than improve them for the people who lived there (Wallace and Wallace 1998; Wunsch 2001). My grandmother lived in the Mitchell Houses on Willis Avenue and 138th Street for over twenty years. The projects are still there, but they are no longer regarded as such a rough or dangerous place to live as they once were. The South Bronx is in the midst of a revival now (Jonnes 1986; Wunsch 2001), and gentrification has brought with it a change in residents. Of course, as property values rise and old buildings are torn down, those who cannot afford to pay market rate rents—people like Miguel's family—will be pushed out.

When I used to visit my grandmother as a boy, we were not allowed to go outside to play on the swings or monkey bars. My father told us that dangerous hoodlums controlled the play areas, and perverts lurked in the stairways and alleys. My cousin, who also lived in the South Bronx, served as a proof that my father's dire warnings were no joke. He was murdered at the age of fourteen, stabbed to death because he made the mistake of refusing to give up his hard-earned leather jacket to a couple of young thieves. There used to be a community center named after him off Gunhill Road, but that too has become a victim of gentrification and has since been torn down.

Times have changed since the bad old days in the 1960s and 1970s, and the gentrification that prompted the makeover of Manhattan in the 1990s has finally hit even this neighborhood. Many of the worst projects and many run-down tenements have been torn down and replaced by single-family homes. The changes are striking, but despite the obvious improvement, they are somewhat disturbing. For someone like me who has been away from the South Bronx for many years, it's easy to get a strange and eerie feeling when walking through the neighborhood. As you observe all of the new construction and the new homes that have been built, you get a clear sense that the neighborhood is being improved for people who do not live there yet, and while there are many sites from the past that are familiar, there is also a lot that is new and strange and that seems out of place. The elevated train still runs along Jerome Avenue, and many of the *bodegas* and White Castles I once frequented are still on Fordham Road. But things look different to me. The neighborhood is still home to some of the poorest people in New York City (Wunsch 2001; Jonnes and Jonnes 2002) and still has a reputation for crime, violence, drug dealing, and gangs. But the Bronx, like the rest of New York City, is changing as property values rise and the middle class moves back to reclaim once-blighted areas.

This kind of change means that for Miguel, his family, and thousands of other recent immigrants, the South Bronx may be a temporary home. Interestingly, Miguel is not unaware of the changes being brought about by gentrification and what it may mean in the long term for his family, but he doesn't feel threatened by it either. He and his family regard the South Bronx as a temporary stop on their journey to progress—a place that served its purpose when they first moved in but not a place to become attached to. His family didn't pick the South Bronx out of a catalogue when they arrived from the Dominican Republic. They moved there because housing was cheap and his mother's cousin was able to help them find a place to live not far from her. They are well aware of the problems in the neighborhood, so for them, the greatest sign of upward mobility would be to leave the South Bronx for good.

When she arrived, Miguel's mother was unmarried and raising six children on her own. She knew she would need family sup-port to get by in this strange new country, so she moved to the South Bronx without a second thought, despite the warnings about danger that she received from others. Like most other immigrants, she came full of hopes and dreams, with high expectations, and a firm belief that life in America would be better—better because that's what everyone had told her about America since she was a child, and better because it would allow her and her children to escape the unhappiness and hardships they knew in the Dominican Republic. She didn't dwell on the fact that when she left, she was leaving behind a whole network of extended *familia* and commu-nity. All she thought about was what she was trading it in for: the possibility of eventual prosperity in the United States of America. For her, the South Bronx was merely a starting point on the way to that better life. Eventually she hoped that she and her children would find a home with a yard in the suburbs of New Jersey or Long Island. But for now, they, like thousands of immigrants before them (Tobier 1998), would find a way to make it in America by starting in the South Bronx. With faith and determination, they could view the hardships they encountered as temporary obstacles—bumps in the road that one day they could look back on, just like life in their hard lives in the Dominican Republic, as another part of what they had overcome.

This is the Faustian bargain that many immigrants embrace. They give up a world they know for one that is completely for-eign based on the belief that they can find a way to make the new country work for them (Portes and Rumbaut 2001). They are overwhelmingly risk takers, brave enough to settle in a strange land where they do not speak the language or know the customs, because they hold on to the tenuous belief that with hard work, good fortune will eventually come their way. Latino immigrants and their children are people of the future. They are a people whose gaze is so firmly affixed on the promise of a better life that it becomes possible for them to endure a host of hardships and inconveniences that might set others back completely. They are a people who manage to hang on to their optimism even in miserable ghettoes like the South Bronx.

Miguel was only eleven when his family arrived from the Dominican Republic. When he arrived, he spoke no English, and he often felt afraid and intimidated at school. On the playground, other Latino kids who barely spoke English themselves teased him because he spoke only Spanish. For years, he felt intimidated when riding the subway with bigger kids from other parts of the city. They were mean and aggressive. They pushed to get a seat, they used foul language, and they knew how to scare a person with little more than a stare. Those days of being scared are over now, and Miguel isn't afraid or intimidated anymore. He's not a big kid, but he knows how to carry himself, and he knows how to stare back and give the look that lets others know he's not a punk. Because he's no longer afraid, Miguel is now at ease in the South Bronx. The many obstacles he has confronted and overcome have made him stronger and have not dampened his optimism about the future in the slightest.

Miguel attends Walton High School, a school that gained notoriety during the 2003–04 academic year because of severe overcrowding. I worked with the school during that academic year and was amazed to learn that it had an enrollment of forty-two hundred even though it was built to accommodate no more than two thousand.[1] The school was in the news on more than one occasion that year because of rising concerns about school violence. In response,

Mayor Michael Bloomberg placed Walton on his list of unsafe schools and promised to do whatever it would take to make it safe again, even if it took placing a police officer in every classroom. As a result of the mayor's posturing, students at Walton were required to wait in long lines each morning, sometimes in subzero temperatures, to pass through metal detectors before entering the school building. Once inside, I was often struck by the irony that while the officials were fastidious in their security screening, they paid little attention to whether students were actually attending class.

Despite less-than-ideal conditions at his school, Miguel is a diligent and dedicated student. He appreciates the importance of getting a good education to achieve his dreams, so he studies hard and strives to do his best. However, as the eldest of six children, Miguel also works thirty hours a week at a local fast food restaurant to help support his family. He works after school, sometimes until 10:00 P.M., and every weekend for eight to ten hours a day, but he never complains. He knows that his mother needs the money to pay the bills, and he likes the fact that he's able to buy clothes he likes to wear with what's left over.

Miguel is well liked by his teachers. They appreciate his positive attitude, honesty, hard work, and the respect he shows to them. These traits, along with the excellent grades he earns, have distinguished him from his peers. On more than one occasion, he has been singled out by the principal as a positive example—a person other students should strive to emulate. He receives ample helpings of praise and encouragement from his teachers, who tell him with great confidence that if he keeps up the good work, his future will be bright. However, his guidance counselor knows better. After his second attempt, Miguel was still not able to pass the English portion of the New York State Regents exam. Though he's lived in this country eight years and attended schools in New York City, his command of English remains weak, and without a Regents diploma, Miguel will not be able to attend a public college. To complicate things even further, Miguel is also an undocumented immigrant.

The combination of his testing troubles and legal complications has caused him to reevaluate his goals.

Instead of college, Miguel plans to stay on at the fast food restaurant. His manager has praised him for his reliability and work ethic, and promised that he would recommend him for an assistant manager's position in six months if he hangs on. This would mean he would be entitled to health benefits and a salary close to thirty thousand dollars a year. For Miguel, the possibility of a stable job and a position of authority is a reward so alluring that he decides it makes far more sense to hang in there rather than work at night school to pass the Regents exam.

In my work with schools, I have met many students like Miguel.[2] Though not all are as studious, as focused, or as disciplined, there's no shortage of promise and potential among the students I meet. This is especially true for those who have recently migrated from the Caribbean and Latin America. In cities like New York, Boston, Oakland, Los Angeles, and Newark, the Latino students I meet, especially those who are recent immigrants, are often ambitious and respectful toward adults. They are also full of hope about the future. Like their parents, they have the drive, the work ethic, and the persistence to take advantage of opportunities that come their way, and unlike so many other urban youth, they have the will to find a way to improve the circumstances they find themselves in.

Of course, it is risky to generalize or to overstate the importance of will and work ethic. As the experiences of young people like Miguel show us, drive and optimism can sometimes take you only so far. When you live in a community like the South Bronx, sometimes circumstances beyond your control—the school you attend, the neighborhood you live in, whether any jobs are available—are far more powerful in determining how far you'll go or where you'll end up. Attitude and drive certainly count too, and the research literature suggests that many immigrant students are willing to work hard and make sacrifices, particularly when compared to U.S.-born youth (Suarez-Orozco and Suarez-Orozco 2001).

As part of a study on high schools in Boston (Noguera 2004a), I conducted an interview with a Honduran honors student from English High School. During the course of our conversation, I asked her about the source of her motivation to succeed in school. With a sense of clear resolve and a wisdom that seemed extraordinary for a person her age, she informed me:

> If I don't do well in school, my mother told me she will send me back to Honduras to wash clothes. That's what she did there, and I know for sure that I don't want to do that. You can hardly live there on the money you make from washing clothes. That's why we had to leave Honduras. People are barely surviving over there. So I try to do my best in school. If I can get into college and become a nurse or something, I'm going to be able to help my family and myself. I definitely don't want to end up washing no clothes.

Of course, not all of the Latino students I meet are so full of drive, determination, or clarity about their goals. Some are angry and sullen, less optimistic about the future, less focused about the purpose of their education, and less inclined to believe in the elusive American dream. These are usually the second- and third-generation Latino students: the ones whose ties to home—Mexico, El Salvador, the Dominican Republic—are more remote. Unlike their immigrant counterparts, these are children of the present—children who are so consumed with surviving, with getting by, with learning how to make it from day to day that they make no plans for the future and often have trouble contemplating life past eighteen. They are also the ones who speak broken Spanish, if they speak it at all, and who identify as Latino, Chicano, Hispanic, or simply claim ties to the clique in their 'hood.

The research literature on the socialization of Latino students has identified this disturbing trend, one that results in the transformation of hopeful Latino immigrant youth into angry and frustrated Hispanic Americans (Portes and Rumbaut 2001; Zentella 2002). In a reversal of past patterns, assimilation no longer serves as the pathway into mainstream American culture and middle-class status for many Latinos, as it once did for European immigrants. Instead, the evidence suggests that the socialization associated with acculturation and assimilation is sometimes harmful to the academic achievement and performance of Latino students (Suarez-Orozco and Suarez-Orozco 2001).[3]

Interestingly, the research also suggests a similar pattern with respect to health and well-being. It turns out that recent Latino immigrants are less likely to smoke; contract heart disease, diabetes, or cancer; or have out-of-wedlock births (Hayes-Bautista 2001). Berkeley anthropologist John Ogbu tried to explain the difference between Latinos, whom he categorized as "caste-like," nonvoluntary minorities, and earlier European immigrants, who were drawn to the United States voluntarily. According to Ogbu, because the nonvoluntary minorities were incorporated through coercion— conquest, colonization, or slavery (Ogbu 1987)—they were more likely to develop oppositional attitudes toward assimilation and, by extension, toward school. Although Ogbu's theory has been widely embraced by scholars of immigration (Noguera 2004b), try as he might, his framework never really worked for Latinos. There is simply too much diversity among Latinos; while some might be categorized as nonvoluntary immigrants (for example, Chicanos, Puerto Ricans, and possibly Panamanians), others (especially those from Central and South America) clearly came to the United States voluntarily—at least if fleeing war, repression, or hunger can be considered a voluntary move.

Once they arrive in the United States, new forces take over in shaping social identities, and Ogbu paid little attention to how variations in social context influence patterns of social adaptation. A Mexican arriving in Los Angeles or a Dominican arriving in Washington Heights in New York can function in a monolithic culture for quite some time. However, for Latinos who settle in a community that is more diverse, new forms of affiliation may emerge, and the significance attached to national identities may melt away, particularly among the youth. For a young person like Miguel, identifying as a Dominican becomes less important when your friends are not just from the Dominican Republic but also from Mexico, Puerto Rico, and Central America. Hybrid identities forged through cultural fusion happen naturally. Perceptions of self invariably become even more complicated when you look Black, at least by U.S. definitions, speak English with an Ebonics accent, and listen to music that is a mix of hip-hop, merengue, reggaeton, house, and rock. Even as the steady arrival of new Latino immigrants gradually begins to change the face and the character of American culture, our presence here also transforms who we are and, more important, who we are becoming.

The patterns evident in education mirror other disturbing trends for Latinos in the United States. Latinos in the United States constitute the youngest, fastest-growing, yet poorest subgroup of American society (Smith 2002). We stand out from other groups because in several states, we are both more likely to be employed and more likely to be poor (Clark 1998). This is because more often than not, Latinos are trapped in the lowest-paying jobs. We are the laborers, the busboys, maids, nannies, gardeners, mechanics, and waiters. We specialize in doing the dirty work—the work U.S.-born Americans reject. We remove the asbestos from buildings, we handle the toxic waste, and we take care of the sick and the aged. In cities across America, we wait patiently on street corners for contractors seeking cheap labor, and we take the subways and buses early in the morning to arrive on time to watch the children of those who earn salaries exponentially greater than our own (Hondagneu-Sotelo 2001).

We are the backbone of the U.S. economy, and we are despised because of it. Instead of gratitude and appreciation for all we do, we are subjected to resentment and scorn and, increasingly, overt hostility and violence. We are accused of taking American jobs, of making neighborhoods unsafe, of causing the quality of life in affluent areas to deteriorate, and spreading communicable diseases (Cornelius 2002). Although American society is historically a nation of immigrants, and although increasingly the U.S. economy is dependent on the labor of Latino immigrants in particular, we are treated as a burden, as unwanted parasites, and problems that must be tolerated or, if possible, removed. Education should serve as our ladder out of poverty. Just as it has for other groups in the past, education should be the source of opportunity and the pathway to a better life. Unfortunately, more often than not, the schools that serve Latinos are not unlike Miguel's Walton High School. Such schools have failed to serve as the vehicle through which our collective dreams and aspirations can be fulfilled. Too many Latino students attend schools that are overcrowded, underfunded, and woefully inadequate in terms of the quality of education they provide (Garcia 2001). More often than not, Latino students are trapped in the worst schools, and more than other ethnic groups, they are likely to attend schools that are segregated on the basis of race and class (Orfield and Eaton 1996). For all of these reasons, Latinos have thus far had limited success in using education as a vehicle to fulfill collective dreams and aspirations.

Of course, our hardships are relative. Compared to those we leave behind in our countries of origin, many of us are far better off. That is why we are able to send money home, to support those who are still struggling and barely surviving. And that is why so many more continue to come. The United States is the land of opportunity, and although there are always sacrifices and costs associated with leaving, for those who risk the journey, there are also often rewards. Our home countries know this too, and increasingly, the governments of Latin America regard us—Latino immigrants in the United States—as a prized resource. The remittances we send home are a stable source of foreign exchange, worth more than oil exported from Mexico, the bananas shipped out of

Central America, or the tourists who visit Puerto Rico and the Dominican Republic (Suarez-Orozco and Qin-Hilliard 2004).

Immigration is a complicated issue, one that does not lend itself to simplistic, dichotomous analysis. In 1996 I participated in a debate over Proposition 187, the first of several wedge issue measures used by conservatives in California to mobilize their base (White voters) against a vulnerable scapegoat, namely us. I was asked to debate an economist from the University of California at Davis about the merits and fairness of the proposed law, which, if passed, would deny undocumented immigrants, or aliens as they preferred to describe us, access to public services such as health care and education. In response to his assertion that the law was not racist but merely a rational response to the fact that immigrants were displacing Americans in the labor market and taking unfair advantage of public services, I pointed out that even if the law was approved by the voters, it would not succeed in curtailing illegal immigration. I suggested that the reason so many immigrants were making the dangerous trip across the border was not in pursuit of education, health care, or other social services but because of the tremendous imbalance in wealth between the United States and Latin America. Certainly it was not the attraction of California's public schools, widely regarded as some of the most inequitable in the nation (Oakes 2002). Rather, immigration is driven by the need to escape poverty and suffering, by the hope that success will make it possible to send money home, and by the often unrealistic belief that by leaving, it will be possible to obtain a small piece of the American dream that has been so creatively marketed to the rest of the world.

Speaking in front of liberal and idealistic undergraduates at the University of California at Berkeley, it was easy to win the debate against a conservative economist, but I knew even then that we would lose the larger battle. Not only was Proposition 187 approved by over two-thirds of California voters, it set the stage for a string of other grassroots initiatives aimed at rolling back gains in civil rights that had been made in previous years. The end to race-based affirmative action policies in higher education, the end to bilingual education under the so-called English-only initiative, the get-tough, three-strikes law, and the juvenile crime initiative that lowered the age at which adolescents could be pros-ecuted as adults all had harmful effects on the status and well-being of Latinos in California.[4] In yet another public debate, this time against Ward Connelly, the African American member of the University of California Board of Regents who has spearheaded the effort to eliminate affirmative action in higher education, I pointed out that if we had to rely on a referendum to bring an end to slavery, forced servitude might still be around. As noted legal philosopher John Rawls has pointed out, democracy in the form of majority rule can be the worst form of tyranny (Rawls 1999). Ironically, but perhaps not surprisingly, this series of race-based ini-tiatives was adopted at just the time that California was becoming a non-White-majority state (Clark 1998), and while the new laws have not deterred the growth of the Latino population in Califor-nia or throughout the rest of the nation, they have made the path to progress much more difficult.

I saw the effects of crushed dreams and vanquished aspirations vividly during a visit to New Bedford, Massachusetts, an old indus-trial town on the southeastern coast of Massachusetts. I was asked to assist the city in a planning effort designed to reduce the num-ber of juvenile homicides. Over the past year, there had been a startling rise in the number of adolescents who had been murdered in the city, startling because none of the community leaders could understand why. They had a hunch that maybe the high unem-ployment in New Bedford might be a factor (the official estimate was 25 percent at the time of my visit in May 2004), or similarly that the high school dropout rate, which officially was listed at 12 percent but unofficially was presumed to be closer to 50 percent, might also have something to do with the problem. But these were factors and not causes, and with no way to link these factors to a strategy that might aid the city in preventing more violence, there was no reason to believe that the carnage would be abated on its own. I was asked to conduct a workshop on youth violence prevention with community leaders to help them gain a better understanding of how various factors were linked to this social phenomenon and, they hoped, to begin to devise a strategy for prevention. With all of the key stakeholders from the city present—school district officials, members of the city council, churches, nonprofits, the police and probation departments, and others—an interesting discussion unfolded about the lack of opportunity for youth in New Bedford. Although no concrete solutions emerged from the meeting, we did leave with an agreement to do two things: (1) include young people in the process of formulating solutions to the problem and (2) keep this group of stakeholders meeting and planning together until there were clear signs that progress was being made.

All of us, myself included, left the meeting hopeful that we had started a process that would have a meaningful impact on this pressing problem. Later that evening, I was asked to speak at a community cultural celebration in a large high school auditorium. I generally don't like being asked to give lectures between performances by local hip-hop artists and Cape Verdean folk dancers, but I obliged with the understanding that I would keep my remarks very short. I knew before I spoke that juvenile homicide was a big issue for the community, because earlier in the day, I had passed by homes where large banners were hung carrying pictures of young people who had recently been killed. Many of the banners and posters carried a simple message, imploring all who would take time to read to "STOP THE VIOLENCE." Aware of how salient the issue was, I tried to speak directly to the problem of youth violence that the community was grappling with, but to do so with a sense of hope about what might be done to address the problem. After my remarks, I was surprised to learn that the emcee wanted to take questions from the floor rather than return immediately to the entertainment. I was even more surprised to see a young Latino male raise his hand immediately without any prodding from the emcee or myself.

Speaking loudly and with no apparent apprehension, the young man declared, "Maybe if there was something for young people to do in New Bedford, we wouldn't be killing each other. It's boring like hell here. No jobs, no colleges, no places to hang out. I think people are killing each other because they're bored to death." It was an interesting thesis, one that hadn't been considered by the group of community leaders earlier in the day and a comment that left me at a loss for a response. Having teenagers of my own who often complain of boredom, I responded by saying that boredom generally emanates from within and that the only remedy for boredom was imagination. I encouraged him not to sit back and wait for someone to offer him a job but to be creative and think of ways that he might create opportunities on his own. Even as I made my suggestion, I knew that if pressed, I might not be able to come up with any creative examples for self-employment, but I still felt that the young man needed a sense of empowerment instead of seeing himself as a helpless victim.

As it turned out, I didn't have to offer any concrete suggestions. The next hand up was that of a middle-aged Mexican immigrant. Although he struggled with English, he readily shared his own story with the audience, directing his remarks to the young man who had spoken first. He explained that he had moved to New Bedford from Mexico five years ago. When he arrived, he knew no one, so he took a job cleaning fish and earning minimum wage. After two years of dirty, backbreaking work, he said he was able to save enough to open a restaurant. He said he now owns two Mexican restaurants in New Bedford and employs twenty people. He then said that the only thing keeping him from doing more to help the community were the young hoodlums who have robbed him several times and recently forced one of his employees to be hospitalized as a result of a beating during a holdup. Sounding not unlike a conservative Republican, the man challenged the young people present not to be afraid of hard work, but to get off their butts and to stop waiting for someone to give them something.

Again I was taken aback by the direction our conversation had taken. Stumbling to figure out what I might say in response to the immigrant's challenge, I was bailed out by a young Latina who was so eager to speak that she jumped out of her seat and demanded the microphone. Speaking with passion and defiance, she blurted out, "I'm sick of hearing people in New Bedford put young people down. I ain't going to clean no fish for minimum wage, and I shouldn't have to. I went to school right here at this high school [the meeting actually took place at New Bedford High School], and I had plans to go to college after graduation. But I got into problems with the law, and now I have a criminal record. A lot of businesses won't hire you if you have a record. I'm willing to work hard, but I need to get a chance."

Her remarks and the passion with which they were delivered prompted several people in the audience to applaud, and now it was up to me to make sense of the exchange. How would I acknowledge the truths inherent in both perspectives: the hopefulness of the new immigrant, the frustration and resignation of the second generation? Given the late hour and the poor setup for an extended conversation, I punted. I encouraged the young woman and the young man who'd spoken earlier to get together with the restaurateur after the meeting to find out about a job and to learn how he managed to do what he had accomplished.

Reflecting on my visit to New Bedford, I was compelled to recognize that the clash in perspectives symbolized a larger division among Latinos: the newly arrived full of hope and expectation, and the fully settled, who understand the reality of dead-end jobs and racial discrimination. Both perspectives are rooted in truth and an understanding of reality, but neither perspective provides a clear way for Latinos as a group to move forward. Can hard work alone help students like Miguel, whose educational opportunities are limited by the kind of school he attends and whose chances for mobility through employment are constrained by the labor market in his community? Will anger and resentment for those who object to their second-class status help? How do we harness the energy and drive of the newcomers but at the same time refuse to accept a permanent place on the lower rungs of American society?

These are the big questions that face Latinos in the United States, but who's providing the answers? We are at a moment of incredible possibility. Latinos are being courted by both major parties as swing voters with the ability to decide state and even national elections. Media moguls, baseball team owners, and fast food restaurants now recognize us as an important consumer market, but to recognize that we can vote and spend money says very little about our potential to alter our status in this country. If we are to move from the lower tiers of society and not become a permanent underclass, and if our communities, schools, and social institutions are to provide the support and nurturing that our children so desperately need, we will need a new direction and a new strategy. Until that time, we will remain like Miguel: industrious and hopeful but trapped in circumstances that stifle our ambitions and dreams. We can and we must do more, and those who have more, our small but growing middle class, have an even greater responsibility to act.

4

How Listening to Students
Can Help Schools to Improve

There is now a broad consensus that our nation's high schools are not adequately serving the needs of students or society and that they are in need of substantial reform. Indicators that many of the nation's high schools are in trouble have been evident for some time, including astonishingly high dropout rates, especially in urban areas (Harvard Civil Rights Project, 2000); widespread concerns about violence and safety (Newman, Fox, Harding, Mehta, & Roth, 2004); pervasive low achievement on most standardized tests, but especially in science and math (Manpower Research Development Corporation, 2002); and a wide and seemingly intractable achievement gap that corresponds disturbingly and predictably to the race and class background of students (Jencks & Phillips, 1998).

These indicators are not new, and in fact, several reports and blue ribbon studies have pointed to such trends to support calls for systemic policy intervention and sweeping reform (Cohen, 2001). Yet despite the growing chorus of calls for change, until recently, the organization and structure of most high schools remained largely unchanged and trapped in traditions that had long outlived their purpose. Several critical studies pointed out that many schools were characterized by pervasive anti-intellectualism, boredom, and alienation among students (Steinberg, 1996); organizational fragmentation combined with a lack of mission and focus (Siskin, 1993); and a curriculum that offered a smorgasbord of courses but little of the intellectual depth and rigor needed to develop substantive knowledge and higher-order thinking skills. Furthermore, the large, comprehensive high school, serving a thousand or more students, has been accused of breeding mediocrity and intellectual laziness, disorder and delinquency, and an inability to provide a personalized learning environment for students (Newman, 1992). According to these critics, the modern high school was inspired by a factory model of education, in which hierarchical management structures, a burdensome and inchoate bureaucratic division of labor, and a control system governed by bells and arcane rules and procedures prevented the typical high school from serving as the enlightened center of learning that was needed (Wasley et al., 2000).

In the past few years, the problems facing high schools have gradually risen to the top of the education policy agenda. Driven by policy reports from the U.S. Department of Education (Lugg, 2005) and critiques issued by various private foundations and think tanks, a new willingness to address the problems confronting high schools has emerged. With this new-found sense of urgency has come a wave of reform with a focus on the organization, size, and structure of schools. With substantial commitments to this effort, the drive to create smaller high schools is sweeping the country.

There is some research to justify the push to create smaller schools and learning communities (Cotton, 1996; Page, 2002), yet there is also good reason to be skeptical about the recent rush to embrace this reform. Smaller schools have been found to offer greater safety, a stronger sense of community, and improved relationships between adults and students (Clinchy, 2000). Yet the clearest evidence that making schools smaller may not be enough to make them better can be seen from the fact that there are already many small schools in existence, and not all of these are examples of academic excellence (Stiefel, Berne, Iatarola, & Fruchter, 2000). Moreover, the much maligned large, comprehensive high school has advantages that most smaller schools will never be able to replicate, such as an ability to offer more elective courses, particularly in foreign language and Advanced Placement; greater resources to serve the needs of populations with special needs such as special education and English as a Second Language students; and a wider offering of extracurricular activities, including sports, music, and theater.

To the advocates of small schools, arguments such as these are easily ignored. Proponents of small schools assert that gains in safety and student learning will more than compensate for any losses that might occur as a result of this change. Despite the fact that the theory of change guiding this reform is highly suspect (that small schools and better student-teacher relations will lead to higher student achievement), the effort to make high schools smaller has taken off and is leading to substantial changes in high schools throughout the United States.

In an effort to contribute to the ongoing discourse over what should be done to improve the nation's high schools, this chapter examines how schools are confronting the challenges that beset them not by seeking answers from a well-regarded think tank or policy center but from students themselves. Drawing on research carried out at ten high schools (both small and large) in Boston through a project known as Pathways to Student Success, the ideas and suggestions students have for how schools can be improved are presented and analyzed. Although no groundbreaking or previously unheard solutions are offered, the reader may be surprised to learn that students do put forward practical, commonsense insights into why certain practices are ineffective and why others should be considered. The goal of presenting these ideas here is to show that solutions to some of the problems confronting our nation's high schools may not be as out of reach as they have seemed, particularly if we have the wisdom and courage to listen to those who bear the brunt of our schools' failures.

Findings: Learning from Student Experiences

The major themes that emerged from the 132 students across ten high schools are presented here briefly as a basis for the suggestions at the end of this chapter on how listening to students can be incorporated into school decision making. The themes that emerged from the students that have implications for improving high schools are (1) relationships between students and teachers (and other adults), (2) the impact of high-stakes testing, (3) discipline and order, and (4) student motivation and goals for the future. In the following sections, I analyze these themes and the lessons they provide to school reformers and practitioners.

Relationships Between Students and Teachers, and Other Adults

Perhaps the most significant, yet hardly surprising, difference that emerged between students attending small and large schools pertained to the issue of anonymity. Whereas only 26 percent of the students at the large schools stated that their teachers knew them well and another 34 percent stated that there was an adult at school they could turn to if they needed assistance with a personal problem, at the small schools the percentages were 92 percent and 84 percent, respectively. Opportunity for greater personalization in the learning experience of students has long been seen as one of the primary advantages of small schools (Wasley et al., 2000). Consistently, students have cited personalization as one of the major advantages of small schools.

Although personalization is a key factor, relatively few students had ideas for how relations between students and teachers could be improved, though several did suggest that if their teachers got to know them better, it might help. However, at all of the schools in the study, students had a clear sense of how teaching could be improved. When asked to describe the characteristics of a school where they would be excited to learn, some of the following suggestions were offered:

- Teachers should be organized and well prepared for the classes they teach.

- Teachers should be patient and ask students if they understand the material. If they don't get the material being taught, the teacher should explain the material in a different way.

- Teachers should have a strong command of the material and a passion for the subjects they teach so that they can get students to be excited about learning it.

- Teachers should show respect to students in the same way that they expect to receive respect.

- Teachers should be firm and not allow students to get away with preventing other students from learning.

These examples of student voice speak volumes to school reformers and practitioners in clear, seemingly simple ways. They provide evidence of the work to be done to help improve schools and the crucial role of students in creating an environment to foster sound relationships as a basis for their achievement.

High-Stakes Testing

At the time of our study, the tenth graders were preparing for the state examination (Massachusetts Comprehensive Assessment of Skills, MCAS). This was the first time that the exam would be used to determine which students would graduate, and all of the schools in the study were under considerable pressure to prepare their students. Among teachers and administrators, some regarded the state examination as a fair benchmark of student learning; others were adamantly opposed to the idea of using a single test to determine whether a student should be allowed to graduate. Interestingly, the attitudes of educators toward the test did not correspond in predictable ways to student performance on the test.

Such sentiments about the MCAS were common among the students. Students in all of the schools overwhelmingly stated that they want their schools to prepare them to be successful in life, not merely to pass a test. They objected to the notion that a single test should be used to determine if they could graduate, and several argued that not enough had been done throughout their years in school to ensure that they could pass the exam. When asked to describe one aspect of their school that they did not like, 36 percent of the students cited the emphasis on test preparation, even though the question made no reference to the test. Yet many students acknowledged that certain aspects of the test were beneficial. For example, several students expressed the view that the state examination makes schools more accountable, because it forces them to make sure that their students are learning.

Discipline and Safety

Concerns related to discipline, safety, and order are increasingly common in public schools (Newman et al., 2004). This was also the case for many of the students in our study, but we found noticeable differences in the perceptions of students at small versus large schools. Students in the small schools were far more likely to report that they felt safe (94 percent), as compared to students at the large schools (46 percent). They were also more likely to respond affirmatively to the question, "If I feel threatened by someone at school, there is an adult I can turn to for support" (92 percent, compared to 38 percent).

Advocates of small schools are likely to seize on these findings to support their claim that small schools are safer and offer a better educational experience to students. Safety and order are essential conditions in any learning environment, and it appears that the small schools in the Pathways study succeeded in creating a more personalized environment that contributed to students' perceptions that their schools were safe. Yet although the small schools in the study were generally perceived as safe, students at some of the schools did experience discipline problems in the classroom that were not unlike those encountered in the large schools.

One of the questions students were asked to address is what they thought it would take to make schools safe and orderly. Following is a list of some of their recommendations:

- Make students who cut class attend Saturday school.

- Require students who disrupt a class to do extra academic work.

- Have administrators observe teachers in classes with frequent disruptions so that they can help them to become better at managing students.

- For kids who fight, find out why they fought before they are punished. If suspension is not necessary, make the students who fought work together to do something to improve the school.

- Ask parents and adults from the community to volunteer to serve as hall monitors.

- Require students who are rude and disrespectful toward teachers to write apologies and do community service, including helping to clean the school.

- Create a panel of students to serve as a jury for students who break school rules. Provide them with training on how to hear discipline cases and advise them on the kinds of punishments that can be assigned.

These ideas might not seem particularly innovative or out of the ordinary, but the fact that they come from students themselves is important. Students recognize the need for safety and order in school, and many of the students interviewed wanted to see disruptive students dealt with in a firm manner. However, it is rare for a school to seek student input on matters related to discipline even though their buy-in is essential if schools are to succeed in creating an environment conducive to learning.

Student Goals and Motivation

Research on student motivation has shown that students who possess clear goals about the future and concrete plans for how they will achieve those goals are more likely to be successful in school (Mickelson, 1990). Students who understand that the hard work they engage in while in school will lead to greater opportunities after graduation are more likely to complete their assignments, even if they regard them as little more than busywork, and more likely to tolerate teachers even if they view them as boring. Students in the Pathways study who had clear plans about the future were also more likely to attend school regularly, more likely to become involved in extracurricular activities, and less likely to get into trouble at school. Unlike their peers whose ideas about the future were ambiguous, the students with clear goals understood that good grades were important, and they were more likely to work hard to attain them.

Yet clarity about future goals and the motivation to attain them rarely comes from a student by himself or herself, particularly when that student comes from a family where there is history of attending college (Steinberg, 1996). We found that the students who had the clearest goals were most likely to cite an adult—a teacher, a counselor, a parent, or a relative—as the source of guidance related to future aspirations. Once again, the students attending the smaller schools in the study, which typically provided more counseling and advising for students, had a clear advantage over the students in the large schools. Although high achievers at all ten schools were generally more likely to articulate clear plans after graduation, even middle and low achievers attending the small schools were likely to have developed a goal that they intended to pursue after graduation.

How Listening to Students Can Be Incorporated into School Decision Making

Students may not have all the answers to the problems plaguing urban high schools. This does not mean that they may not have ideas on improving schools on a wide variety of issues, including school safety and student achievement. Students may very well have ideas and insights that adults are not privy to and could prove to be very helpful to improving schools if adults were willing to listen.

I saw this personally while carrying out research in five high schools in the Bay Area of Northern California. I was trying to understand the causes of racial violence within schools that had been plagued by racial conflict, some of which posed a serious threat to the safety of adults and students. Prior to my involvement, all five schools responded to the problem in the same way: calling police after a violent incident. Despite the severity of the problem—several students had been seriously injured at two of the schools—the police publicly stated that they could not solve the problem because it was an issue that extended well beyond law enforcement, and they pointed out that it was neither cost-effective nor plausible to deploy dozens of officers to the campuses. Unlike the police, school administrators could not dodge their responsibility to address the problem. At a loss for how to proceed, the schools turned to me for assistance in figuring out what could be done. I suggested that we start by convening small groups of students from the conflicting ethnic groups to get their sense of what was causing the violence and to solicit their ideas for how to respond to the problem. These meetings turned out to be extraordinarily effective. Not only did the students have insights into what was causing the conflicts (most incidents started outside school) that the adults were oblivious to, but they also had practical ideas for addressing the problem, which included involving students in the implementation of solutions (Noguera & Bliss, 2001).

Given how poorly so many past reforms in our nation's high schools have fared with respect to delivering lasting improvements in student achievement and overall quality, it certainly could not hurt to solicit student perspectives on what they believe might be done to make their schools better from a variety of perspectives. Of course, a willingness to listen to students implies that adults actually want to hear what students think, that they respect them enough to listen and learn, and that they will be open to suggestions they might make. In schools where decisions about reform are made in a top-down manner by administrators with little, if any, input from teachers, it is highly unlikely that such an approach to listening to students would ever be embraced. Insecure leaders are likely to regard soliciting student opinions as an admission that they do not know what they are doing, and being exposed in that way would undoubtedly be more than they could bear.

Others who are more courageous and secure in their positions might recognize that one of the benefits of engaging students in discussions about the state of their schools is to get them to take their own education more seriously. Too many schools operate under the false assumption that the quality and character of schools can be shaped by adults alone. In so doing, they assume that the actions and behavior of students are less important than those of adults, even though the decisions and choices students make about how hard to study, or whether to take their education seriously, have considerable bearing on the quality of their educational experiences. A substantial body of research has shown that student norms and attitudes have influence on the quality and character of schools (Steinberg, 1995; Valenzuela, 1999). The question is, How can schools influence student attitudes and behavior so that they reinforce the importance of learning and positive social development rather than undermining it?

One part of the answer to this question is finding ways to include students, on a regular basis, in discussions about their school experiences. Such discussions can occur in formal settings, such as on established committees or decision-making bodies, and they can occur informally at the classroom level. The main thing is that they occur regularly and that adults respond respectfully to what they hear. Students can tell if adults are genuinely interested in their opinions, and if they discern that no one is listening when they share their perspectives, they will quickly lose interest in a meaningless exercise. To be effective, it is also important that these conversations not be limited to students who have been handpicked by adults because they occupy a leadership role within the school. It is important not to omit those who might know more because they are better connected to their peers, even if it means including students who are not models of ideal student conduct.

This project illustrates that students may sometimes have criticisms of the way things are done at their schools, and when invited to share their thoughts, they may also say things that may offend some adults. This should not deter educators from listening to what students have to say. The best schools in this project used the ideas they received through the research to find ways to make their schools better. These schools show us that success is achieved not by their ability to implement a particular reform, but rather to the quality control they exercised in implementing the reform. Soliciting and responding to the perspectives of students can serve as another means of ensuring quality control, and unlike so many other reform strategies, this one cost nothing. Given the importance of what is at stake in our efforts to reform the nation's high schools, it may be time to try an approach that allows us to learn about how to improve schools without expending additional resources, yet engaging those with so much at stake: students.

Part II

The Search for Equity

5

Latino Youth

Immigration, Education, and the Future

Immigrant Latino youth are here to stay. Many have U.S. citizenship and, in contrast to their parents, who may continue to hold onto dreams of returning to their homelands one day, the United States is their home. Whether or not they are embraced as legitimate U.S. citizens, they will stay because for many, the United States is the only land they know. Therefore, understanding how Latino immigrant youth acculturate and adjust to life in the United States and how they are being affected by the political backlash against immigrants must be seen as an important issue for educators today.

Unlike their parents, immigrant Latino youth often find themselves caught between two worlds, neither fully American nor fully part of their parents' country. Many arrive without having experienced formal education in their countries of origin or literacy in their native Spanish language. Consequently, there is growing evidence that immigrant youth are susceptible to a variety of hardships and pressures that many adults, including their parents, do not fully understand. These challenges and hardships encountered by Latino immigrant youth living in a society where hostility toward their presence is growing must be of concern to educators, service providers, and policymakers. Through constructing culturally relevant educational policies, programs, and pedagogy, we can assist Latino immigrant youth to avoid the pitfalls that often beset this vulnerable population. Helping educators to find ways to assist immigrant youth in making the adjustment to this strange and often hostile land is a central preoccupation of my reflections here.

Push and Pull Factors and Their Impact on Latino Families

Certainly not all immigrants who come to the United States do so voluntarily. While it is hard to distinguish between the factors that pull immigrants to this country and the forces that push them to leave their countries of origin, there is no doubt that many who come to the United States do so because they believe they have no alternative. The great imbalance in wealth between the nations to the north and those to the south of the Rio Grande, created to a large degree by a history of U.S. domination in the region—colonization and military intervention, unequal trade and unabashed exploitation of people and resources, and the subsequent legacy of widespread poverty and underdevelopment—has created conditions that make immigration from the South to the North virtually inevitable.

Many Latino immigrants leave to escape the ravages of political violence, to flee the suffering caused by unrelenting poverty, or in the wake of a natural disaster that has destroyed jobs, communities, and possibilities for advancement. There are also those who come as political refugees to escape war, persecution, and torture. Even though they must overcome tremendous obstacles—barbed-wire fences, Coast Guard vessels, or armed militias—they still come because, for many, immigration offers the only possibility of hope.

Immigration forces those who emigrate to make tough choices that often take a toll on families. The development of transnational families, separated by borders and thousands of miles, often results in children experiencing disruptions in school attendance (Ada, 1998). To ensure that relationships are maintained, it is not uncommon for Latino parents to send a child to Mexico or the Dominican Republic for six weeks during the middle of the school year. For educators who are concerned with academic progress, such a choice might seem nonsensical and even negligent, but to a family that is coping with the hardships caused by separation, such choices may be the only way to maintain the bonds of family.

Migrant workers often return to Mexico for several weeks during the winter because there is no work available during the nongrowing season. Although they consistently return to their jobs, it is often the case that their children lose their seats in classrooms because of adjustments that are made during their absence. Those interested in supporting Latino immigrant youth and their families must at the minimum demonstrate a capacity to understand the difficult choices transnational families face (Olsen, 2000). Finding ways to help reduce the strains caused by separation, while minimizing the losses in learning associated with extended absences, is an important pedagogical consideration for schools that serve large populations of Latino immigrant youth.

A growing number of schools have adopted strategies to support Latino youth who miss extended amounts of time because they are part of transnational families. For example, one elementary school in Los Angeles modified the academic year so that students could take off four weeks at the end of December and beginning of January. An additional two weeks of school is added to the end of the year to make sure that students do not miss instruction. A school in Texas located near the Mexican border established a cooperative relationship with a Mexican school across the border to enable its students to enroll in school while they are in Mexico. Finally, several schools in Miami and New York that serve immigrant youth whose parents reside in the Caribbean have hired social workers who are familiar with students' living arrangements and who can provide additional social and emotional support to youth in need (Ada, 1988). Such measures do not eliminate the difficulties experienced by immigrant youth who are separated from their families, but they do help to lessen the hardships they endure and demonstrate that the school is not interested in punishing students for a situation they cannot control. Employing staff with language and cultural skills to work effectively with immigrant youth and their families is also of vital importance if trust and respect between home and school are to be established (Valdez, 1999).

Of course, there are limitations to what schools can do to mitigate the effects of long absences. Obviously students would be better off if they had minimal disruptions in learning and they could remain in the same school, assuming of course that it is a good school, for longer periods of time. However, children cannot control whether parents or grandparents will be granted visas, and their parents often cannot control the factors that compel them to move or make sacrifices to keep their families together. Families that are forced to make tough choices between stability for their children and the need to retain contact with relatives who live elsewhere should receive support, advice, and understanding from educators rather than belittlement and condemnation. Working closely with families and assuring them that the educators who serve their children have their best interest at heart is essential for creating a partnership that can lead to creative solutions to complex transnational arrangements.

Race, Assimilation, and Social Mobility

Like many other immigrants today, earlier generations of European immigrants encountered hardships: the Irish experienced decades of unrelenting discrimination and harassment (Roediger, 1991); Italians were crowded into ghettos and tenements of northeastern cities and forced to take the worst jobs (Gans, 1967); Jews were denied access to middle-class professions and seats at prestigious universities by admissions quotas (Brodkin, 1999). Nonetheless, each of these groups gradually improved their social conditions and experienced the social mobility promised by the American dream.

Of course, social mobility came with a price and some sacrifice. Many European immigrants found it necessary to abandon their native languages, to give up their cultures, and in many cases to "Anglocize" their names (Jiobu, 1988; Fass, 1989). During the nineteenth century, many German immigrants sought to have their language taught in public schools and in communities where they constituted the majority. These German immigrants managed to do so for years, long before *Lau* v. *Nichols* required the federal government to support bilingual education (Katznelson and Weir, 1994). Ultimately, however, most groups relinquished many of their ethnic and cultural distinctions to embrace a more socially acceptable American identity. With assimilation came social mobility, and over time, early stigmas and hardships were gradually overcome as differences were erased (Glazer and Moynihan, 1963). Over generations, Irish, Italians, Jews, and others who were once perceived as ethnically inferior were gradually accepted as full-fledged White Americans (Roediger, 1991; Brodkin, 1999).

In sharp contrast, the situation is very different for Latino immigrants and their children. Although Latinos represent the fastest-growing segment of the U.S. population and are now the largest minority group, it is not clear that the future will be as bright and promising for them as it was for European immigrants of the past. Globalization and deindustrialization have contributed to a worsening of circumstances for low-skilled Latino immigrants. Ironically, Latinos now constitute the ethnic group least likely to be unemployed but most likely to be impoverished (Smith, 2002). This is so because Latinos are concentrated in the lowest-paying jobs, and many lack the skills and education needed to seek better-paying alternatives (Smith, 2002). Unlike European immigrants whose offspring reaped the rewards of their sacrifices, Latinos are not experiencing a similar degree of success (Portes and Rumbaut, 2002).

The pervasiveness of racialized inequalities, particularly within education, at least partially ensures that Latino youth are more likely than any other ethnic group to be enrolled in schools that are segregated not only by race but by class as well (Orfield and Easton, 1996). In cities such as New York, Los Angeles, and Chicago, where they comprise the majority of the school-age population, Latinos are disproportionately consigned to schools that are overcrowded (Oakes 2002; Noguera, 2003, 2004). For years, Latino youth have had the highest high school dropout rates and lowest rates for college attendance (Garcia, 2001). In general, they are overrepresented in most categories of crisis and failure (for example, suspensions and expulsions, special education placements), while underrepresented in those of success (honors and gifted and talented classes) (Meier, Stewart, and England, 1990). Outside school, Latino youth find themselves more likely to be arrested and incarcerated than White youth, more likely to have children as teenagers, and less likely to graduate from college (Hayes-Bautista, 2002). In short, if the old adage that youth are our future is correct, then current trends suggest that the Latino population in the United States is in deep trouble.

Latino Immigrant Students and Prospects for the Future

Yet in my work with schools, I often hear from administrators who speak favorably of the conduct of Latino immigrant students. Although not all are described as studious, most are characterized as well behaved, courteous, and deferential toward adults. These comments are often made with a comparative reference to African Americans and second-generation Latinos, who are more likely to be described as undisciplined, unmotivated, and at risk (Ogbu, 1988). While passive, compliant behavior may win praise, the positive statements made about Latino immigrant students usually do not mean that they are succeeding academically. In fact, Latino immigrant students are overrepresented in remedial classes and special education, are more likely to be placed in English as a Second Language classes that effectively bar them from courses that prepare students for college, and are more likely to drop out of school.

Like their parents, many Latino immigrant youth have the drive, the work ethic, and the persistence to take advantage of opportunities that come their way. And unlike so many urban youth, they have the will and determination to find a way to improve the circumstances in which they live (Kao and Tienda, 1998). Of course, it is risky to generalize or to overstate the importance of will and work ethic. For Latino youth who live in communities where economic and social opportunities are limited and who have no ability to control basic circumstances that shape the opportunities available to them—the schools they attend, the neighborhoods where they live, or whether any jobs are available—will and determination may not suffice. In fact, research on the socialization of Latino immigrant youth shows that in a reversal of past patterns, assimilation no longer serves as the pathway into mainstream American culture and middle-class status as it once did for European immigrants (Portes and Rumbaut, 2002). Instead, the evidence suggests that the socialization associated with acculturation and assimilation often results in a lowering of the academic achievement and performance of Latino students (Suarez-Orozco and Suarez-Orozco, 2001).[1]

Berkeley anthropologist John Ogbu (1988) tried to explain the difference between Latinos, whom he categorized as "caste-like," nonvoluntary minorities, and earlier European immigrants, who were drawn to the United States voluntarily. According to Ogbu, since nonvoluntary minorities were incorporated through coercion (conquest, colonization, or slavery), they were more likely to develop oppositional attitudes toward assimilation and, by extension, toward schooling. Although Ogbu's work has been widely embraced by many scholars in the field of immigration, his framework has failed to accurately reflect the Latino condition. There is simply too much diversity among Latinos; while some might be categorized as nonvoluntary immigrants (for example, Chicanos, Puerto Ricans, and possibly Panamanians), others (especially those from Central and South America) clearly came to the United States voluntarily—if fleeing war, repression, or hunger can be considered a voluntary move.

Once they arrive in the United States, new social, political, and economic forces take over in shaping social identities. Ogbu's work does not address how variations in social context could influence patterns of social adaptation. A Mexican arriving in Los Angeles or a Dominican arriving in Washington Heights in

New York can use Spanish in most of their day-to-day interactions and function in a monolithic culture for quite some time. However, for Latinos who settle in a community that is more diverse, new forms of identity and affiliation may emerge, and the significance attached to national identities may melt away, particularly among Latino immigrant youth. Hybrid identities forged through interaction and familiarity with others develop naturally. Theoretically at least, education should serve as a means out of poverty. As it has for other groups in the past, education should be the source of opportunity and a pathway to a better life. Unfortunately, more often than not, schools that serve Latino immigrant youth fail to become vehicles through which their dreams and aspirations can be fulfilled. Too many are trapped in the worst schools and are treated as though their inability to speak fluent English is a sign of cognitive and cultural deficit. What will it take for education to serve immigrant Latino youth and become a genuine resource for Latino immigrants? How can educators help students make the transition to a new society less painful, particularly for those who lack family support? How can we make sure that the needs of Latino immigrant students are not ignored because their parents lack the power and voice to make their needs heard? The answers to these questions could potentially help reshape educational opportunities for Latino immigrant youth in this country.

We are at a moment of incredible possibility. Latinos are a growing political force with the ability to decide local and even national elections. They are recognized by business owners and media moguls as an important consumer market. However, votes and dollars alone won't guarantee gains in the status of Latinos in this country. Unless we develop a new educational direction and a new political strategy, our communities, schools, and social institutions will find it hard to provide the support and nurturing that our youth so desperately need. Until that time, many Latino youth will remain like so many immigrant youth of the past, hard-working and hopeful but caught in circumstances that erode their dreams of a better future.

Preventing and Producing Violence

A Critical Analysis of Responses
to School Violence

The problem of violence in schools, which is part of the overall problem of violence in society, has become one of the most pressing educational issues in the United States. In many school districts, concerns about violence have even surpassed academic achievement, traditionally the most persistent theme on the nation's education agenda, as the highest priority for reform and intervention.[1] Public clamorings over the need to do something about violence in schools have brought the issues to a critical juncture; if schools fail to respond decisively to this problem, popular support for public education may be endangered. The escalation of violent incidents and the apparent inadequacy of traditional methods to curtail them have led to a search for new strategies to ensure the safety and security of children and teachers in schools.[2]

Accepting the fact that it may not be realistic to expect that schools can ever be completely immune from the violence that plagues our society, this chapter seeks to understand why schools may be especially vulnerable to its occurrence. Current efforts aimed at combating violence may in fact have the opposite effect, particularly given the weakening of the moral authority schools once enjoyed. Following a brief critique of popular strategies used to curtail school violence, my analysis begins by examining how the early preoccupation with social control influenced the design and operation of schools at the turn of the twentieth century. From there I consider the practical and symbolic effects of the ways in which discipline is typically exercised in school and analyze the race and class dynamics among the population that is most frequently targeted for punishment. Finally, I discuss alternative approaches to addressing the problem of violence and strategies that have been shown to be effective alternative routes to school safety.

The search for solutions to the problem of violence in schools has generated a package of remedies that closely resembles those used to combat the threat of violence and crime in U.S. society.[3] Some of the more popular measures include the installation of metal detectors at school entrances to prevent students from bringing weapons onto school grounds;[4] the enactment of zero-tolerance policies that guarantee the automatic removal of students (through either suspension, expulsion, or transfer) who perpetrate acts of violence;[5] and the use of police officers and security guards to patrol and monitor student behavior while school is in session. Accompanying such measures has been an increased tendency of school officials to treat violent incidents (and sometimes nonviolent incidents) involving students as criminal offenses to be handled by law enforcement officials and the courts rather than by school personnel. In their desire to demonstrate toughness and reassure the public that they are in control, school officials have become increasingly rigid and inflexible when meting out punishment to students who violate school rules, even when the infractions are not of a violent nature.[6]

Less punitive approaches have been introduced to reduce the incidence of violence in schools. Conflict resolution programs have been promoted as a way of teaching children to settle disputes non-violently. Mentoring programs that pair students with adult role models have also become popular in school districts across the country, serving to reduce violence by providing students perceived to be at risk with the attention, support, and counseling of an adult.[7] Teachers have been encouraged to design curricula that teach children how to avoid violent situations and explore in their classrooms the ethical and moral issues related to violent behavior.[8] Finally, a variety of counseling programs have been implemented by establishing partnerships between schools and social service agencies to provide direct services to students.[9]

Although some of these less coercive strategies for reducing violence have proven relatively successful in particular schools, the overall momentum of school policy has been biased in favor of the get-tough approach. In response to the pervasive fear of violence among parents and students, politicians and school officials have pledged to quell the tide of violence by converting schools into prison-like, lockdown facilities and by increasing the penalties incurred for committing violent acts. Yet despite the tough talk, the track record of these methods provides little reason for optimism. For example, in California, law enforcement officials have attempted to reduce gang activity by increasing penalties against juvenile felons who are alleged to be gang members. While such measures have contributed to a sharp increase in the prison population, there has been no reduction in gang activity in targeted communities. In addition, gang activity has become such a major problem in state prisons that gang affiliation must now be considered when convicts are being assigned to correctional facilities.[10]

Relatively speaking, young people may in fact be far safer in school than they are in their neighborhoods or, for that matter, at the park, the roller rink, or even in their homes.[11] For many parents and students, the fact that schools are "relatively safe" provides little solace, given the expectation that schools should be absolutely safe and therefore should not be judged by the same standard that we use to gauge security in other public, or even private, places. Schools are controlled institutions, public spaces where individuals sacrifice a measure of individual liberty in exchange for the opportunity to learn. In such a setting, the threat of violence constitutes more than just a threat to personal safety. It represents a fundamental violation of the social contract between school and community, an abrogation that could easily hasten the collapse of popular support for public education.[12]

To address the problem of violence in schools effectively, I believe we must begin by asking ourselves why schools are vulnerable to the occurrence of violence. What is there about the structure and culture of schools that has, in recent times, increased the likelihood that acts of violence will be perpetrated within them? In the following pages, I demonstrate why I believe that many of the popular strategies for disciplining students and curtailing violence in schools are ineffective. I focus on urban schools, where violence tends to occur more frequently, because I believe that social and economic conditions in urban areas add considerably to the extent and degree of the problem.[13] I believe that it is in the context of fulfilling goals that have traditionally prioritized maintaining order and control over students, as opposed to creating humane environments for learning, that schools have become increasingly susceptible to violence. As an alternative approach, I argue that schools must seek ways to create more humane learning environments, both to counter escalating violence and to transform social relationships within schools, so that those who spend their time there feel less alienated, threatened, and repressed. As I argue for this alternative, I will also consider the ways in which issues related to the symbolic representation of violence, and the fight against it, influence interaction between adults and children within school, paying particular attention to the ways in which race and class inscribe these images.

This chapter draws heavily from my years of working directly with schools in the San Francisco Bay Area in a variety of capacities: as a classroom teacher, a school board member, a university-based researcher, and a consultant. My experience leads me to avoid offering specific remedies or to claim that I know what should be done to address a problem that is so complex and multidimensional. Still, it is my hope that suggesting new ways of approaching the question, "What is to be done about violence in schools?" will enable educators to open the door to new strategies, based on a different conceptual framework, for dealing with the issues of violence in schools throughout this country.

Waging the Fight Against Violence

The phrase *fighting violence* might seem to be an oxymoron. For those concerned with finding ways to prevent or reduce the occurrence of violence, "fighting" might seem to be the wrong way to describe or to engage in the effort to address the problem. The choice of terms, however, is not accidental. The prevailing wisdom among policymakers and school officials is that you must counter violence with force;[14] that schools can be made safe by converting them into prison-like facilities;[15] and that the best way to curtail violence is to identify, apprehend, and exclude students who have the potential for committing acts of violence from the rest of the population.[16] Therefore, it is important to examine the ideological stance held toward violence when critiquing the methods used to fight it, for without doing so, it is not possible to understand why failed strategies remain popular.[17]

In the campaign against school violence, school officials often point to statistics on the number of weapons confiscated and to the number of students suspended, expelled, or arrested for violent reasons as evidence that something is being done about the problem. The number of reported violent incidents is also used to demonstrate that while valiant efforts are being made to reduce violence, the problem persists, and therefore the fight against violence must continue.[18] The compilation of such data plays an important role in rationalizing the expenditure of resources on security-related services, resource allocations that often result in the elimination of other educational programs and services. Such data are also instrumental in framing the public discourse about violence, for as long as it can be shown that quantifiable results are obtained as a result of the fight against violence, combatants in the war can be assured of continued financial backing.[19]

For parents and students who live with the reality of violence and who must contend with the threat of physical harm on a daily basis, data on how many students have been arrested, expelled, or suspended do little allay their fears. When engaging in once ordinary activities such as walking to school or playing in a park evokes such extreme anxiety so as to no longer seem feasible, news that arrests or suspensions have increased provides little reassurance.

In my capacity as a consultant to a local school district, I attended a meeting with school officials from an urban school district on the West Coast at which we were discussing the problems of violence and what could be done about it. While reviewing data from the past year on the incidence of violence, I remarked sardonically, "Here's some good news: homicides are down 100 percent from last year." To my amazement, an administrator replied, "Yes, the news isn't all bad. Some of our efforts are beginning to pay off." What surprised me about the comment was his apparent belief that since there had been no murders at any of the schools in the district at the midpoint of the school year, compared to the two that occurred the previous academic year, there was reason for hope and optimism. I found it hard to believe that district administrators, who generally have little contact with the school sites on a regular basis, could accept a statistical analysis as evidence that the schools had in fact become safer. And even if data on crime show that homicides are down, statistics don't tell us whether teachers or students feel any safer.

Within the context of the fight against violence, symbols such as crime statistics take on great significance, although they have little bearing on how people actually feel about the occurrence of violence.[20] Pressed to demonstrate to the public that the efforts to reduce violence are effective, school districts often pursue one of two strategies: either they present statistics quantifying the results of their efforts, or they go to great lengths to suppress information altogether, hoping that the community will perceive no news as good news.[21] Metal detectors, barbed-wire fences, armed guards and police, and principals wielding baseball bats as they patrol the halls are all symbols of tough action. And while most students whom I have spoken to during my visits to schools realize that a student who wants to bring a weapon to school can get it into a building without being discovered by a metal detector or that it is highly unlikely that any principal will hit a student with a baseball bat, the symbols persist, masking the truth that those responsible for school safety really don't have a clue about what to do to stem the tide of violence. Rather than looking to solve this problem through increased security or improved technology, school administrators must begin to ask more fundamental questions as to why these institutions have become so vulnerable to violence. I believe that this is a question that must be answered in the context of the purpose and social function that schools have historically performed.

The School as an Agent of Control

To understand why violence has become rampant and how a climate of fear and intimidation gradually has come to be the norm in so many schools, we must examine the influences that guided the creation of public schools and consider the social role that they were expected to perform. When public schools were being developed in northeastern cities during the latter part of the nineteenth century, their architecture, organization, and operation were profoundly influenced by the prevailing conception of the asylum.[22] Whether designed to house the indigent, the insane, the sick, or the criminally inclined, the asylum served as the model for human service institutions. Although the client base of the early prisons, almshouses, and mental hospitals differed, those who developed and administered the institutions shared a common preoccupation with the need to control those held in custody. The custodial function of the institution should not be confused with rehabilitating or reforming, for in postcolonial America, crime, immorality, hunger, and poverty were seen as inherent in society.

David Rothman writes, "Although eighteenth century Americans were apprehensive about deviant behavior and adopted elaborate procedures to control it, they did not interpret its presence as symptomatic of a basic flaw in community structure, nor did they expect to eliminate it."[23]

The role of the asylum was to regiment, control, and discipline the social outcasts who were housed there. These goals were accomplished through the routinization of every aspect of life within the asylum and through the imposition of a set of rules and regulations that were rigidly enforced.[24] A military tone characterized life in the asylum, as did a focus on sanitation, orderliness, punctuality, and discipline. Since the goal of these institutions was not to prepare inmates for readmission to society but to eliminate the threat they posed to the safety and security of others, the managers of the institutions believed that this could best be done by enforcing rigid discipline and removing undesirables indefinitely from the community.

Although schools were designed with a different purpose in mind, Rothman suggests that it was logical for the architects of the first large urban schools to turn to the asylum as the blueprint for these new public institutions.[25] Although schools were never envisioned as asylums for the young, the need for them to serve as a vehicle for controlling the minds and bodies of youth helped to convince many of those who questioned the merits of public education that it was an enterprise worth supporting.[26] Educational historian Lawrence Cremin identifies three dominant and distinct agendas among the many influences shaping public education at the turn of the century that were pursued in relation to the public schools: (1) the need to provide a custodial function for children and thereby serve as an agent of social control, (2) the need to acculturate and "Americanize" large numbers of children born of European immigrants, and (3) the need to prepare future workers for U.S. industry. At times overlapping and at other times conflicting, these goals influenced the content of school curriculum, the training of teachers, and, most important for the purposes of this analysis, the way in which the schools were to be administered.

Although the goals of education tended to be framed in humanitarian terms, the need to regiment and control the behavior of students dominated the educational mission.[27] Motivated by a combination of benevolence related to child welfare and fear related to the perceived threat of crime and delinquency, schools were called on to assume greater responsibility for the rearing of urban children. Defining the problem in moral terms, reformers felt that "raised amid intemperance, indulgence, and neglect, the lower-class urban child began life predisposed to criminality and unprepared for honest work."[28] Educators such as G. Stanley Hall called for the creation of pedocentric schools, which were to be designed so that the school's central mission was to treat the social and psychological needs of children.[29] Although child rearing was seen primarily as a responsibility of the family, social reformers feared that many poor and immigrant parents were unfit to raise the children properly.[30] For this reason, public schools were seen as the vehicle through which poor children could be "saved." Regarding this point, Cremin writes:

> It was to the school that progressives turned as the institution that would at least complement familial education and in many instances correct it and compensate for its shortcomings. The school would rear the children of ordinary families, it would provide refuge for the children of exploitative families, and it would acculturate the children of immigrant families. . . . The school would deliver whatever services children needed to develop into healthy, happy and well-instructed citizens—it would provide meals for the poorly fed, medical treatment for the unhealthy, and guidance for the emotionally disturbed. . . . Though progressives asserted the primacy of familial education, they advanced the pre-eminence of schooling.[31]

To carry out these social goals, reformers promoted efficiency in the organization and operation of schools. These reformers borrowed from the writings of Frederick Taylor, an engineer who championed the idea that industrial production could be made more efficient through the application of scientific techniques. His ideas were later applied to the operation of schools, where the need for order and efficiency was perceived as essential to effective management.[32] Supported enthusiastically by many of the business-men who served on local school boards, efficiency and routiniza-tion of school activities were emphasized as ways to bring order to city schools. The combination of rising enrollments—due to the steady influx of immigrant and rural children into eastern cities—and inadequate facilities had gradually transformed urban schools into little more than warehouses for children. Cremin's descrip-tion of schools during this period is helpful in understanding why a focus on order might have seemed warranted:

> Whatever the high-minded philosophies that justi-fied them, the schools of the 1890s were a depress-ing study in contrasts. . . . In the cities, problems of skyrocketing enrollments were compounded by a host of other issues . . . school buildings were badly lighted, poorly heated, unsanitary, and bursting at the seams; young immigrants from a dozen different coun-tries swelled the tide of newly arriving farm children. Superintendents spoke hopefully of reducing class size to sixty per teacher, but the hope was most often a pious one. Little wonder that a desire for efficiency reigned supreme.[33]

Acting under mandates issued by authorities who were almost always far removed from the direct management of schools, super-intendents and principals employed a variety of strategies to con-trol the students and teachers in their charge. In many school districts, teachers and students were tested on a regular basis "to see if the program was being followed."[34] Specific instructions were given to teachers that addressed not only curriculum and methods, but ways to discipline and control the bodies of their students as well.[35] Describing this preoccupation with disciplining the body, one observer wrote that students were required to comply with the following set of instructions when asked to recite memorized text: "Stand on the line, perfectly motionless, bodies erect, knees and feet together, the tips of shoes touching the edge of a board in the floor."[36]

To ensure that students were trained appropriately for the kinds of work they would perform after graduation, specialized high schools were created in several cities. Vocational high schools were set up to cater to lower-class immigrant youth, and academic high schools were established to prepare middle-class students for higher education and professional careers. At the vocational schools, the curriculum was designed to provide the skills and training needed to obtain industrial employment on graduation. In this respect, David Tyack's comment that "urban education in the nineteenth century did more to industrialize humanity than to humanize industry" is helpful in understanding how the relationship between education and the economy influenced the character of schools.[37] Although many of the newly created urban secondary schools sought to provide vocational training, what the expanding industrial sector primarily required was an ample supply of low-skilled, cheap labor. Schools helped to meet this demand by emphasizing citizenship training for the children of newly arrived immigrants and offering a curriculum that placed greater weight on punctuality and obedience than on the acquisition of technical skills.[38]

While students were sorted and educated differently to satisfy the needs of industry, educators still wanted them to undergo a common socialization process to prevent fragmentation and to ensure that "American" values would remain dominant and undiluted. Fearing that the arrival of this "illiterate, docile mass" would "dilute tremendously our national stock, and corrupt our civic life," educators were called on "to assimilate and amalgamate these peo-ple as part of our American race, and implant in their children, so far as can be done, the Anglo-Saxon conception of righteous-ness, law and order, and popular government."[39] An important part of the assimilation process included conforming to an assortment of rules governing student behavior and to values promoting the vir-tues of hard work, punctuality, and obedience.[40]

Although there is some evidence that schools were challenged in their attempts to fulfill their role as the keepers of children, in most cases it seems they succeeded in producing "docile bodies": students who could be "subjected, used, transformed, and improved."[41]

Discipline as an Exercise of Power

With concerns about order, efficiency, and control dominating the thinking that guided the early development of schools in the United States, we must ask ourselves how this legacy has influenced the current character of public schools. As the demographics of cit-ies began to change in the 1950s and 1960s with the arrival of new immigrants (for example, West Indians, Puerto Ricans, and other Latinos) and the migration of Blacks from the South,[42] and as social and economic conditions within urban areas began to deteriorate,[43] the character and condition of schools also began to change. How-ever, this shift did not produce immediate changes, for while the student population changed, in many cases the teachers remained the same, with most still relying on methods of control that had proven successful in the past.[44] Writing about the conditions of schools in what he described as "slum areas," James Conant spoke of the need to impose a harsher standard of discipline to ensure that discipline and order prevailed:

> Many educators would doubtless be shocked by the prac-
> tice of on-the-spot demotion of one full academic year,

with no questions asked, for all participants in fights. In one junior high school I know of, a very able principal found so intolerable a situation that he established that very rule. As a consequence, there are fewer fights in his school among boys, many of whom at one time or another have been in trouble with the police. The school must attempt to bring some kind of order to their chaotic lives. . . . This formal atmosphere appears to work. School spirit has developed. . . . Children must stay in school till they are sixteen or till graduation to prevent unemployed, out-of-school youth from roaming the streets.[45]

By the mid-1960s, however, the situation had changed. Students' insubordination and aggression toward teachers were becoming increasingly common, and violence within schools, especially among students, was widely seen as the norm.[46] Some educators made the connection between the difficulty schools were having in maintaining control over students to the political turmoil that accompanied the civil rights movement and the riots that took place in many cities across the country.[47] Describing the political dimension of this problem and advising teachers about how to respond to it, Allan Ornstein wrote: "Some Negro children have newly gained confidence, as expressed in the social revolution sweeping across the country. Some see themselves as leaders, and not helpless, inferior youngsters. This new pride is evidenced by their tendency to challenge authority. The teacher should expect, encourage and channel this energy toward constructive goals."[48]

With control and compliance increasingly difficult to obtain, many urban schools lowered their expectations with respect to student behavior.[49] The preoccupation with enforcing rules was gradually replaced with a desire to maintain average daily attendance, since this was the key funding formula for schools. As teachers have come to realize that they cannot elicit obedience through the "terror of degradation,"[50] concerns about safety have led more of them to think twice about how to reprimand a student, lest their attempt at chastisement be taken as a challenge for a physical confrontation, for which most are unprepared.[51]

Still, schools have not given up entirely on the goal of exercising control over students; although the task may be far more difficult now than it ever was, schools are still expected to maintain some form of order. Beyond being a threat to the personal safety of students and teachers, violence in schools challenges the authority and power of school officials. In carrying out their duties as caretakers of youth, school officials serve as both legal and symbolic representatives of state authority. With the power vested in their position, they are expected to control the behavior of those in their charge. When violence occurs with impunity, a loss of authority is exposed. Therefore, the issue of violence is seldom discussed in isolation from other control issues. More often, violence is equated with insubordination, student misconduct, and the general problem of maintaining order in school. The way the issues become melded together is indicative of how schools perceive their role in relation to the social control function that schools have historically performed in the United States.

The Disciplining Event

The exercise of discipline in schools takes on great importance because it serves as the primary means through which symbols of power and authority are perpetuated. In analyzing the symbolic issues associated with discipline and violence in schools, it is helpful to consider the work of Michel Foucault. Writing about the role of punishment meted out to criminal offenders in France during the nineteenth century, Foucault describes what he calls the "juridico-political" function of the act:

> The ceremony of punishment is an act of terror. . . . The
> practice of torture was not an economy of example . . . but

a policy of terror; to make everyone aware, through the body of the criminal, of the unrestrained presence of the sovereign. The public execution did not re-establish justice; it reactivated power. . . . Its ruthlessness, its spectacle, its physical violence, its unbalanced play of forces, its meticulous ceremonial, its entire apparatus were inscribed in the political functioning of the penal system.[52]

While the kinds of public executions and tortures carried out in France during the nineteenth century may seem far removed from the forms of discipline carried out in schools today, Foucault's focus on the relationship between the disciplining act and the "reactivation" of power is relevant to understanding the symbolic role of discipline. The disciplining event, whether it occurs in public or private, serves as one of the primary means through which school officials send a message to perpetrators of violence, and to the community generally, that the authority vested in them by the state is still secure. Particularly within the current political climate created by the fight against violence, the disciplining event provides an opportunity for school authorities to use those accused of committing acts of violence as an example to others.

From a symbolic standpoint, within the context of the school, the student expulsion hearing is perhaps the most important spectacle at which the meting out of punishment to those accused of violence can be used for larger political purposes. As a quasi-judicial ceremony, the formality of an expulsion hearing often contains all of the drama and suspense associated with a courtroom trial. Although the event itself is closed to the public, news of the decision rendered by the school board or hearing officers often travels quickly, particularly when the student is charged with committing an act of violence.

I had the opportunity to attend an expulsion hearing at an urban school district for which I was working as a consultant.

I describe what happened because I think it helps to illuminate important dynamics of power and knowledge embedded within the disciplining event. The accused in this case was charged with bringing a loaded gun to school. The education code in this particular state called for automatic expulsion hearings whenever students were apprehended for bringing weapons to school. When asked to explain why he had brought the weapon to school, the student informed the board members that his father and mother had recently separated, and that his father, who was distraught over the separation, mentioned that he was thinking of killing himself. He instructed his son to remove his handgun from the house so that he wouldn't harm himself or anyone else.

The boy informed the board that during the summer, his grandmother had attempted to commit suicide by slashing her wrists and that he and his father had to apply pressure to her bloodied arms in order to prevent her from bleeding to death while they waited for an ambulance. With vivid memories of that traumatic event in his head and fearing that his father might follow through on his threat to take his own life, the boy placed the gun in his backpack and took it with him to school. He explained that he later showed it to a friend at school because he wanted to talk to someone about what was going on, but that he had not shown the weapon to anyone else, nor had he brought the gun back to school after that day.

In questioning the student about his actions, one board member noted that the student possessed an exemplary academic record and that all of his teachers spoke highly of him, referring to him as "respectful, honest, hard working, etc." He was then asked whether in retrospect he would have handled the situation differently. The student explained that he still wasn't sure what he should have done, but thought that maybe he could have hidden the gun in the bushes near his house instead of bringing it with him to school. Upon hearing this, one of the board members proceeded to lecture the student and his father, who had accompanied him to the hearing, about the danger of guns. One board member commented that the student didn't seem to have learned a lesson from this serious error in judgment. Exasperated by their doubts, the student claimed he had learned a lesson and promised never to bring a weapon to school again. A board member then asked what punishment the school principal recommended and was told that the principal wanted to see the student expelled so that "we send a clear message that guns on campus will not be tolerated." After deliberating for several minutes, the board responded with a unanimous vote for expulsion.

As an observer of this event, I was struck by several aspects of what took place. First, all five board members judging this student, as well as the principal who presented the evidence against him, were White and middle class, while the student was Black and from a low-income family.[53] From the questions they asked and the lectures that they directed at the student and his father, it seemed evident that they were unable to identify with the student and the situation that he was in. While I felt uncomfortable hearing the student and his father divulge the problems they were having in their personal lives, there was no apparent consternation among board members over the imbalance of the situation, and no attempts were made to communicate that they could empathize with the anguish and pressure that either the student or his father must have been experiencing. After hearing one board member ask the student if he would have handled the situation differently in retrospect, I wanted to ask how she would have handled it, or if she or any of the others had ever experienced anything similar. The gulf in experience between the board members and the student seemed to be compounded by the obvious differences of race, class, and age. However, I sensed no indication that the board regarded this as a problem, nor did I sense any effort on their part to understand the student's actions from his point of view.

Second, despite evidence that this incident represented an aberration from this student's "normal" behavior in school, and despite the fact that no one at the school was actually threatened by the presence of the gun, the board members and principal seemed primarily concerned with using the case to communicate a message about guns in school. No effort was made to try to figure out an appropriate way of responding to this student's particular situation. In this respect, the hearing provided an occasion through which the district's power could be communicated. By ignoring the circumstances of the offense and focusing exclusively on the issue of the gun, the board could demonstrate its toughness and intolerance for those who threatened the security of others. While there was no evidence that the punishment of this individual student would have any influence on the behavior of others, his expulsion reinforced the institutional authority of the district leadership by serving as an example of their prerogative and power to punish. In a setting where most perpetrators of violence are not apprehended and where most efforts to ensure the safety of students and teachers are ineffective, the act of punishment becomes an important exercise for showing who has control.

Finally, the disciplining moment also reveals the way in which the adult professionals, and to a lesser extent the student and his father, were constrained by the "discipline" embedded in the roles each party occupies within the institution. To the extent that the board members and the principal have power or authority, it is derived from their relation to an institutional structure—a structure whose history is rooted in nineteenth-century preoccupations with social control. In their roles as prosecutor and judge, their sense of how to discipline this youngster is profoundly influenced by a body of knowledge of "discipline" that is rooted in the power relations that exist between the state and the school as a social institution. This power-knowledge limits the ability of the board and administrators to identify with the student on a human level, for to do so would open up the possibility that there might be other ways to understand his actions.[54] To recognize that there might be another way of viewing this behavior that goes beyond a focus on crime, violence, and misconduct might lead to a different type of intervention.

However, school board members and administrators typically see their job as protecting the institution and the staff, students, and teachers in their charge. The state provides explicit guidelines on how this is to be done, but there are also implicit guidelines pertaining to notions of how schools are supposed to operate and function and how students are supposed to behave. To explore alternative ways of responding to violent, or potentially violent, behavior would necessarily require a fundamental change in how the institution and the provision of educational services were conceptualized by those in authority, a prospect that at the disciplining moment often seems unimaginable.

Although a less sympathetic case could have been selected for analysis, I chose this one because I feel it demonstrates how the act of violation is in many ways irrelevant to the form of discipline that is employed. Beyond their real-life effects, violence and discipline take on a symbolic life of their own, symbols that play heavily on interactions within schools and that ultimately influence how schools and violence are perceived by others. In the pages ahead, I will pursue further how a preoccupation with control limits the ability of administrators to respond creatively to the crisis created by the increase in violence in schools.

Race, Class, and the Politics of Discipline

In many school districts across the country, considerable controversy has been generated over the disproportionate number of African American and, in some cases, Latino students who are subjected to various forms of school discipline.[55] In California, legislation was proposed to limit the ability of school districts to use suspensions and expulsions as a form of punishment, in response to the imbalance in the number of Black and Latino students subjected to these sorts of penalties.[56] Although the legislation was not approved by the state legislature, the fact that it was proposed indicates the depth of feeling in many Black communities that

Black children are being treated unfairly. In Cincinnati, Ohio, the disproportionate number of Black students who are suspended and expelled in public schools prompted a judge to call for teachers and administrators to be held accountable for "student behavior management" as part of a court order monitoring desegregation in the district's schools.[57]

Although there is evidence that schools that serve White middle-class students in the suburbs also have problems with violence, this is downplayed in the public media.[58] Just as the threat of violent crime in society is characterized largely as a problem created by Black perpetrators, violence in schools is also equated with Black, and in some cases Latino, students.[59] While the correlation between race and who gets arrested, suspended, or expelled in schools is so consistent that it is impossible to deny that a linkage exists, the issue tends to be avoided in public discussions due to the controversy and tensions surrounding racial issues in U.S. society. To avoid the charge of racism, many school officials argue that the connection between race and punishment disguises what is really more an issue of class than an issue of race, since most of those receiving discipline come from lower-class families.[60] While this may be true, the correlation between race and class is also high in many school districts, and so the three variables—race, class, and violence—tend to be associated.

The unwillingness to confront the implications of these kinds of correlations is replicated in the general refusal of most policymakers and school officials to place the problem of violence within the broader context of race and education. Not only is school punishment consistently correlated with race, it is also highly correlated with academic grouping and high school graduation rates. Those most likely to receive punishment in school are also more likely to have been placed in classes for Educationally Mentally Retarded or Trainable Mentally Retarded students.[61] The consistency of these trends is more than mere coincidence. Such patterns point to what some have described as a "second-generation discrimination effect":

"In every case where policy reflects positively on a student, black students are underrepresented. In every case where policy reflects negatively on a student, black students are overrepresented. . . . That a pattern similar to the one revealed here could occur without some discrimination is virtually impossible to believe."[62]

The Role of Teachers

While police officers, security guards, and administrators generally assume primary responsibility for managing and enforcing school discipline, in most cases teachers make the first referral in the discipline process, and therefore have tremendous influence in determining who receives discipline and why. In my work with urban schools, the most frequent concern I hear from teachers is that they have trouble disciplining and controlling their students. This has been especially true in schools at which the majority of students are Black and the majority of teachers are White. Having taught in urban public schools, I am familiar with what teachers are up against and recognize that some semblance of order and safety is essential if teaching and learning are to take place. However, whenever I conduct workshops in schools, I generally try to shift the focus of talk about discipline to discussions about what teachers know about their students. I do this because I have generally found that teachers who lack familiarity with their students are more likely to misunderstand and fear them.

Once I had the opportunity to conduct a workshop on student discipline for a multiracial group of teachers at an urban middle school located in an economically depressed community. Before addressing what I knew to be their primary concern—a recipe for controlling student behavior in the classroom—I wanted to impress on the teachers the importance of knowing the students with whom they worked. These teachers, like many others in urban school districts, did not live in the community where they worked and knew little about the neighborhood in which the school was located. From our discussions at the workshop, it was clear that most of the teachers also knew little about the lives of the children they taught, and most assumed that the majority of children came from deprived, dysfunctional, and impoverished families.

In an effort to increase the awareness of the group about the importance of knowing the community in which they worked, a community with which I was familiar, I presented them with a hypothetical situation: If you were invited to teach in a foreign country, what kind of information would you want to know before leaving? The teachers responded by generating a long list of what they felt was relevant information that would assist them in teaching in a land that they did not know. The list included information about politics, culture, the economy, history, and geography. After discussing why they felt this information was important, I asked how much of this information they knew about the community in which they worked.

Two of the teachers said that they didn't need to know this sort of information in order to teach effectively because the school was located within the United States, and therefore was part of familiar territory. Most of the others, however, recognized the inconsistency in this perspective, particularly after being primed by the previous discussion, and acknowledged that a lack of knowledge might pose a problem for them in their work with students.

I suggested that we visit some of the housing projects and neighborhoods where their students lived, the stores where families shopped, the health clinics, libraries, parks, and some of the noteworthy historic landmarks in the community. I pointed out that a brief tour of the community would provide them only limited useful information, but that it could be a start at becoming better acquainted with their students.

They agreed to go, and the following day we piled into my van for a four-hour tour. Interestingly, after the tour, nearly all of the teachers told me that they resented me for taking them on this excursion because it made them feel like tourists. "Didn't you see the people staring at us?" one teacher commented. "They were probably wondering why we were there." Only one teacher disagreed with the group's reaction and expressed appreciation for being exposed to the community in this way. As it turned out, this teacher had lived in this community when she was a child, and the trip had served as a reminder to her that most of the residents in the area were working-class home owners. The winos and crack addicts who were visible on certain street corners, and whom many other teachers believed were typical of a majority of the residents, actually constituted a small minority. However, the other teachers took up the position espoused by two of their colleagues earlier, insisting that they did not need to know the community in order to teach effectively. One asserted that "a good teacher can work with any child. I don't have to become an anthropologist to each." I responded by asking if it was possible to be an effective teacher if you did not know your students, but by this point, most of the teachers were unwilling to pursue this line of inquiry.

For me, this experience illustrated, in a profound way, the gulf in experience between teacher and student, which is typical in many urban schools. The pretense operating in many schools is that teachers should treat all students the same, although numerous studies on teacher expectations have shown that race, class, and gender have considerable influence over the assumptions, conscious and unconscious, that teachers hold about students.[63] Although multicultural education and student diversity have become popular topics of discussion among teachers, understanding how the politics of difference influences teacher-student interactions generally remains largely unexplored, except at the most superficial level.[64]

When teachers and administrators remain unfamiliar with the places and the ways in which their students live their lives outside the school walls, they often fill the knowledge void with stereotypes based on what they read or see in the media, or what they pick up indirectly from stories told to them by children. Many teachers, like others who live outside poor urban communities, tend to hold negative views toward these areas, views that are rooted in a fear of violence and in media representations of the people who reside in the inner city as less than civilized. This fear invariably influences the interaction between teachers and administrators and their students. In the eyes of these teachers and administrators, who are "foreigners" to the school's community, the students often seem to embody the traits and exhibit the behavior of the hoodlums and thugs they have heard about or seen from afar. Many of the teachers with whom I have worked in urban schools seem to fear the children whom they teach; more often than not, where the students are aware of it, they may attempt to use the teacher's fear to their advantage.

This is not to say that violence in schools is an imagined problem. I do believe, however, that it is a problem exacerbated by fear. A teacher who fears the student that she or he teaches is more likely to resort to some form of discipline when challenged, or to ignore the challenge in the hope that she or he will be left alone. Rather than handling a classroom disruption on their own, teachers are also more likely to request assistance from the central office.

My work with teachers and students at a number of urban schools has shown me that students often know when their teachers fear them. In many cases, I have seen students use a teacher's fear to assert their control over the classroom and, if possible, the entire school. I have visited schools where children openly gamble and play dice in the hallways, and where the presence of an adult is insufficient reason to put out a cigarette or a joint. When adults are frightened or intimidated, disorder prevails, and acts of crime and violence become the norm. Moreover, when fear is at the center of student-teacher interactions, teaching becomes almost impossible, and concerns about safety and control take precedence over concerns about teaching.

From speaking to students and teachers at such schools, I have found that they typically share a common characteristic: the adults don't really know who their students are. Their sense of what the children's lives are like outside school is either distorted by images of pathological and dysfunctional families or simply shrouded in ignorance. School personnel who hold such views may make little effort to increase parental participation in school because they can't see any benefits that might be gained through parents' involvement. School staff and faculty may also be reluctant to reach out to the community to establish partnerships with community-based organizations and churches that are interested in providing services to youth, because all they can see in the neighborhood are problems that are best kept out of the school. Fear and ignorance can serve as a barrier greater than any fence and can be more insulating than any security system.

In many schools, differences in age and life experience make it difficult for students and teachers to communicate and understand one another. When such differences are compounded by race and class differences, a huge gap can be created that can easily be filled by fear and suspicion. Anonymity and ignorance create shields that protect the identities of those who perpetrate acts of violence and crime. In such an atmosphere, adults and students may welcome armed guards, metal detectors, and barbed-wire fences because they can't envision another way to ensure their safety. Even if they come to find the prison-like conditions depressing and oppressive, they are likely to cling to such measures because chaos is worse, and no other alternative seems imaginable.

Humanizing the Environment: Alternative Approaches to Violence Prevention in Schools

In critiquing the approach to discipline that is most widely practiced in the United States today, I in no way want to belittle the fact that many teachers and students have been victims of violence and deserve the right to work at and attend safe schools. In many schools, violence is real, and the fear that it produces is understandable. Still, I am struck by the fact that even when I visit schools with a notorious reputation for the prevalence of violence, I can find at least one classroom where teachers are working effectively with their students and fear is not an obstacle to dialogue or even friendship. While other teachers in the school may be preoccupied with managing their student's behavior, an endeavor at which they are seldom successful, I have seen the same students enter other classrooms willing to learn and comply with their teacher's instructions.

Many of these "exceptional" teachers have to "cross borders" and negotiate differences of race, class, or experience in order to establish rapport with their students.[65] When I have asked students in interviews what makes a particular teacher special and worthy of respect, the students consistently cite three characteristics: firmness, compassion, and an interesting, engaging, and challenging teaching style.[66] Of course, even a teacher who is perceived as exceptional by students can be a victim of violence, particularly because of its increasingly random occurrence. I have, however, witnessed such teachers confront students in situations that others would not dare to engage, boldly breaking up fights or dice games, or confronting a rude and disrespectful student, without showing the slightest bit of apprehension or fear.

What is there about the structure and culture of the institution that propagates and reproduces the destructive interpersonal dynamics evident in so many schools? The vast majority of teachers whom I meet seem genuinely concerned about their students and sincerely desire to be effective at what they do. Even those who have become cynical and bitter as a result of enduring years of unrewarded work in underfunded schools generally strike me as people who would prefer more humane interactions with their students.[67]

What stands in the way of better relations between teachers and students, and why do fear and distrust characterize those relations rather than compassion and respect? My answer to these questions focuses on the legacy of social control that continues to dominate the educational agenda and that profoundly influences the structure and culture of schools. The pervasive dysfunction that characterizes social relations in urban public schools is not accidental, but is due to the severity of social and economic conditions in the inner city. However, it is also not unavoidable. There are a few important exceptions to this norm—schools where teachers and students support each other in pursuit of higher personal and collective goals.[68] Such schools, however, are not typical or common. Rather, the average urban high school tends to be large, impersonal, and foreboding, a place where bells and security guards attempt to govern the movements of students and where students more often than not have lost sight of the fact that education and personal growth are ostensibly the reasons that they are required to attend this anonymous institution five days a week.

I have visited urban schools that have found ways to address effectively the problem of violence, ways that do not rely on coercion or excessive forms of control. At one such school, rather than hiring security guards, a grandmother from the surrounding community was hired to monitor students. Instead of using physical intimidation to carry out her duties, this woman greets children with hugs, and when some form of punishment is needed, she admonishes them to behave themselves, saying that she expects better behavior from them.[69] I have also visited a continuation high school,[70] where the principal was able to close the campus, not permitting the students to leave at lunchtime, without installing a fence or some other security apparatus but simply by communicating with students about other alternatives for purchasing food so that they no longer felt it necessary to leave for meals.[71] Now the students operate a campus store that both teachers and students patronize. Such measures are effective because they make it possible for children and adults to relate to one another as human beings rather than as anonymous actors playing out roles.

I believe that we have a variety of ways in which to humanize school environments and thereby reduce the potential for violence. Improving the aesthetic character of schools by including art in the design of schools, or by making space available within schools for students to create gardens or greenhouses, can make schools more pleasant and attractive. Similarly, by overcoming the divide that separates urban schools from the communities in which schools are located, the lack of adults who have authority and respect in the eyes of children can be addressed. Adults who live within the community can be encouraged to volunteer or, if possible, be paid to tutor, teach, mentor, coach, perform, or just plain help out with a variety of school activities. These examples are meant to begin a discussion of alternative practices for building humane school communities. There are undoubtedly a variety of ways this can be done, and while such efforts may not eliminate the threat of random violence, they can help to make schools safer, less impersonal, and better able to provide students with a sense of stability in their lives.

The goal of maintaining social control through the use of force and discipline has persisted for too long. While past generations could be made to accept the passivity and constraint such practices engender, present generations will not. Most urban youth today are neither passive nor compliant. The rewards dangled before them of a decent job and material wealth for those who do well in school are seen by too many as either undesirable or unattainable. New strategies for providing an education that is perceived as meaningful and relevant and that begins to tap into the intrinsic desire of all individuals to obtain greater personal fulfillment must be devised and supported. Anything short of this will leave us mired in a situation that grows increasingly depressing and dangerous every day.

The urban schools that I know that feel safe to those who spend their time there don't have metal detectors or armed security guards, and their principals don't carry baseball bats. What these schools do have is a strong sense of community and collective responsibility. Such schools are seen by students as sacred territory, too special to be spoiled by crime and violence, and too important to risk being excluded from. Such schools are few, but their existence serves as tangible proof that there are alternatives to chaotic schools plagued by violence and controlled institutions that aim at producing docile bodies.

Schools, Prisons, and Social Implications of Punishment

Rethinking Disciplinary Practices

Throughout the United States, schools most frequently punish the students who have the greatest academic, social, economic, and emotional needs. An examination of which students are most likely to be suspended, expelled, or removed from the classroom for punishment, reveals that minorities (especially Blacks and Latinos), males, and low achievers are vastly overrepresented. The enactment of zero-tolerance policies related to discipline in school districts has contributed to a significant increase in the number of children who are being suspended and expelled from school. This chapter explains why this has occurred and puts forward an alternative approach to discipline that is aligned with the educational mission of schools.

Not long ago, I was taken on a tour of an elementary school in Northern California by an assistant principal. The purpose of my visit was to learn more about the ways this school was implementing a grant designed to increase the provision of social services to students, most of whom came from a low-income, economically depressed neighborhood. As we came to the end of the tour and walked toward the main office, the assistant principal shook his head and pointed out a boy, no more than eight or nine years old, who was standing outside the door to his office. Gesturing to the child, the assistant principal said to me, "Do you see that boy? There's a prison cell in San Quentin waiting for him." Surprised by his observation, I asked him how he was able to predict the future of such a young child. He replied, "Well, his father is in prison; he's got a brother and an uncle there too. In fact, the whole family is nothing but trouble. I can see from how he behaves already that it's only a matter of time before he ends up there too." Responding to the certainty with which he made these pronouncements, I asked, "Given what you know about him, what is the school doing to prevent him from going to prison?"

I could tell by his flustered response that the assistant principal was surprised by my question. He did not think it was his responsibility to keep the child from following a path that would lead to prison. In fact, he informed me that he was preparing to put this child on an indefinite suspension from school. This was an extreme form of punishment used in a small number of cases for children with persistent behavior problems. It allowed the school to remove difficult children to be schooled at home while still collecting funds from the state for their average daily attendance. Under the plan, work would be sent home, and occasionally a teacher or counselor would make visits to monitor the academic progress of the student. I asked if he thought that such a plan would work for this child given what he had said about the difficulty of his situation at home (the child was being raised by an elderly grandmother). He responded by telling me that there was nothing more the school could do: "Kids like him just can't be helped. They take up so much of my time and keep teachers from serving the needs of other children who are here to learn. It may not be the best thing for him, but right now, it's the best thing for the school."

I begin with this vignette because I believe that while it may seem extreme, it is indicative of the ways many schools handle the discipline of troubled students. Throughout the United States, schools most frequently punish the students who have the greatest academic, social, economic, and emotional needs (Johnson, Boyden, & Pittz, 2001). In most schools and districts, an examination of which students are most likely to be suspended, expelled, or removed from the classroom for punishment reveals that minorities (especially Blacks and Latinos), males, and low achievers generally are vastly overrepresented (Meier, Stewart, & England, 1989). An even closer examination of disciplinary practices reveals that a disproportionate number of the students who receive the most severe punishments are students with learning disabilities, students in foster care or under some form of protective custody, and students who are homeless or on free or reduced-price lunch (Skiba, 2000a).

Often it is the needs of students and the inability of schools to meet those needs that cause them to be disciplined. Children who are behind academically and who are unable to perform at a level commensurate with grade-level expectations often engage in disruptive behavior, out of either frustration or embarrassment (Hirschi, 1969). Likewise, children who suffer from abuse or neglect, and children who are harassed by their peers because they are different, are sometimes more likely to act out and get into trouble (Singer, 1996). Too often, schools react to the behavior of such children while failing to respond to their unmet needs or the factors responsible for their problematic behavior. In so doing, they contribute to the marginalization of such students, often pushing them out of school altogether, while ignoring the issues that actually cause the problematic behavior. Schools also punish the neediest children because in many schools, there is a fixation with behavior management and social control that outweighs and overrides all other priorities and goals.

Understanding why many schools have a preoccupation with control is essential to understanding why it is that certain children are more likely to be targeted for punishment than others. This is the central focus of this chapter, and such a focus is particularly pertinent because available evidence suggests that the adoption of zero-tolerance policies related to discipline and order by school districts across the United States has contributed to a significant increase in the number of children who are being suspended and expelled from school (Skiba, 2000b).

What is it about the way schools throughout the United States operate—without any apparent orchestration or uniform code— that results in the consistency of these patterns and their recent acceleration? And why is it that the drive for order and safety has resulted in the neediest and most disadvantaged students being the ones most likely to be punished?

By attempting to answer these questions and analyzing some of the factors that influence the approach schools take toward maintaining order and control over students, I hope to make the case that alternative methods for producing safe and orderly environments are possible.

Social Control and the Social Contract of Schooling

Disciplinary practices in schools often bear a striking similarity to the strategies used to punish adults in society. Typically schools rely on some form of exclusion or ostracism to control the behavior of students. Chastising a child who has misbehaved or broken a rule with a reprimand, or placing a child in the back of the room or out in the hallway for minor offenses, are common disciplinary practices. For more serious infractions—fighting, defiance, cutting class—removal from the classroom or removal from the school through suspension or even expulsion serve as standard forms of punishment employed by schools throughout the United States. Increasingly, behavior that violates the law (for example, drug use or drug trafficking, assault against a teacher or another student) results in intervention by law enforcement and school sanctions. Consistent with the way we approach crime in society, the assumption is that safety and order can be achieved by removing "bad" individuals and keeping them away from others who are presumed to be "good" and law abiding. Not surprisingly, those most frequently targeted for punishment in school often look—in terms of race, gender, and socioeconomic status—a lot like smaller versions of the adults who are most likely to be targeted for incarceration in society (Singer, 1996).

As social institutions charged with the task of preparing and socializing young people for adult roles, schools generally reflect many of the characteristics of the society in which they are located.

As is true in society, an implicit social contract serves as the basis for maintaining order in schools. In exchange for an education, students are expected to obey the rules and norms that are operative within school and to comply with the authority of the adults in charge. Like the social contract that serves as the basis of order in most democratic societies (Durkheim, 1961; Rawls, 1971), students are expected to relinquish a certain degree of individual freedom in exchange for receiving the benefits of education. For the vast majority of students, this arrangement elicits a relatively high degree of compliance. Despite surveys that suggest a growing number of teachers and students fear violence in school, schools in the United States are generally safe places (Pollack, 1999). Although children significantly outnumber adults, students largely conform to adult authority and, through their compliance, make it possible for order to be maintained.

Not surprisingly, this arrangement tends to be least effective for students who are not receiving the benefits of an education. Once they know that the rewards of education—namely, acquisition of knowledge and skills and, ultimately, admission to college and access to good-paying jobs—are not available to them, students have little incentive to comply with school rules. As the vignette I described at the beginning of this chapter illustrates, at a relatively young age, students may have so many negative experiences in school that they soon begin to recognize that education is not working for them and will not provide them with access to socially desirable rewards. Such students are more likely to be labeled defiant, maladjusted, and difficult to deal with (Brookover & Erickson, 1969), and they are more likely to internalize these labels and act out in ways that match the expectations that have been set for them (Johnson, 1995). Because they violate school rules more often, they are more likely to be punished and subjected to various sanctions. A large body of research has shown that labeling and exclusion practices can create a self-fulfilling prophesy and result in a cycle of antisocial behavior that can be difficult to break (Casella, 2001; Gottfredson, 2001). As the children get older, the rule violations perpetrated by such students often increase in frequency and severity, resulting in a steady escalation in the sanctions that are applied. For many, the cycle of punishment eventually leads to entanglement with law enforcement and the criminal justice system. This is why the assistant principal's prediction about the future of the misbehaving youngster in his charge is disturbingly prophetic; administrators like him often play a significant role in matriculating young people from school to prison.

Students who get into trouble frequently are typically not passive victims; many of them understand that the consequences for violating school rules can be severe, particularly as they grow older. However, as they internalize the labels that have been affixed to them and as they begin to realize that the trajectory their education has placed them on is leading to nowhere, many simply lose the incentive to adhere to school norms.

This dynamic is illustrated quite vividly in Willis's *Learning to Labor* (1977), a study carried out in a decaying industrial city in northern England. The troublesome youngsters he refers to as the "lads" boldly flaunt school rules, harass their teachers and peers, and even break the law with reckless abandon. They do so with full knowledge that their antisocial behavior will guarantee their failure in school, largely because they have already concluded that their education will not lead them to college or middle-class jobs in the future. Willis argues that the boys' behavior constitutes more than just "acting out." He suggests that their blatant noncompliance is rooted in an active rejection of middle-class norms; the students understand that their education will lead them to the factories where their parents have worked, and they deliberately engage in behavior that will ensure their educational failure.

Willis focuses his analysis on students in secondary schools, but chances are that signs of trouble for the lads were present during their earlier school experiences. In my many years of teaching in and working with schools, I have seen this phenomenon played out repeatedly. Schools struggle to maintain order and discipline while a relatively small number of recalcitrant students wreak havoc in classrooms and hallways until they are pushed out or drop out of school on their own accord. Before they exit, the administrators charged with handling discipline engage in a futile game of cat and mouse with them. They desperately try to apprehend, contain, and control incorrigible students even as the students conjure up new ways to violate school rules. The repeated violations suggest that the students understand completely that the social contract underlying their education has been broken. By their actions, it appears they have decided to make the lives of adults and other students miserable as their way of obtaining retribution for a failed education.

Discipline and the Social Purposes of Education

To break the cycle of failure and restore the social contract that underlies schooling, I believe it is necessary to revisit the purpose of education. In American society, schools carry out three primary functions. First, schools sort children based on various measures of their academic ability and place them on trajectories that influence the economic roles and occupations they will assume as adults. In so doing, they play a role in determining who will lead and manage corporations and government and who will be led and managed by those in charge (Bowles & Gintis, 1976; Oakes, 1985). Second, schools play an important role in socializing children by teaching the values and norms that are regarded as central to civil society and the social order (Apple, 1982; Durkheim, 1961). They do this by teaching social conventions (for example, obedience to authority) through implicit and explicit means and by instilling in students a sense of what it means to be "normal" (Gottfredson, 2001). Finally, schools operate as institutions of social control, providing an important custodial function with respect to the care and movement of children. Operating as surrogate parents, schools exercise considerable authority over students, and many of their basic civil rights are suspended while they are in school (Casella, 2001).

Each one of these functions is important and central to the operation of most schools, but without the third—maintaining order and control—the other two functions cannot be easily accomplished. Without a relatively orderly environment where the authority of adults is respected and rules are followed, it is difficult to sort and socialize students. Of course, there are some schools where adults experience considerable difficulty in maintaining order and where control of students is tenuous at best. Such places are generally regarded as educational wastelands and schools of last resort, and placement in these schools constitutes the ultimate sorting and socializing on the path to nowhere (Devine, 1996).

While important in their own right, each of these functions also serves an overlapping and related purpose. By sorting children on the basis of their presumed academic ability or behavior, children learn whether they are in the educational pipeline and develop expectations regarding where they will end up on the social hierarchy. Some paths lead to success and prosperity or, at the minimum, economic security. Other paths lead to dead-end jobs, low wages, and subordination. The socialization process that accompanies the sorting makes it possible for students to accept the educational trajectory set for them and to see their future adult roles as positions they have earned. For this reason, there is surprisingly little objection to the sorting process because students come to believe that their grades, test scores, and behavior have created a future for them that they deserve.

Yet the fact that the process seems to work does not mean that there isn't any resistance. In fact, most often it is the students who understand that school is not working for them and who know that education will not lead to admission to college or access to a promising career who typically cause the most trouble and disturbance in school. With the rewards of education largely unavailable to them, we must realistically ask ourselves why we would expect that students would comply with the rules and adhere to school expectations. When the social contract of schooling is broken or no longer operative for certain students, should we be surprised that they become more likely to disrupt the educational process?

Experience shows that the answer is no. Although it is almost never stated as official policy, school officials are generally aware that students on an educational path that leads to nowhere will cause more trouble and will therefore have to be subjected to more extreme forms of control. This is especially true for schools that serve disproportionate numbers of academically unsuccessful students (such as alternative schools for students with behavior problems, some vocational schools, and many inner-city high schools). Such schools often operate more like prisons than schools. They are more likely to rely on guards, metal detectors, and surveillance cameras to monitor and control students, restrict access to bathrooms, and attempt to regiment behavior by adopting an assortment of rules and restrictions. Although such measures are more likely to be imposed on high schools, I have observed a number of elementary schools that have adopted similar measures. In any educational setting where children are regarded as academically deficient and where the adults view large numbers of them as potentially bad or even dangerous, the fixation on control tends to override all other educational objectives and concerns.

Of course, carrying out the three functions of schooling—sorting, socializing, and social control—is not what attracts most educators to the field of education. Most are drawn to teach and work in schools because they believe education should serve a higher moral purpose. Many are drawn by ideals like those espoused by Rousseau or Dewey, who envisioned schools that would instill values that result in enlightenment, intellectual growth, compassion, and appreciation for human dignity (Fishman & McCarty, 1998; Rousseau, 1974). Others are inspired by the possibility that education can serve as a means to empower and open doors of opportunity to those who have been disadvantaged by poverty, racism, and injustice. Noble ideals such as these catalyzed support for public education in the early nineteenth century (Katznelson & Weir, 1985) and continue to generate support for education among the American public today (Metropolitan Life, 2001).

The majority of my students who seek to become teachers and the vast majority of teachers I have worked with did not enter the profession because they wanted to serve as sorters and gatekeepers. They also did not choose to teach because of the high status the profession enjoys or because they believe it will lead to financial security. Most are motivated by the idea that education can transform lives by inspiring young people and exposing them to knowledge that makes it possible to dream, aspire, and imagine new possibilities for themselves and the world.

The fixation on control is antithetical to many of these ideals. When children are presumed to be wild, uncontrollable, and potentially dangerous, it is not surprising that antagonistic relations with the adults who are assigned to control them develop. The fact that such assumptions and the disciplinary practices that result from them are commonplace and deeply embedded in the routines of so many schools makes one wonder why so many educators could allow themselves to become complicit in this unfortunate subversion of educational ideals.

Does Sorting Out the Bad Apples Work?

The story I began with at the outset of this chapter about the assistant principal and the little boy serves as a useful anecdote for understanding why schools rely so heavily on punishment to deal with the needs of their most disadvantaged students. This example also serves as a useful means of showing why these strategies generally fail to produce the results they seek: safety and order. Even before finding out why the student had been sent to his office, the assistant principal assumed that the boy had once again done something that warranted his removal. It is ironic and telling that schools typically punish children who are behind academically by depriving them of instructional time. Particularly if the misbehaving student is behind academically or missing school frequently, it would seem illogical that the punishment for misbehavior should be denial of school time. But more often than not, schools treat the removal of students as though it were the only form of punishment available. In so doing, the factors that give rise to misbehavior go unexplored, ignored, and unaddressed, while the penchant to punish proceeds with little thought given to the long-term consequences on students.

Schools typically justify using removal through suspension or expulsion by arguing that such practices are necessary to maintain an orderly learning environment for others. The typical rationale given for such practices is that by sorting out the "bad apples," others will be able to learn. This is the only justification that seems even remotely plausible, because there is very little evidence that such practices actually change or improve the behavior of offending students. I often point out to teachers and administrators that the only students whose behavior is likely to improve if they are suspended are students who care about school and who believe their participation in school will help in meeting goals they have set for themselves. The strongest indication that such practices are ineffective at changing behavior is the fact that students who get into trouble and are suspended most frequently rarely change their behavior for the better because they are periodically not allowed to attend school for a few days.

But does excluding the troublemakers and those who misbehave actually make it possible to provide a better learning environment for others? Keeping in mind that one of the primary functions of schools is to sort students according to some measure of their ability by separating those with promise from those without, it might seem that excluding the most vulnerable and difficult students would make perfect sense. Administrators who mete out punishments typically rationalize their actions by suggesting that removal of difficult students is beneficial for those who want to learn. This form of sorting, or what I often call the triage approach to schooling, requires that we accept the fact that not all students will succeed and that some students must be deemed expendable so that others can be saved.

I saw how this approach played itself out while I was working with a middle school in Oakland, California (Noguera, 2001b). The school was under pressure from the district leadership to raise its abysmally low test scores. In response to this pressure, teachers at the school asserted that they were unable to produce higher levels of student achievement because they simply had too many disruptive and misbehaving students. Tired of the school's excuses, the district leadership responded by providing the school with a specially trained teacher who was assigned to work with the most disruptive students in the school. Teachers identified the most difficult students, who in turn were assigned to the new teacher. The teachers welcomed the plan, and twenty-two students were placed in a separate classroom for the entire school day in an isolated part of the school building. In this racially diverse school, all but two of the identified students were Black males (the other two were Black females). To gain their parents' permission for the placement, the students were promised mentors, field trips, summer jobs, and an enriched Afrocentric curriculum that would be taught by a gifted, young African American male teacher. The students and their parents were assured that the classroom was designed to help them and would not serve as some form of isolation unit.

Within a week, it became clear to the students and the new teacher that the class was in fact an isolation unit. The atmosphere in the classroom degenerated quickly as the students realized that the district would not fulfill its promise of providing additional services. The students took out their resentment on their new teacher, who quickly went from being enthusiastic about the experiment and the prospect of working with this group of students to being bitter toward both the students and the district.

The most interesting thing about this story is not what happened in the classroom but what happened in the rest of the school. When I spoke with teachers about the state of their classrooms now that the most disruptive students had been removed, the responses from the teachers were surprisingly similar. In nearly every case, I was told that while they appreciated the absence of the troublemakers, new students had emerged to take their place. Several teachers informed me that they were still experiencing disruptions in their classrooms, and some even suggested that the school needed one more teacher and one more isolated classroom to handle the remaining problem students.

A few weeks after the experiment was terminated, I attended a faculty meeting where we discussed what had happened and what should be done next. During the discussion, I pointed out that I had visited several classrooms and noticed that not all teachers had trouble with disruptive students. I then suggested that we ask these teachers to talk about what they were doing in their classrooms that made it possible for them to experience few disruptions and keep all of their students academically engaged. This turned out to be a truly radical idea because the teachers had never talked with each other before about how to handle discipline issues in the classroom.

This example illustrates why it is problematic to assume that better learning environments can be created by excluding students who misbehave. In most schools, the number of referrals made by teachers for discipline is very uneven; some give many, others very few. In most cases, what separates those who experience frequent behavior problems from those who do not is their ability to keep their students focused on learning and intellectually engaged. Ultimately I believe that unless we focus on how to do this in more classrooms, we will continue to have a revolving door for students who are bored, restless, and behind academically—the kids we typically sort out and push out of school. Moreover, when we locate discipline problems exclusively in students and ignore the context in which problematic behavior occurs, we run the risk of overlooking some of the most important factors that give rise to the behavior.

Disorder and Disengagement in High Schools

In schools where suspension rates are high, sorting out the "bad" students rarely results in a better education for those who remain. This is not because order is not a necessary precondition for teaching and learning; rather it is because there are several other factors that must be addressed in order to improve the quality of education. A large body of research on high schools shows that many students are bored, academically unengaged, and deeply alienated in school (Newmann, 1992; Steinberg, 1996). Many students have weak and even antagonistic relationships with the adults who serve them, and many students report that they have very few teachers who they believe care about them (Metropolitan Life, 2001). Schools that suspend large numbers of students, or that suspend small numbers of students frequently, typically find themselves so preoccupied with discipline and control that they have little time to address the conditions that influence teaching and learning.

I have been engaged in research at ten high schools in Boston and Cambridge, Massachusetts. The purpose of the research is to understand how the reforms carried out by schools are affecting the achievement and social development of students. Many of the schools in the study have been engaged in some of the most popular reforms sweeping the country today: the adoption of small learning communities, block scheduling, and career academies, for example. The types of schools in the study include charter schools, pilot schools (the equivalent of charters that are still part of the school district), vocational schools, magnet schools, and traditional comprehensive high schools. With two exceptions, the schools in the study have high suspension rates, even though concerns about safety are an issue for only three of the schools.

The research approach we have taken is relatively unique: we are studying schools through the perceptions and experiences of students. We are doing this by collecting qualitative and quantitative data on approximately 150 students (15 students at each of the participating schools). Working with the school staff, we have selected a sample at each school comprising five high, five medium, and five low achievers. Each student in the study is interviewed several times throughout the course of the school year and observed in the classroom and in out-of-school settings. In addition, we have interviewed teachers, parents, coaches, and employers in order to develop a complete profile of each student in the sample.

Preliminary findings from the research are both surprising and disturbing. At most of the schools, students routinely report that their teachers have low expectations for them and allow them to get away with doing minimal amounts of work. In our own observations, it was not uncommon to find students sleeping or playing cards in class, courses where students were made to watch videos that were unrelated to the subject of the class, and students who roamed the hallways freely without concern that they would get into trouble. One of the highest-achieving students in our sample informed us that he was going to drop out of school at the end of the tenth grade because he felt he wasn't learning anything. He had obtained the highest possible score on the state exit exam, but he was opting to quit school so he could take the exam that would provide a general equivalency degree. He then planned to enroll in a junior college. Another student in the study, who was widely regarded as one of the best students in her school due to her high grades and good behavior, had been unable to pass the exit exam. When we probed further to find out why, we discovered that despite her high grades, she actually had very low skills in literacy and math. Her high grades, it seemed, were largely attributed to her good behavior.

Conditions like these were not present in all ten schools in the sample. In two of the schools—the ones that happened to have the lowest suspension rates—there was considerable evidence that students were being challenged by rigorous courses and supported by caring teachers. But at the other eight schools, maintaining order and discipline was the priority of the administrators, and relatively little attention was paid to the quality of education being provided. Some of these were large schools with elaborate security systems. However, even two of the smaller schools showed evidence of a preoccupation with discipline and had high suspension rates due to rigid enforcement of rules and regulations. At the larger schools, the focus on security appeared to be largely superficial. These schools had metal detectors at the entrances and an assortment of guards patrolling the hallways. Yet beyond these symbols of order, a disturbing chaos prevailed, particularly in classrooms taught by disorganized or unmotivated teachers.

At each of the schools, we reported our findings to the site administrators at the end of the first year of data collection. In the majority of cases, the principals were neither surprised nor disturbed by our findings. At one school where two-thirds of the senior class was at risk of being denied a diploma because they had not passed the exit exam, we explained to the administration that students felt their teachers had low expectations of them. The principal readily acknowledged the problem but said there was nothing he could do about it because he was preoccupied with raising test scores. When we asked him how he would raise test scores without addressing the quality of instruction, he informed us that he was requiring all students who failed the exam to take a double period of test preparation. Another school had a very rigid tardy policy that required students who arrived at school five minutes after the starting time (7:30 A.M.) to be denied access to school unless they could present a letter from a parent. I arrived one morning at 7:45 A.M. to find dozens of students pleading with security guards to be allowed into the school. When I pointed out to the principal that he now had a tardy policy that was creating a truancy problem, he responded by telling me that at least he had solved the tardy problem.

Research on urban high schools suggests that our findings are not anomalous (Newmann, 1992). While the preoccupation with order and control is widespread, particularly since the school shootings of the past ten years, relatively little attention has been paid to finding ways to increase academic engagement and the intellectual challenge students experience in school. I frequently visit schools in suburban communities and private schools that serve affluent students and see quite clearly that poor children in the inner city are more likely to receive an education that places greater emphasis on order and control than academic rigor. I have also conducted research in schools that are racially and socioeconomically diverse and seen how a single school can provide affluent students with a quality education, while disproportionately punishing its poorer and needier students and providing them with an education that leads to nowhere (Noguera, 2001a).

Breaking the Connection Between Prisons and Schools

Sociologist Loïc Wacquant has argued that there is a growing correspondence between inner-city schools and prisons and that the similarities are not an accident. He suggests that the linking of the two institutions is a by-product of what he terms a "deadly symbiosis" between ghetto and prison (2000). He argues that since colonial times, the United States has been trapped in a quandary over what to do about the Black people captured in Africa and enslaved. Slavery was motivated and rationalized by the desire to exploit Black labor, but there was also a competing desire to exclude Black people—except for those in servile roles—from all facets of public life. A series of strategies—beginning with slavery, which was followed by legally sanctioned segregation, which in turn was followed by de facto segregation in ghettos—were designed to make it possible for American society to accomplish these contradictory and competing goals. However, over time, each of these strategies proved to be untenable, either because they were morally indefensible or, for practical reasons, difficult to sustain. He argues that in the current period, the melding of ghetto and prison through various carceral strategies is the latest method devised for achieving these long-standing objectives. Wacquant (2000) suggests that ghettos became more like prisons in the 1970s and 1980s as poverty became more concentrated, Black labor became redundant, and state institutions of social control replaced communal institutions that previously served community needs. He cites inner-city public schools as one of the primary examples of community organizations that have gradually been transformed into "institutions of confinement" (p. 15).

Public schools in the hyperghetto have similarly deteriorated to the point where they operate in the manner of institutions of confinement whose primary mission is not to educate but to ensure custody and control: "Like the prison system, their recruitment is severely skewed along class and ethnoracial lines. . . . Like inmates, children are herded into decaying and overcrowded facilities built like bunkers, where under-trained and under-paid teachers . . . strive to regulate conduct so as to maintain order and minimize violent incident" (p. 15).

Wacquant's characterization of inner-city schools and his attempt to link their deterioration to historical forces that have shaped the urban environment and the conditions under which poor Black people live is disturbing. It is disturbing because the accusations are almost conspiratorial, implicitly if not explicitly. My own experience as a researcher and educator in urban public schools leads me to reject the possibility that the correspondence between patterns of punishment in prison and schools is the product of a conspiracy. If we were dealing with a genuine conspiracy, it would be relatively easy to identify the conspirators; figure out when, where, and how they hatch their plots; and put a stop to them or at least expose them.

In many ways, the problem is actually far worse. The tendency to punish the neediest children, especially those who are Black and Brown, occurs without conscious planning and deliberate orchestration. For those like the assistant principal in the opening vignette who enforce disciplinary measures, it is simply the way things are done. The fact that he is a Black man is irrelevant to how he responds to this child. When he contemplates the course of action to take to discipline the student, removal is the only option that comes to mind, even though he knows this will not help him and may in fact make matters worse.

Like the ballooning prison population that disproportionately comprises poor Black and Brown men, those who are punished and disproportionately pushed out of school have few advocates and defenders in American society. Particularly since the advent of zero-tolerance discipline policies in the 1990s (Ayers, Dorhn, & Ayers, 2001), relatively few educators are willing to question the fact that we disproportionately punish our neediest students.

However, if we remind ourselves of the noble ideals that served as at least a partial impetus for the creation and proliferation of public schools in the United States, it may be possible for alternative approaches to discipline to be considered. In the early part of the twentieth century, many educators called for schools that functioned like an extension of families (Cremin, 1988). They were envisioned as places where the education of children was to be as concerned with the mastery of basic subjects as with the development of character and the inculcation of values and ethics conducive to a moral and just society (Fishman & McCarty, 1998). Some of these ideals are still present in private and public schools for affluent children, but they are less evident or common in schools for the poor.

This should not be the case. Poor children are no less deserving of nurturing and kindness and in fact may require them even more. A small number of urban schools understand this and try to embody these principles in their operation. Not surprisingly, they tend to be extremely popular and academically successful. One such school, Phyl's Academy in Fort Lauderdale, Florida, has been praised simply for adhering to principal Monica Lewis's admonition to "treat children with kindness." In describing her school, she reports, "We don't have a rigid hand. We show them values. Once you give a child reasons, you get them to follow directions" (Shores, 2003).

It sounds so simple because it is. Finding ways to produce safe and orderly schools need not compel us to turn schools into prisons or detention centers. It should be possible to create more schools like Phyl's Academy where high academic achievement is the norm and discipline problems the exception. It should be possible if we realize that the children of the poor are no less deserving than the children of the affluent. Perhaps what is needed even more than a revival of ideals is a recruitment of educators who will question the tendency to punish through exclusion and humiliation and who see themselves as advocates of children, not as wardens and prison guards. Without such personnel, the drive to punish will undoubtedly be difficult to reverse and abate.

8

Racial Politics and the Elusive Quest for Excellence and Equity in Education

The relationship between race and academic achievement is once again the focus of national attention. Periodically this issue has become the subject of debate in the national news media, and on each occasion, various experts are called on to put forward explanations of racial differences in academic performance, preferably one that can be summed up in two minutes or less. As the current debate over the relationship between race and student achievement has heated up, the performance of Black middle-class students in particular has been the subject of intense scrutiny. Despite their relative privilege, middle-class Black students typically lag behind White and Asian students of similar and even lower socioeconomic status (Jencks and Phillips 1998; Spencer 2000). Similar patterns can be seen among Black and Latino students who attend well-financed, integrated schools in affluent communities (Jencks and Phillips 1998). For such students, arguments related to inequities in funding and access to educational opportunities, which are relevant to poor students, do not seem pertinent. As such, the search for explanations to this apparent paradox has inspired renewed interest in the relationship between race and academic performance, but once again there is more confusion than clarity in public discussions of the issue.

The last controversy surrounding the racial achievement gap was triggered by the publication of *The Bell Curve* by Herrnstein and Murray (1994). In this case the authors argued that genetic differences between Blacks and Whites accounted for unequal outcomes in academic performance, and much of the controversy related to their book centered on whether there was actual proof that African Americans were genetically inferior.[1]

In the current period, cultural factors figure more prominently in the explanations that are proffered by experts and touted in the media. Scholars such as John Ogbu (1987) and John McWhorter (2000) attribute the lower performance of Black students generally, and the middle class in particular, to an "oppositional culture" (Ogbu 1978), "anti-intellectualism," and "a culture of victimology" (McWhorter 2000). Despite the fact that such arguments tend to be based on generalized descriptions of "Black American culture" rather than intensive investigations into the experience of Black students in school settings, such theories have been widely embraced by scholars and educators. Like the genetic theories of intelligence that preceded them, cultural theories that attempt to explain the link between race and academic performance generally locate the cause of the problem within students (lack of motivation, devaluing academic pursuits, and others) and, in so doing, effectively absolve educational institutions of responsibility for finding solutions.

With the hope of shedding some light on the complexities surrounding the relationship between race and academic performance, this chapter examines the factors that influence the development of educational policies and practices designed to ameliorate the achievement gap in relatively affluent school districts. To provide a context for understanding the issues surrounding efforts to promote educational equity, the chapter begins by describing initiatives undertaken by schools in the Minority Student Achievement Network (MSAN). The remainder of the chapter draws on research collected from a four-year study carried out at Berkeley High School (BHS) to illustrate how racial disparities in academic outcomes are influenced by the structure of opportunity within schools and how efforts to address inequities often become politicized. The goal is to use the case of BHS to show how political factors complicate efforts to reduce racial disparities in student achievement and to make it clear why political rather than educational strategies alone are needed to respond to the racial achievement gap.

The Minority Student Achievement Network

In February 1999, the superintendents of fourteen urban and sub-urban school districts came together to form the Minority Student Achievement Network (MSAN 1999). This newly formed consortium was created for the purpose of providing the districts with strategic support in tackling a common problem: the racial gap in student achievement. Although racial disparities in student performance are recognized as a national phenomenon (Jencks and Phillips 1998), the fourteen districts believed that they might be better positioned than most others to eliminate or significantly reduce the gap, because of the favorable conditions present within each of the member districts. All fourteen districts in MSAN were located in affluent communities where per pupil expenditures generally exceeded the state average (MSAN 1999). In addition, each of the districts has a record of high achievement among many of their White students as measured by performance on standardized tests and college enrollments (MSAN 1999). This record of success led many to believe that it should be possible to produce similar outcomes among students of color. Finally, all fourteen districts are in communities known for their liberal political values and their support for public education, and several of the districts are located in close proximity to major research universities. Since its inception, MSAN has hoped university-based researchers could be enlisted to support this effort.[2]

Despite the relative advantages of school districts in cities such as Berkeley, Cambridge, Chapel Hill, and Ann Arbor, past efforts to elevate the academic performance of minority students had yielded little success. Moreover, in each of the districts, clear direction with respect to future steps that could be taken to raise student achievement was lacking. Lack of success could not merely be attributed to institutional indifference or a lack of effort. Each district had a long history of developing innovative programs and enacting a variety of measures to boost the academic performance of students of color (MSAN 1999). Moreover, at varying points in the recent past, several of the districts had been led by an African American, and in all of the districts, people of color occupied significant leadership roles. However, good intentions and the presence of an ethnically diverse leadership has not been sufficient to keep any of the districts from becoming mired in bitter political disputes that have arisen as a result of their failure to significantly improve the performance of minority students.

Conflicts over what could broadly be termed "educational equity issues" have plagued the districts within MSAN. Most often, these conflicts take the form of hostility from impatient and frustrated minority parents directed at district administrators. However, affluent parents whose students are generally well served by the schools are not disinterested parties in these disputes. Occasionally some of these parents also enter the fray when they believe their interests are endangered. Although by no means monolithic in their sentiments, this constituency has the ability to exert tremendous influence over district policies through its political and economic resources, which can be deployed whenever it believes high academic standards are threatened. While it is unlikely that any interest group will ever directly oppose efforts to improve the academic performance of minority students, occasionally the interventions that are proposed require a reallocation of resources or the restructuring of educational programs. Such changes often encounter fierce opposition from the parents of high-achieving students if or when they are interpreted as compromising the educational interests of their children. Examples of the kinds of measures that might evoke the ire of this constituency include efforts to eliminate or reduce tracking or to open up access to gifted and talented or Advanced Placement courses (Wells and Serna 1996).

Faced with frustrated minority parents who believe their children are not well served and well-organized affluent parents who are prepared to do whatever it takes to defend the educational interests of their children, the leaders of MSAN find themselves stuck between a rock and a hard place. They must find ways to respond to the pressing concerns raised by the parents of low-achieving minority students, while at the same time scrupulously avoiding any measure that might provoke the wrath of parents of high-achieving White students. The perception that the pursuit of academic excellence and the pursuit of educational equity are goals that are fundamentally at odds and exist within a zero-sum scenario is at the crux of many of the conflicts experienced by the districts in MSAN. The stakes are high in these conflicts because in most cases, they take on an unfortunate racial character, and if they escalate, the ensuing polarization can have an injurious effect on intergroup relations in the broader community and the job security of district administrators.

Hence, the districts that came together to create MSAN faced a common need. All were searching for educational strategies that would enable them to make measurable progress in the performance of their minority students but would not arouse opposition from their affluent parents. Moreover, with the adoption of high-stakes testing in several of the states where MSAN districts are located, there was even greater need for such strategies. Many of these districts were faced with the prospect that high percentages of their minority students were at risk of failing state-mandated assessments. The likelihood of such an outcome added to the urgency associated with the search for solutions to the racial gap in student achievement.[3]

However, after nearly three years of meetings and conferences, it is becoming clear that a common experience with failure in past efforts to raise minority student achievement, and a common need to demonstrate genuine progress on the issue, may not be enough to serve as a useful basis for new direction and insight. Despite sharing research and information on their programmatic interventions among themselves, there is still no sign that the districts in MSAN have discovered ways to close the achievement gap or to reverse these disturbing academic trends. MSAN members continue to hold meetings several times a year at which information on best practices and research findings is shared, but the optimism that was present when the consortium was first established is gradually beginning to fade. Already it is becoming increasingly clear that MSAN is largely a support group and that the organization is not able to provide its members with clear answers or direction.

I am one of several university-based researchers who was asked to serve on an advisory board of MSAN. Since the consortium was created, I have attended their meetings, and on occasion I have been asked to deliver presentations on research that I have done that relates to the MSAN effort. Having been a researcher and parent of four children who were enrolled in the Berkeley public schools and having served as an elected member of the school board in Berkeley, I am intimately familiar with the problems and issues confronting these kinds of schools and communities. From the beginning, I was intrigued by the ideas that had influenced the establishment of MSAN, and I believed, or at least hoped, that the theory of change guiding its work had merit and could lead to improvements in patterns of academic achievement. My hope was that if we could show that change was possible, the efforts of MSAN would have national ramifications for the education of students of color. For me, such a prospect was very compelling.

However, even as I hoped for the best, my experience in the Berkeley public schools left me with nagging doubts and skepticism. Having worked over several years on an intensive effort to raise minority student achievement at Berkeley High School, I was left with the realization that even when an objective analysis of conditions suggested that change should be possible, well-thought-out plans could easily be thwarted by obstacles that have more to do with politics and relatively little to do with educational practice. I felt strongly that unless members of MSAN were prepared to confront the political challenges that arise from zero-sum thinking on issues related to educational equity and excellence, their good intentions would fail to produce the results that were hoped for. In the absence of a strategic vision that could provide guidance on how to attain this balance, I was sure that MSAN would eventually be dismissed as yet another good idea that had not lived up to expectations.

In October 2000, I was invited to speak on a panel to address the subject of the achievement gap before an audience of program officers from major foundations. Also on the panel was Ron Ferguson, an economist at the Kennedy School of Government at Harvard University, and like me, a research consultant to MSAN. Accompanying us on the panel were two superintendents from districts within MSAN. Because the creation of MSAN had generated national media attention,[4] the audience was packed, and those present eagerly awaited information that might be shared from our work.

Instead of revealing findings, much of the panel discussion focused on the goals of MSAN and the initiatives that had been undertaken by the consortium to date. Ron Ferguson started out discussing his research, much of which had been carried out in Shaker Heights, Ohio. His work, which was based on surveys with students, showed significant differences in study habits and attitudes toward school between African American and White students. Though it produced few recommendations for action, his research did shed further light on some of the factors influencing the lower academic performance of minority students (Ferguson 2001). The two superintendents described efforts that had been undertaken in their districts to raise minority student achievement, and they explained why they invested a great deal of hope in MSAN.

I started my presentation by suggesting that the lack of progress in minority student achievement in MSAN districts was a paradox in need of an explanation that went beyond a focus on the attitudes and study habits of minority students. Using language that made both superintendents visibly uncomfortable, I argued that the lack of progress on student achievement in MSAN could be attributed largely to the difficulty inherent in serving the educational needs of two different constituencies: affluent Whites and low-income African Americans and Latinos. I pointed out that middle-class Black and Latino students were more likely to identify with lower-class members of their racial group, and that based on my experience in Berkeley, it would be difficult to raise their academic achievement unless it was possible to move beyond the zero-sum terms that framed how this issue was perceived. Particularly if the districts intended to initiate major changes in educational programs, fierce opposition was likely and should be expected.

Given that affluent White parents were typically more powerful and politically influential, I posited that it would be nearly impossible to bring about significant change in student outcomes unless the educational leaders in MSAN found a way to address the concerns they were bound to raise. Specifically, I suggested that MSAN had to find a way to deal with the perception that advances in educational equity would necessarily come at the expense of the educational interests of affluent White students. To the discomfort of the superintendents who were present, I also pointed out that in some communities, superintendents had been fired and school board members recalled when the pursuit of educational equity ignited the wrath of powerful and privileged parents.[5] I concluded by arguing that the solution to the achievement gap in MSAN districts would be based on political more than educational strategies and that unless the political solution could be found, there would be no progress.

The Role and Significance of Race in the Achievement Gap

My pessimistic prognosis on the efforts of MSAN is rooted in my experience with the Berkeley public schools, where for years I have worked with others to find ways to raise minority student achievement. In the beginning, I could not understand why schools that possess a track record of success in educating affluent White students are largely unable to produce similar success with students of color from low- or middle-class backgrounds. However, after years of experience and research in the Berkeley public schools I have come to the conclusion that the explanation is complicated because it cannot simply be answered within the context of educational practice. Certainly part of the answer lies in the difficulty educators experience in responding to the different needs of poor and affluent students; educational strategies that work for some students simply are not effective for others.[6] However, a closer examination of the issues reveals that much more is involved.

The complexity surrounding the relationship between race and achievement is particularly evident when we consider what appears to be a paradox in the performance of two broad categories of students: recent immigrants and middle-class Black and Latino students. Several studies reveal that immigrant students of color, many of whom are from low-income families, are often academically successful (Ogbu 1987; Stepick and Castro 1991; Suarez-Orozco and Suarez-Orozco 2001).[7] In contrast, many middle-class Black and Latino students tend to be less successful even though their families are relatively privileged (Jencks and Phillips 1998; Ferguson 2000). While several factors directly and indirectly influence these patterns, it is my contention that both phenomena are largely related to the ways in which identities related to race and gender are constructed in school settings and to perceptions and expectations that develop among adults and students in response to these perceived identities.

For many years, a number of researchers have recognized the significance of the link between identity and academic performance. The subjective positioning of students has been found to have bearing on motivation and persistence (Newman 1992), relationships with peer groups and teachers (Steinberg 1996; Phelan Locke Davidson, and Cao Yu 1998), and overall self-esteem (Williams 1996). Yet despite the substantial body of research in this area, there is far less agreement among scholars about how the development of racial identities among adolescents influences the stance and orientation that is adopted in relation to schooling. Despite overwhelming evidence of a strong correlation between race and academic performance, there is considerable confusion about the process through which students come to perceive a linkage between their racial identities and their academic ability and how these in turn shape their aspirations and behaviors toward education.

Scholars such as John Ogbu (1987) and Signithia Fordham (1996) have suggested that Black students from all socioeconomic backgrounds develop "oppositional identities" that lead them to view schooling as a form of forced assimilation. They argue that Black students and other "nonvoluntary minorities" (such as Chicanos, Puerto Ricans, and Native Americans) come to equate academic success with "acting White" which leads to the adoption of self-defeating behaviors that inhibit possibilities for academic success. The few who manage to achieve academically pay a heavy price for success. According to these researchers, Black students who perform at high levels are compelled to adopt a "raceless" persona so as to avoid the stigma associated with membership within their racial groups (Fordham 1988).

In contrast, Ogbu and others (Gibson 1988; Suarez-Orozsco 2001; Matutu-Biachi 1986) have argued that immigrant students of color are largely immune to the insidious association between race and achievement that traps students from domestic minority backgrounds. So-called voluntary minorities, whether they be Mexican, Asian, African, or West Indian, are more likely to perceive schooling as a pathway to social mobility, and for that reason they are also more likely to adopt behaviors that increase the likelihood of academic success. Moreover, having been raised in societies where people of their race or ethnic group are in the majority, they have not been subjected to socialization processes that lead them to see themselves as members of subordinate or inferior groups. Less constrained by the history of racial oppression in the United States, these students are more likely to accommodate the dominant culture and conform to the prescriptions that are integral to the social experience in schooling (Spring 1988). Even if they avoid complete assimilation, they are more likely to adopt behaviors that contribute to school success (Ogbu 1987; Gibson 1988).

When the work of these authors is viewed in combination with Claude Steele's work (1997) on the effects of racial stereotypes on academic performance, a compelling explanation for the identity-achievement paradox begins to emerge. Through his research on student attitudes toward testing, Steele has shown that students are highly susceptible to prevailing stereotypes related to intellectual ability. According to Steele, when "stereotype threats" are operative, they lower the confidence of vulnerable students and negatively affect their performance on standardized tests. According to Steele, "Ironically, their susceptibility to this threat derives not from internal doubts about their ability but from their identification with the domain and the resulting concern they have about being stereotyped in it" (p. 614). For Steele, the debilitating effects of stereotypes can extend beyond particular episodes of testing and can have an effect on overall academic performance. In his other work, Steele suggests that schools and universities can adopt strategies to reduce the stigma experienced by women and racial minorities and thereby militate against the effects of stereotype threats (Steele 1992).

If we attempt to combine Ogbu's arguments with those of Steele, one could extrapolate that recent immigrant students are less likely to be susceptible to the threat associated with negative racial stereotypes because their newness to the American social landscape protects them. Having not been socialized to see themselves as inferior, immigrant students are less likely to "resist" aspects of schooling that require conformity and assimilation to values and norms that domestic minorities regard as White and middle class. In contrast, middle-class Black and Latino students are more likely to identify with the styles and behaviors of lower-class members of their racial/ethnic group (Portilla 1999). Rather than risk being ostracized for differentiating themselves from their peers, these students may adopt attitudes and behaviors that undermine their possibilities for achieving academic success.

My own research on this topic suggests that the racial identity development process is not nearly so dichotomous (Noguera 2001); a range of possibilities for expressing one's identity exists. Racelessness or "acting White" is just one possibility. There are also many examples of Black and Latino students who manage to do well in school while retaining a sense of pride in their racial and cultural identity. In addition, there are many who achieve by adopting multiple personas: they adopt the cultural norms that are valued in school settings while embracing the speech, style of dress, and larger identity construct associated with their racial group outside of school.

Understanding the process through which racial identities are constructed in school is essential if we are to devise strategies that can transform the ways in which race and achievement become linked. In the following section, I draw on data from four years of research at Berkeley High School to demonstrate how the link between racial identity and student performance becomes operative. However, in departure from both Ogbu and Steele, I also show how the structure and culture of this school and, I argue, others like it contribute to the creation of this linkage. That is, rather than treating racial identities as fixed categories, I maintain that oppositional identities and an antiacademic orientation (for example, an unwillingness to enroll in challenging courses) are social products that are directly related to the school experience of many Black and Latino students. Furthermore, I show that political factors related to the protection of privilege serve to maintain and reinforce structural and cultural barriers that obstruct efforts to improve minority student achievement. Without a strategy for confronting these barriers, lasting gains in student achievement at BHS, or the schools in MSAN, cannot be made.

Good Intentions Are Not Enough: The Failure of Integration at Berkeley High School

To the unknowledgeable outsider, Berkeley would seem to be one of the most likely places to find excellent schools available for all children. Home to a world-class public university, the people of Berkeley tend to be highly educated and socially progressive. In fact, the liberalism and idealism of the citizenry have consistently placed the city at the forefront of various social movements and at the vanguard of innovation in American politics. From the movement against the Vietnam War to the movement to promote recycling of household goods, Berkeley has been at the forefront of progressive change in the United States. Not surprisingly, the liberal political inclinations of the community have historically also had a profound influence on the character of the public schools.

In 1968 Berkeley was one of the first cities in the nation to voluntarily desegregate its public schools (Kirp 1982). This it accomplished through a novel system of shared busing, which called for minority students from the flatlands to be bused to predominantly White schools in the hills in the early grades, and for older children from the hills to be bused to flatland schools in the later grades. Berkeley's progressive stance toward education did not stop there. Even as the rest of California embraced a revolt against property taxes in the 1970s and 1980s, Berkeley voters demonstrated a willingness to adopt a variety of local tax measures to provide additional funding to public education (Noguera 1995).

Yet despite this impressive track record of public support, Berkeley schools are characterized by extreme disparities in academic outcomes among students from different racial/ethnic backgrounds. At every school in the district, patterns of student achievement on most standardized tests adhere to a bimodal distribution of scores (see Table 8.1). The majority of White and Asian students score at or above the eightieth percentile on most norm-referenced tests, while the scores of Black and Latino students are generally closer to

Table 8.1. 1999 Report on Student Performance on the Stanford 9

National Percentile Ratings	Black	Asian	Hispanic	White
60th to 90th	18	47.7	24.9	81.2
1st to 30th	63.1	37.9	61.4	8.6

the thirtieth percentile (Noguera 1995; Berkeley Alliance 1999). Similar patterns emerge when the composition of special and compensatory education programs is compared to the composition of gifted and talented and Advanced Placement courses: Black and Latino students overwhelmingly comprise enrollment in the former, while affluent White students populate the latter. Similarly, wide disparities are evident in the grades assigned to students, in attrition rates, and suspension and expulsion rates at all schools in the district (Diversity Project 2000).

Given its long history of liberalism and its reputation for embracing progressive causes, one might expect that Berkeley citizens would have eventually become outraged at the persistence of such glaring disparities. Yet a careful analysis of the political dynamics that have shaped policy in Berkeley's schools reveals that the community has been willing to tolerate a degree of racial inequality in student academic outcomes that any objective analysis would indicate is quite extreme. The most obvious example of this tolerance can be seen at Berkeley's continuation school, which was renamed Berkeley Alternative High School. Serving approximately 160 students, most of whom have been sent there because of poor grades, poor attendance, or poor behavior, the school is almost entirely composed of African American students, with a smattering of Latinos and an even smaller number of Whites and Asians. Although the school was recently moved to a new facility, in almost every sense imaginable, this racially segregated school has been marginal to the district. In fact, the academic performance of students at the school has received so little attention that basic information such as graduation, dropout, and college attendance rates is not even maintained.[8]

Yet my own experience as a former school board member, parent, and researcher in the Berkeley schools leads me to reject the idea that there is a conspiracy to deny Black and Latino students educational opportunities. To understand how these disparities are rationalized and thereby come to be tolerated and maintained, it is necessary to understand how efforts to do something about them tend to become politicized. In the following section, I examine two elements of the structure and culture of the school: the practices used to assign and sort students into courses and the informal practices that shape voluntary association in clubs and other extracurricular activities. It is my contention that research on the organization of academic opportunity in schools can serve as a means to reveal the practices through which racial inequality is produced and maintained. Critical discussion of these practices must be the first step in the process of closing the achievement gap, for without such careful scrutiny, issues related to race and student achievement become obfuscated. As I will show, lack of clarity about the nature of the problem limits the possibility that action can be taken to improve academic outcomes for failing students.

Two Schools in One: Sorting Students at BHS

BHS is a relatively large school, with approximately three thousand students and nearly two hundred teachers, counselors, and administrators. According to the district's data, approximately 40 percent of the students at BHS are White, 40 percent are African American, 10 percent are Latino, and 10 percent are Asian American (Berkeley Alliance 1999). These numbers may be inaccurate because approximately 10 percent of the students who responded to a survey administered by the Diversity project to the class of 2000 identified themselves as mixed race (Diversity Project

2000). Racial differences tend to correspond closely to class differences. The vast majority of White students reside in middle-class and affluent neighborhoods in the hills and North Berkeley, while the majority of African American and Latino students come from low-income communities in the flatlands of South and West Berkeley. In addition, approximately 25 percent of students do not reside in Berkeley at all. They enroll in BHS either through interdistrict transfer or by surreptitiously claiming Berkeley residence, and the vast majority of these are Black students from poorer neighborhoods in Oakland (Diversity Project 1999).

On the basis of almost every significant indicator, BHS is a school that does not serve its Black and Latino students well. Nearly 50 percent of Black and Latino students who enter BHS in the ninth grade fail to graduate, and among those who do graduate, few complete the course requirements necessary for admission at the University of California or the state college system (Berkeley Alliance 1999). African American students constitute the overwhelming majority of students who are suspended or expelled from the school for disciplinary reasons (Diversity Project 2000), and they comprise the majority of students enrolled in special education classes. Finally, the English as a Second Language (ESL) program functions as a distinct school within the larger school, and its students, most of whom are Latino and Asian, are effectively denied access to college preparatory classes and resources available at BHS.

In contrast, for most White and some Asian students, BHS is a highly successful school offering a vast array of educational opportunities and enriching experiences. The vast majority of White students graduate and matriculate to four-year colleges and universities, and a significant number are admitted to Ivy League colleges and the University of California (1996 Report on College Admission 1996). BHS consistently produces several National Merit scholars, most of whom are White, and the jazz band, debating club, and school newspaper (all of which almost exclusively White) have received several national awards. With its rich and innovative curriculum, BHS is one of few public schools that actually draws White students away from private schools.[9] Their parents, many of whom are professionals with advanced university degrees, know a good thing when they see it, and as a result many have refused to abandon this urban public school in the way that many White middle-class families have done elsewhere (Nocera 1991). In fact, many White parents and students perceive the diversity of the school as an added benefit, and some regard sending their children there as an inherently progressive political act.[10]

When Berkeley schools were desegregated in 1968, issues related to race and schooling seemed so simple and clear-cut that the advocates for desegregation merely argued that "it was the right thing to do" (Kirp 1982, p. 67). However, addressing racial disparities in the postintegration period has been far more difficult. With the advent of Black nationalist movements in the 1970s, "the right thing to do" became more ambiguous. In 1969 Black students at BHS demanded and were granted the first African American studies department established at a high school in the United States. The logic behind this concession was rooted in the notion that separate and distinct approaches to educating Black and White students were necessary and desired. Such thinking led to the creation of several smaller separate high schools in the mid-1970s, including the UMOJA House for Black students seeking a culturally defined educational experience and the Raza House for Chicano students seeking something analogous for themselves. Ultimately these experiments in racial separation were brought to an end by the U.S. Department of Education, which determined that maintaining racially separate schools was a violation of several civil rights statutes and was therefore illegal.[11]

Despite this setback, the underlying philosophical premise that produced the racially defined schools retained its influence. Over time, BHS effectively became two schools within the same facility: an elite college preparatory school serving affluent White students and an inner-city school serving economically disadvantaged Black and Latino students. Officially there was only one school, with one principal, one faculty, one football team, and so on. But for students and anyone else who spent their days at the school, the fragmented nature of BHS, where divisions occurred along racial and class lines, was evident and ever present in nearly every aspect of the school.

Patterns of racial separation are most evident when one enters the school grounds at the beginning of the school day. Across the sprawling campus, students can be seen huddled in racially distinct groupings. Black students gather in front of the administration building, congregating near a map of Africa that has been painted on the asphalt. White students gather on the steps of the Community Theater. Along Martin Luther King Way on the periphery of the campus, groups of Latino students come together near and around a Mexican mural. Smaller groups of Asian students find their place along a wall adjacent to the Science Building. Each grouping is racially distinct, but the lines between them are permeable, as can be seen from the significant number of students who mingle in mixed groups or who cross over to interact with individuals from another group.

While this form of separation may be most noticeable and such voluntary associations create the sense that this is what students prefer, the separation that occurs in classrooms throughout the school is largely involuntary and substantially less visible, yet the impact on student outcomes is far more profound. During the course of a four-year study carried out at the school,[12] the Diversity Project analyzed course enrollment patterns and the trajectories they create for students. Our analysis of the data revealed that White students are concentrated in the honors and college track courses, while African American and Latino students are predominant in less demanding remedial courses. These patterns are set in place starting from the time a student enters the school in the ninth grade, and for this reason this is where our initial research efforts were focused.

Since 1993, reports on the number of the D's and F's received by students in major courses were produced and released to the public at the end of each semester. Because these reports disaggregated the student population by racial status, release of the reports tended to elicit considerable controversy and finger-pointing. Underlying the controversy were profound disagreements over the causes of academic disparities. Finger-pointing by those who attributed the problem to indifferent teachers, negligent parents, lazy and unmotivated students, or even society as a whole only contributed to further paralysis and inaction. More significant, the lack of change in student outcomes over time contributed to a perception that racial dichotomies in patterns of student achievement were normal or even "natural," and their consistency gave them a fixed and unchangeable quality.

To challenge assumptions about the link between race and school performance within the school and community, the Diversity Project used two research strategies: an annual survey administered to students in the class of 2000 (approximately 750 ninth graders who entered BHS in the fall of 1996) and an analysis of grades and course selections made by the same ninth graders using student records as the database. The purpose of choosing these two data collection strategies was to find ways to show the school and community how students were being separated as they entered BHS.

Over the course of the 1996–97 academic year, data on course enrollment and student perceptions of their BHS experience were collected and analyzed. Once this process was completed, we contemplated ways of presenting the data to the school's faculty for a discussion of the issues related to student achievement. Our goal was to move the conversation beyond an assignment of blame to a more constructive focus on potential solutions. To facilitate such a discussion, the faculty were divided into four groups and assigned to rooms where large graphics were displayed that illustrated findings from our investigation. In the first room, the charts illustrated how the assignment of students to math courses in the ninth grade influenced their trajectory into other academic courses and electives within the school. For example, it showed that students who were placed in honors geometry, 87 percent of whom were White and who disproportionately had come to BHS from private schools, were on track to complete the advanced math and science courses needed for admission to the University of California. We also displayed graphics that showed these students were more likely to be enrolled in higher-level foreign language courses, (for example, second-year or above French or Spanish or first-year German or Latin) and honors biology.

In contrast, another set of graphics showed that students who had been placed in the lowest-level prealgebra class, 83 percent of whom were African American and Latino, were not on track to complete the university's science and math requirements. With nearly 80 percent of the students who had been enrolled in this course failing it in the fall semester of 1996, the graphics made it clear that it would be highly unlikely that more than a handful of these students would be able to complete the math and science course sequence needed to fulfill university entrance requirements. Moreover, students placed in prealgebra were not likely to be enrolled in a college prep science course, and if they had a foreign language class, it was most likely to be beginning Spanish or Swahili (Diversity Project 1999). Most surprising of all was the fact that nearly all of the students who had entered BHS through interdistrict transfer or under caregiver status had been assigned to prealgebra.

The course enrollment charts were followed by the presentation of a map of the City of Berkeley broken down by ZIP code. Within each ZIP code, the average grade point average (GPA) for students residing within the area was indicated. As might be expected, the map revealed a clear and distinct pattern: students from homes in South and West Berkeley, the poorest sections of the city with the highest African American and Latino populations, had the lowest GPAs, while students in North Berkeley and the affluent

Berkeley Hills had the highest GPAs. Interestingly, though the map revealed patterns that anyone associated with the school would expect, reaction to the map was striking. Teachers viewing the map were amazed by the consistency of the pattern and wondered aloud why such a pronounced trend existed. The comment of one veteran teacher captured the sentiment of many of the teachers: "I expected kids from the poorer sections of the city to do less well, but I'm amazed that it's this blatant. Something must be going on." The map turned out to be such a powerful illustration of the relationship between social class and academic achievement that the *San Francisco Chronicle* featured a copy of the map in a front-page article describing the research that was done by the project (Olszewski 1998).

As teachers discussed the findings from the research, no one argued about the accuracy of the data, nor did the conversation about the data deteriorate into a debate over who was to blame for these patterns. Instead, those present wanted to know more about what could be learned from the data, and they asked questions to probe the information that had been collected. How did the grades students obtained in math compare to those in English and history? How did a student's grades correlate with his or her attendance in school? How effective were the academic support programs that had been set up to help students who were struggling academically?

There were similar reactions to the data derived from the survey that was presented in another classroom. The survey data provided information on what students liked and disliked about BHS, as well as information about how often they studied, whether they were employed and for how many hours a week, and where they went when they needed academic support. Many teachers reacted with surprise when they discovered that a majority of students indicated that the diversity of the student body was one of the things that students liked best about their experience at BHS. Students also expressed considerable support for the "freedom" they enjoyed at BHS, which they identified as the opportunity to set their own course schedule and the ease with which they were able to cut classes without being caught.

Discussion of the data generated from the student survey and course enrollment patterns opened the door to a more difficult discussion about the implications of the findings for students and the school as a whole. Confronted with evidence that course assignments in the ninth grade would determine the trajectory students were on over the next four years, some teachers began to question the fairness of the course assignment process. As teachers learned that course assignments in math were made by counselors who based their decision on a review of student transcripts and without a formal assessment of student ability, questions about the fairness of the process were raised. Concerns about the lack of structure at BHS (for example, the absence of a coherent tardy policy and the inconsistent application of penalties for cutting) led to a discussion about the permissive culture of the school, which effectively allowed large numbers of students to fail and slip through the cracks.

The presentations in the third and fourth rooms focused on how patterns of separation extend beyond the classroom and show up in areas of the school where membership is based on voluntary association. Our data showed that nearly every club, sports team, and extracurricular activity offered by the school had a racially exclusive makeup. Even more disturbing was the fact that any activity that might be regarded as having the potential to enhance one's academic performance (such as academic clubs and the debating team) was composed almost exclusively of White students.

Because they have been in place for so long, such patterns of separation have been rationalized as the product of choices made freely by the students. Some adults at the school consciously condone these practices as a way of accommodating the diverse cultures and interests present within the school, and they argue that these patterns of separation provide a form of cultural affirmation. However, what some regard as a benign and voluntary form of racial separation actually masks the ways in which these patterns rein-force the racialized nature of academic failure and success at the school. Because many students and teachers have come to accept this form of racial separation as voluntary and therefore unavoid-able, there has been relatively little willingness to take responsi-bility for the wide disparities in academic outcomes and the social tensions that accompany these patterns. Nor has there been much acknowledgment that these patterns profoundly influence the future opportunities available to students once they leave BHS. Several studies on extracurricular activities have shown that students who are involved in sports, music, the arts, and other clubs generally per-form better in school than students who are uninvolved (Steinberg 1996). Students who participate in extracurricular activities are also more likely to be engaged academically. In this way, school activities often counter alienation, antisocial behavior, and an orientation toward school that devalues the importance of academic pursuits. In addition, students who are involved in extracurricular activities are more likely to feel connected to and identify with their schools. Studies have shown that the psychological effects of such a connec-tion can positively influence academic performance (Steele 1992).

Our discussions with teachers about the factors that pro-duce racially distinct clubs and sports teams made it possible for the adults who had long come to accept these patterns as unavoid-able to consider actions that might be taken to alter them. Perhaps with some encouragement, Latino students who frequently can be seen playing soccer on their own time in unstructured pickup games could be recruited to the school's soccer team. Similarly, with a concerted outreach plan and even some arm-twisting, minority stu-dents could be recruited to write for the school newspaper, try out for a part in a school play, or join one of the predominantly White athletic teams such as golf, fencing, or tennis. It was acknowl-edged that in order to increase minority student participation, it might also be necessary to be open to their suggestions for how these activities might become more appealing to their interests and tastes. However, given the social benefits the school might gain from improved intergroup relations and the long-term academic benefits that might result from increased student engagement, several of those participating in the discussion indicated a willingness to take extra steps to make increased involvement from minority students possible.

Conclusion: Making Steps Toward Educational Equity by Overcoming the Institutional Obstacles

As is true in all of society, the other side of racial inequality at BHS is racial privilege. Just as certain institutional practices contribute to the concentration of African American and Latino students at the bottom rungs of educational performance, other policies and practices work to ensure that high-achieving, upper-middle-class White students retain their academic advantages. Of course, a key point to be made here is that institutional bias is generally not based on overtly racist behaviors and intentions on the part of school personnel. Rather, the policies and practices that reinforce academic disparities appear on the surface to be race neutral, even though close analysis of their impact reveals clear and distinct costs and benefits that break down along racial lines.

At BHS, and at most other schools, disparities in student achievement are most likely to be attributed to factors related to student motivation. The various ways in which the operations of schools serve to reproduce and maintain racial disparities in academic achievement are less likely to be considered in discussions about the achievement gap. Unless educators are willing to examine organizational practices that facilitate the perpetuation of the gap in academic opportunities and unless they are willing and able to take actions to undo them, reducing the racial gap in student performance will not be possible.

This is obviously easier said than done, for the structural mechanisms through which racial inequality is reproduced tend to be subtle and complex. This is especially likely to be the case in the schools within MSAN, where the official discourse consistently appears to support efforts to raise the achievement of minority students. Until educators in these districts are willing to move beyond good intentions to address the institutional practices that reward academically motivated students and harm the interests of underachieving students, little progress can be made.

At the schools within MSAN and in many others as well, there are undoubtedly numerous ways in which race and class differences are maintained within the organizational culture and structure. At BHS, the Diversity Project initiated conversations with teachers first and used research to create a context in which the structure of opportunity could be discussed and challenged. However, even at BHS, changing these practices has been difficult. The difficulty comes from the fact that those who benefit most from existing institutional practices are generally able to mount fierce resistance to any effort aimed at reducing the benefits they enjoy.

To counter such a reaction at BHS, the Diversity Project found ways to provide Black and Latino parents with information about how the school operates so that they could be in a better position to advocate effectively for the educational rights of their children. Organizing African American and Latino parents was not an easy task because these parents have historically not been involved in making decisions at the school. To increase the involvement of Black and Latino parents and bring greater balance to the political forces that exert pressure on the school and district, the parent outreach committee of the project organized a series of focus group discussions for Latino and African American parents designed to elicit their views on the school. Specifically, we wanted to know what concerns they had about the education their children were receiving, what kinds of obstacles parents encountered when interacting with school officials on behalf of their children, and what kinds of changes they felt would help make BHS more receptive to their concerns.

Over the course of six months, over seventy focus groups were conducted with over four hundred parents. To ensure that maximum opportunity was provided for open communication, all of the sessions with Spanish-speaking parents were conducted in Spanish. Food and child care were also provided as an added incentive to attract high levels of participation. The parent outreach committee recruited parents to join them in conducting the focus groups and carrying out the research. This was important because the core group of the committee is now playing an active leadership role at the school. As a result of these efforts, the parent outreach group has already gotten the BHS administration to designate a surplus classroom for use as a parent center, and with the support of grants from foundations, two part-time parent organizers have been hired.

Confronted with the demands of an organized constituency, administrators at the school and the district have been forced to find ways to respond to the educational needs of underserved students. In the spring of 2001, Black parents succeeded in getting the administration to establish a new section of algebra classes for students who had failed the subject in the first semester. Although the initial reaction was that such an intervention would be too costly, when confronted by sustained pressure from organized parents, the administration eventually gave in and found a way to support the new initiative.

Much more must be done before a genuine balance between academic excellence and equity can be achieved at BHS, but for the time being, at least there is a climate in which a debate over these goals can occur. An active debate in which the concerns of all parties can be aired and openly discussed is undoubtedly the most that can be hoped for at this time. In an ideal situation, excellence and equity would not be regarded as competing goals. However, for now, the history of polarization on these issues makes it unlikely that a broad consensus will be achieved any time soon. The debate has at least allowed the school and district to move beyond the paralysis that previously characterized discussions of these issues—a paralysis that leaves so many other schools mired in acrimony and trapped in a zero-sum framing of the issues.

Even with changes intended to promote equity under way, it will undoubtedly take some time before significant reductions in the achievement gap are evident. Still to be addressed are the more difficult to address cultural factors that influence the orientation students adopt toward school. Primary among these is student motivation. Even as new tutoring and support services are provided to low-achieving students, it is not clear that students will seek these out, nor is it clear that they will enroll in more challenging courses once the opportunity is provided. Student motivation does have an impact on student achievement, and while it is essential that opportunities to learn are expanded, it is also necessary for schools, parents, and the community to find ways to motivate students who have come to see schooling and education generally as unimportant. In addition, it will take some time before we know if efforts to change BHS succeed in removing the rigid connection between racial identity and school performance that exist in the minds of some students of color. If students regard Blackness as being equated with playing basketball and listening to rap music but not with studying geometry and chemistry, then it is unlikely that changing the school alone will do much to change achievement outcomes for students. Certainly it would help if similar efforts to change the structure and culture of school were initiated in the lower grades, when students are more impressionable. But it is also important to recognize that in their efforts to challenge the insidious relationship between racial identity and academic performance, schools are up against powerful cultural forces in the media that often reinforce the opposite message (McCarthy and Crichlow 1993).

Despite the odds against success, the challenge that has been taken on by the fourteen districts in MSAN is extremely important, not just for the schools involved but for public education in the United States generally. Throughout the country, integration as an ideal and practice is under attack. Over the past twenty years, the courts have steadily weakened the legal basis for desegregation, and several communities have withdrawn their commitment to its goals (Orfield and Eaton 1996). The failure of MSAN to produce significant improvements in minority student performance would further undermine support for the goals of school integration.

Yet the experiences of places like Berkeley High School offer a glimmer of hope. When educators demonstrate a willingness to accept responsibility for their role in maintaining school structures that foster inequality and when local discussions of these issues move beyond a search for blame to a search for concrete solutions, the possibility for genuine progress in raising student achievement can be significantly increased. Of course, even that possibility must eventually yield measurable results, and obtaining these results will take much more than good intentions.

Part III

The Schools We Need

9

Reclaiming the Promise of Public Education

With Alan Blankstein

T he pressure is on. For the first time in our nation's history, schools are being required to produce measurable evidence that all students are learning, and they are being asked to do so amid fiscal crises at the state and local levels.

While several legitimate criticisms have been made about No Child Left Behind and its unfunded mandates, few can argue that it does not serve as a robust lever for change.

The demand that schools ensure that all students make adequate progress challenges even the most successful schools for many reasons, not the least of which is that educators never have been expected to do this before. Some don't even believe it is possible, others don't know where to begin, and still others know more than they have the courage to act on.

High Performance

The attitudes, skills, and beliefs of the adults who work in a school are the most important factors distinguishing schools where high levels of academic achievement are the norm for all students. School professionals who succeed in elevating student achievement accept responsibility for student outcomes. They avoid attributing student performance to factors they cannot control and pointing their fingers at others.

It is true that students whose basic psychological, physical, and emotional needs have not been addressed often experience greater difficulty in school. Nonetheless, there are schools and entire districts where recent immigrants, children of color, and poor children are more likely to excel, and external factors are treated as challenges to be addressed rather than as immutable reasons for failure. It is to these schools and districts that we must look for real ways to help all students succeed.

An examination of the research on effective schools and professional learning communities and the U.S. Department of Education's criteria for excellent schools confirms that high-performing schools share six elements:

- *A common mission, vision, values, and goals.* Collectively developing a mission statement that articulates what students should learn, how they will learn it, how we will know whether they have learned it, and what will happen if that learning does not occur is the first major pillar for school success. The vision provides a compelling and achievable long-term direction. Values describe how school personnel will behave in moving toward that vision. Goals break that vision into manageable, time-bound, results-driven pieces.

- *Systems for prevention and intervention to ensure achievement for all students.* High-performing schools adopt comprehensive systems for prevention and intervention that accelerate learning opportunities for students who are behind academically rather than separating them and slowing them down.

- *Collaboration among staff to maintain a focus on teaching and learning.* In high-performing schools, staff members take collective responsibility for the success of every student. This entails developing and adhering to a coherent and deliberate approach to educating children.

- *The use of data to guide decision making and continuous improvement.* High-performing schools rely on data to evaluate programs and to monitor initiatives implemented to help children. They reflect on the efficacy of their practice and assess their efforts to continually make modifications and improvements toward their students' progress.

- *The active engagement and participation of family and community members.* High-performing schools make efforts to involve parents as partners in helping children learn. They work collaboratively with community agencies to address needs that they have neither the capacity nor the expertise to serve.

- *A commitment to building leadership capacity at all levels.* Given the high rate of turnover among principals and superintendents, successful schools and districts develop a deep bench by cultivating leadership teams, creating alternative paths for teachers to demonstrate leadership, and developing succession plans.

High Standards

Emerson Elementary School in Berkeley, California, and the Newport News, Virginia, school district provide concrete examples of how successful schools and districts promote achievement and demonstrate the power of a genuine commitment to serving the needs of all students.

For more than ten years, Emerson Elementary School has had the highest test scores among elementary schools in the Berkeley district. One of us (Noguera) came to know of Emerson and its accomplishments while serving as an elected member of the Berkeley board of education from 1990 to 1994 while enrolling two children at the school. Emerson consistently has been a high-performing school, and despite changes in leadership, it continues to produce high levels of achievement among all of its students.

In 2000, it received an Academic Performance Index score of 9 out of a possible 10, and a 10 when compared to schools with similar demographic populations. All students score above national norms in literacy and math on standardized tests. What makes this accomplishment so significant is that like other elementary schools in Berkeley, 60 percent of the children at Emerson are minority and qualify for free or reduced-price lunch.

All adults associated with Emerson—teachers, administrators, and parents—work together to ensure that students who are behind academically do not slip through the cracks. This requires a thoughtful and deliberate approach to serving the needs of all students and a high level of collaboration among stakeholders.

At the beginning of the school year, each child is assessed in math and literacy so that teachers have a clear sense of each child's learning needs. At the first parent-teacher conference, an individualized learning plan for the student is presented and discussed. The plan includes details about monitoring student progress and using the school's supplemental resources to reinforce classroom instruction, as well as giving explicit guidance to parents on what they can do to support learning at home.

Parents are actively involved at Emerson even though most do not live in the school neighborhood. Their children are bused to the school, and they must travel across town to get there. Consistent outreach to parents takes place throughout the year. Activities aimed at encouraging participation include family math and literacy nights, family fun night, a special event for Black History Month, and workshops on various challenges faced by parents such as discipline and setting limits and talking to children about sex and drugs.

Parents respond to the support they receive by supporting the school. In response to concerns about safety caused by traffic in the morning as children are dropped off at school, parents volunteer to coordinate traffic and to serve as safety monitors.

Perhaps Emerson's most impressive feature is its consistent focus on delivering quality instruction. Every staff meeting focuses on professional development. Teachers share their expertise and materials, and they discuss ways to ensure they reach all students. They discuss how to align instructional strategies to the curriculum and state-mandated assessments in creative, compelling ways.

The goal of faculty meetings is to ensure that each teacher understands what the academic standards are and how to teach to the standards. The meetings also serve as a time to discuss the needs of individual students known to be struggling. Strategies for providing these students with the additional support they need are devised, and plans for monitoring their performance are implemented.

The key to Emerson's success seemed to relate to the strength of its leader, Laura Monroe, who served as principal for ten years. She was a resourceful and innovative leader who constantly sought to enrich the educational experience of her students through the continuous pursuit of best practices. A taskmaster and stern disciplinarian, she found ways to get teachers and parents to put out extra effort in support of children and the school by providing a clear and compelling vision that all could understand and identify with.

In the middle of the 1999–2000 academic year, Monroe was forced to take an extended leave of absence due to illness. Fearing that the district might assign a replacement who would undermine all their hard work, the faculty notified the district that they would not need a replacement while she was away. Instead, a senior teacher at the school stepped in to serve as the acting principal, and a frequently used and respected substitute assumed responsibility for her classroom.

Although Monroe had been a fixture at the school for years and a source of strength for students, teachers, and parents, Emerson did not falter during her absence. Because she had taken time to cultivate shared leadership with her staff, they knew what to do when she was gone, and the system of academic support continued to operate.

Ultimately the success of the school was confirmed once again when the scores on the Stanford 9 achievement tests were released in the fall of 2000. Emerson was again among the highest-ranked schools in California.

In the pursuit of high achievement at Emerson, nothing is left to chance.

Systems for Success

The professionals in the Newport News, Virginia, school district, a diverse, K–12, urban system of thirty-three thousand students, half of whom are on free or reduced-price lunch, are uniformly committed to the success of each student. Since 1982, the district has won twelve Blue Ribbon School awards from the U.S. Department of Education, more than any other district in Virginia.

Each school in the district systematically ensures student success through an approach similar to the "pyramid of interventions" used by mental health professionals. Staff collectively evaluate existing preventions and interventions and create new ones as part of a coherent continuum of support to ensure that all children get what they need to succeed.

Every teacher along with the school administration within a school is involved with determining the following:

- What preventions and interventions do we currently have in place in this school?

- Which of these are working well, and which could work well if modified?

- If we were to place them in a pyramid such that the lower-level intensity preventions (such as summer orientation) were at the base and more intensive interventions (such as referral to a school psychologist for individual counseling) were at the top, what holes would we have within this pyramid?

- What changes to current programs and additional pro-grams are needed to ensure success for all students?

When teachers have weekly grade-level meetings (in the elementary schools) and department-level meetings (in high schools), the pyramid is used as a tool to determine appropriate interventions for students who are falling behind. In most schools in the district, the efficacy of many of the programs within the pyramid is evaluated quarterly. On an annual basis, the entire pyramid is reviewed as both a means to orient new teachers to the options they can access for low-performing students, as well as to improve programs within the pyramid.

The base of the pyramid (level 1) consists of prevention strategies and activities. Level 1 programs typically involve a large number of students in widely implemented prevention activities. For example, the Pals Program in the Newport News middle and high schools matches all incoming students with upperclassmen who serve as mentors. This reduces the number of students who get lost in the system.

Other level 1 prevention strategies include a summer orientation for all incoming freshmen to teach them survival skills (how to study, how to avoid getting into trouble, whom to see for information on everything from questions on picking appropriate classes to what to wear for the prom and using the automated homework hotline system). Part of this orientation is taught by upperclassmen.

Those students who are "red-flagged" as likely needing more support coming into high school become part of ninth-grade teaching teams that carry through on the middle school team concept. The same four teachers work with about eighty students in English, math, science, and social studies for one year. This helps ease the transition for these middle schoolers while affording teachers more time to evaluate each student's progress.

The remaining levels of the pyramid include increasingly intensive interventions needed by fewer students, such as after-school study halls, reading and math support classes, and counseling groups formed by guidance counselors to address the needs of specific groups of students.

The pyramid of interventions involves coordination among feeder schools, support from families and the community, and systematic application by each teacher. This reduces the stress on any one member of the faculty to single-handedly ensure student success. When a teacher can't meet the needs of a student, she or he takes the concerns along with performance data to the team meeting, at which point the student's needs become a group effort.

The pyramid becomes an organized way of looking for appropriate interventions based on data. It was developed collectively, to support a mission statement created by all stakeholders, and the collaborative team focused on learning then jointly solves the challenge posed by the student needing additional support.

Generating the Will

Schools such as Emerson and districts such as Newport News prove it is possible to serve the needs of all students. Such success stories must become the norm.

The greatest obstacle preventing schools from raising achievement and closing the gap is not a lack of resources or technical expertise but rather a lack of will. If we are to make success more common in schools across the United States, the question we must ask ourselves is, "What will it take for everyone involved to resolve that failure is not an acceptable option for public education?"

The fact that we have schools where academic achievement is not the norm and where large numbers of children are written off as unteachable is unacceptable.

The changes necessary to close racial, economic, and second-language-learner achievement gaps are not easily made. The toughest among them, however, is mustering the courage and will to commit to real success for all children. The rest becomes the far easier task of determining how to go about it, a task clearly being handled effectively in districts genuinely committed to the success of all learners.

10

Standards for What? Accountability for Whom?
Rethinking Standards-Based Reform in Public Education

With the passage of the No Child Left Behind (NCLB) Act, public schools across the United States are for the first time required to show evidence that all of the students they serve are learning. For those unfamiliar with the ways in which the educational system has operated and functioned prior to the enactment of the new law, this may come as a surprise. For many years, the great shame of public education in the United States was that large numbers of students graduated from school possessing limited skills and knowledge. The new law is intended to ensure that all students demonstrate measurable evidence of academic achievement, and the slogan—Leave No Child Behind—dramatically captures this intention.

NCLB and the Promise of American Education

As noble and important as such a goal might seem, accomplishing it will be far more difficult and complicated than President Bush and supporters of the law may have imagined. Across the country, there are thousands of schools that have never shown any evidence that they can educate the majority of children they serve (Maeroff, 1988). Under the new law, such schools will be labeled "failing," and if they are unable to improve within a fairly narrow time frame, they face the prospect of being shut down or subjected to various negative sanctions (Schwartz & Robinson, 2000).

For the most part, the most troubled public schools have traditionally served the children of the poor. This is especially true in large cities such as New York, Chicago, and Los Angeles, but it is also true in small cities like Compton, Poughkeepsie, and East St. Louis. In fact, wherever poor children are concentrated, especially poor children of color, public schools are almost always very bad. Of course, part of the problem is that owing to local financing, considerably less money is spent on the education of poor children (Barton, Coley, & Goertz, 1991), but it is also true that poor children are more likely to attend schools with fewer qualified teachers and inferior facilities (Darling-Hammond, 1997).

Middle-class and affluent children have almost always received a better education, one designed to ensure that they would retain and perhaps even surpass the achievements of their parents. But for poor children, especially minority children in the inner city, public education, like public housing and public hospitals, has rarely been associated with exceptional service and excellence. Rather, public schools that serve the poor have been more often associated with a litany of problems—high dropout rates, low test scores, discipline problems, and the like—and rarely have they been a source of home and genuine opportunity for the children served.

Given the dismal state of so many public schools, the president's call to "leave no child behind" would seem to be a bold and significant development in educational policy. How could any reasonable person oppose the idea that schools should be required to show some measure of success in carrying out the function for which they were created and produce evidence that children are learning? Such a goal is, after all, a central element of the "great promise" of American education, a promise that was first enunciated by Horace Mann, one of the early architects of public education from Massachusetts. Mann called for schools that would serve as the "great equalizer of opportunity" and "the balance wheel of the social machinery." He envisioned this great leveling process occurring in a "common school," where the children of farmers and bankers, commoners and aristocrats would be educated together (Cremin, 1988, pp. 8–10). His vision called for schools that would ensure that an individual's status at birth would not determine what he or she could accomplish or become later in life. It is a vision and promise that has been intimately connected to the American dream, and it was so powerful a source of inspiration that over time, it led this nation to be the first modern democracy to create a system of public schools (Katznelson & Weir, 1985).

Taking the Easy Way Out

Advocates of the new law argue that it aims to make this promise real (Schwartz & Gandal, 2000). In compliance with NCLB, states across the country have adopted new academic standards and assessments designed to hold schools and students accountable for academic achievement. To ensure that a high school diploma is regarded as a legitimate indicator of educational accomplishment to colleges and employers, students in several states are being required to pass "high-stakes" exit exams prior to graduation. In the lower grades, students will not be allowed to advance from one grade to the next unless they have demonstrated minimal competence on standardized tests. In addition, schools with high rates of failure will be targeted for various forms of intervention and face the prospect of being taken over by state governments if they fail to improve (Elmore, 2003).

In many states, the new standards constitute a significant increase in the academic expectations that students are required to meet. They are rigorous and demanding, and, not surprisingly, many schools and districts are struggling with the challenge to meet them. They are struggling in part because they have never been expected to use high academic standards as a basis for teaching all children before, and they are struggling because many schools lack the essential ingredients to meet the needs of the children they serve. For example, schools serving recent immigrants who speak little or no English are held accountable to the same standards as schools serving native-born English speakers. The same is true for schools serving poor children with significant social and psychological needs (for example, housing, nutrition, health, and learning disabilities) and schools that are faced with shortages in essential resources (such as certified teachers, capable administrators, adequate facilities, and learning materials). In the name of equity and goal of "ending the tyranny of low expectations," all schools are being held to the same standards.

For obvious reasons, schools that were struggling before the new law was enacted are under the greatest pressure. Such schools are now required to demonstrate steady improvement in test scores on state exams, or they face the prospect of being subjected to various sanctions imposed by the state. Under the new law, there is no provision to provide assistance to struggling schools or to ensure that they will receive help developing the capacity needed to meet the needs of their students. Instead, what they will receive is pressure, and lots of it. The operating assumption behind the new law is that pressure and, in some cases, public humiliation are effective ways of forcing schools to improve.

In contrast, most schools serving affluent student populations begin this process with designations as higher-performing schools. They too must produce evidence of incremental improvements for all of their students, but they are less likely to be threatened with punitive sanctions. In several areas of the country, it is now customary for local newspapers to rank school districts by the test scores of students. In most cases, the districts serving the most privileged students are at the top, whereas those serving the poorest children are at the bottom of the test scores ladder. This is hardly surprising. In fact, school rankings often follow a form of race and class profiling: if you know the demographic composition of a school or district, it is easy to predict where that school or district will fall on the rankings. This was true before NCLB, so it is not surprising that it is true now. However, never before have policymakers construed labeling schools and districts as "failing" as a strategy for improvement and reform (Noguera & Brown, 2002).

The advent of standards-based reform has drawn greater attention to the so-called achievement gap: the gaping disparities in student performance that correspond closely with racial, linguistic, and socioeconomic differences among students. Such patterns have been evident in school districts throughout the country for many decades, but because NCLB requires that test scores be disaggregated by race and released to the public, the issue has garnered considerably more attention recently (Noguera & Akom, 2000). Gaps in achievement are particularly noticeable in affluent suburban districts. As their scores have been released to the public, it has become evident that many communities that have had a reputation for sending large numbers of students to elite colleges and universities have a far worse track record with their minority students, even when there are very few of them and most of them are middle class (Noguera, 2001a). The achievement gap is now widely regarded as one of the major challenges confronting public education today, but once again, relatively little is being done to provide concrete assistance to the schools that need the most help.

As a result of NCLB, we now have high standards imposed on students but no standards for schools. State governments have not set minimal standards that schools must meet with respect to the qualifications of teachers, the state of facilities, or access to learning materials. Moreover, there is no effort afoot to ensure that schools provide students with an education that meets the new high standards. Although students are required to pass rigorous exit exams, schools are not required to ensure that all students have been adequately prepared so that they have the opportunity to learn the relevant material.

The irony of this situation warrants close examination. It would be analogous to the Food and Drug Administration's setting standards for product quality by punishing individuals who consume faulty products, or the Federal Transportation Commission's setting new standards for air safety and enforcing them by punishing passengers for security violations at airports. The absurdity of such an approach is obvious when we apply the logic of standards and accountability to other areas of service. Yet there has been relatively little outcry over the fact that students, who have no control over the quality of education they receive, are the primary individuals held accountable under the new law. In Florida, where numerous reports have exposed severe overcrowding in schools serving the poorest children, the state has taken the bold step of placing letter grades on the front of school buildings so that all can know a failing school even before they enter. Of course, the state still allows failing schools to operate, but they pretend that by labeling such schools with a D or an F on the front door (I actually visited a school with an FF grade in Miami), they have taken tough action. In Florida and several other states, governors and state legislators have taken credit for raising standards without doing anything to improve the quality of education provided to students in schools where they know conditions are most severe.

Similar arguments can be made about the accountability strategy built into the new law. We now have tough systems of accountability for students but none for adults—teachers, administrators, governors, and legislators. I once asked the superintendent of a large urban school district who is a leading proponent of standards-based reform how many adults in his district would lose their jobs if hundreds of students did not receive a diploma in June 2003. With a puzzled look, he responded, "Perhaps a principal or two from one of the failing schools." I posed the same question to members of the state legislature and to some of the individuals who have been the architects of these reforms, and on each occasion, my question was met with the same puzzled look. How could it be that the only constituency that is being held accountable and that stands to lose something vital—a high school diploma—is made up of students, whereas the only thing at stake for most adults is the possibility that they will be embarrassed by low test scores? At a time when teachers and qualified administrators are in short supply in many areas of the country, it is unlikely that mass firings could be used as a threat for pervasive failure. I would argue that given the difficulty involved in improving schools, such a strategy would not even be fair or productive. But how fair is it that students—the only constituency that lacks lobbyists and representation in the state legislature—are being held accountable by the new law? Perhaps it is because some students are actually regarded as expendable.

At the high schools I work with in Boston, where in some cases half or two-thirds of the seniors will be denied a high school diploma, I hear anger and resignation among students and teachers. I speak with principals who readily admit that most of their students have not been adequately prepared to pass these exams. I also hear from anxious parents who hope desperately that at the last minute, public officials will come to their senses and reverse the policy as they recognize the folly of their actions and the devastating consequences that will befall many students.

However, it now appears increasingly unlikely that there will be any reversal in policy. When the results of the last exam were released in March 2003, Massachusetts state superintendent of instruction David Driscoll announced triumphantly that 90 percent of high school seniors had passed the exam, and he boldly declared victory (Feddeman and Perlman, 2003). Boston College researchers, however, pointed out that the actual percentage is closer to 78 percent if one calculates the passing rate by measuring how many students entered the ninth grade in 1999 and how many will graduate with diplomas in 2003. Moreover, even if we accept the state's figures, the results mean that one out of every four Black students, one out of every three Latinos, and just over a third of all special education students will not receive high school diplomas in 2003 (Haney, Madaus, & Wheelock, 2003).

Similar practices with similar results have been obtained in places such as Texas and Chicago where high-stakes exams have been in existence longer (Hubert & Hauser, 1999). Mass failings in these places have not led to backpedaling or a change of course from policymakers. It is not a stretch to conclude that because the casualties of this policy are overwhelmingly poor children of color, politicians are generally not troubled by the outcomes. Although large numbers of students will leave school lacking the skills and certification to obtain meaningful employment, there has not been much concern expressed. Certainly some wring their hands and publicly lament the failure of so many students, but many others seem to find solace in their belief that only the undeserving—the lazy, the unmotivated, and the dumb—have been affected.

Doing the Right Thing: Addressing the Needs of the Toughest Schools

Although politicians, corporate leaders, journalists, and others have generally hailed standards-based reform as the tough medicine needed to cure the ills of public education, those closer to the neediest schools and students have typically been less supportive about the effects of the new law. As thousands of students in states such as California, Massachusetts, Texas, and Florida are faced with the prospect of being denied high school diplomas, a growing chorus of opposition is emerging to what some regard as a gross injustice against poor students. Will our society truly be better off if thousands of students are denied high school diplomas, unable to go to college and significantly less able to find decent jobs? This is one of many questions that the advocates of NCLB have not answered, except through their silence.

Opposition to standards-based reform should be not equated with a desire to return to the past, to the time when it was possible for students to graduate with meaningless diplomas, or to when too many schools showed little interest in promoting higher levels of learning and achievement. Rather, many of those who oppose the new law and the way it has been implemented want to see state governments do more to assist struggling schools and would like to see measures of achievement broadened beyond a narrow focus on test scores.

One frightening result of NCLB is that in pursuit of the goal of raising test scores, "failing" schools have been compelled to enact a number of measures that have actually undermined the education and social well-being of students. Faced with cutbacks caused by declining state revenues, many schools and districts have been forced to eliminate subjects such as art, music, and even science if they are not covered on standardized tests. Some have eliminated field trips, recess, and physical education to increase the amount of time available for test preparation (Kohn, 2000). In secondary schools, several students have been required to enroll in test preparation courses, some of which meet for nearly two hours per day, in the hope that such a strategy will make it possible for more students to pass the exams. Rather than taking steps to ensure that students in failing schools are taught in enriched learning environments and exposed to creative and effective teachers and stimulating curricula, the narrow pursuit of higher test scores has reduced the focus of education to test preparation in too many schools.

What many advocates of standards-based reform fail to see is that it is possible to raise academic achievement and improve public education without compromising the quality of education that children receive. For this to happen, the scope and purpose of NCLB would have to be broadened considerably so that a variety of approaches could be taken to address the needs of poor children and struggling schools. In the remaining pages, I outline what some of the approaches might include in the hope that the debate over standards-based reform can move beyond critique to consideration of measures that might genuinely make a difference.

Respond to the Nonacademic Needs of Poor Children

There are a few things that we know from research about the achievement gap. For example, disparities in achievement correspond closely with other disparities that exist in our society (Miller, 1995; Noguera & Akom, 2000). The students who are least likely to achieve in school are the students from the poorest families—the kids who are least likely to have educated parents, stable housing, or adequate health care. Put more simply, the achievement gap is a reflection of the socioeconomic gap, the health gap, and the gap in opportunity.

If we want to ensure that all students have the opportunity to learn, we must ensure that their basic needs are met. This means that students who are hungry should be fed, that children who need coats in the winter should receive them, and that those who have been abused or neglected receive the counseling and care they deserve. If the commitment to raise achievement is genuine, there are a variety of measures that can be taken outside of school that will produce this result. For example, removing lead paint from old apartments and homes and providing students in need with eye exams and dental care are just some of the steps that could be taken. This may seem obvious, but although the new law is called No Child Left Behind, many of these needs have been ignored, and consequently many children are being left behind.

Even without a major change in social welfare policy, it should be possible to use several successful models of full-service schools to provide poor students with the services they need (Dryfoos, 2001). Such schools provide a variety of services to the children and families they serve, including preschool, after-school programs, health services, and job counseling for adults (Eccles & Gootman, 2002). Given that schools that serve the poorest children are most likely to need assistance in providing these kinds of services, policymakers will have to take the lead in forming partnerships with social service agencies. It is not fair or reasonable to expect schools to meet these needs or to do this work on their own. This is a wealthy nation, and as in other affluent societies, it should be possible to ensure that all children here have access to the services they need so that they can concentrate on learning in school.

Hold State Governments Accountable for Maintaining High Standards in Schools

Just as we do for the maintenance of highways and the public water supply, we should ensure that common standards of service are upheld at all public schools. Unlike the state of Florida's government that affixes letter grades on schools as a symbol of the quality of education provided there, state governments should be required to ensure that no students attend schools staffed by unqualified teachers or learn in buildings that are falling apart. State governments should be required to establish minimal operational standards for public schools, and they should be held accountable for the quality of education provided to all children.

Historically, there has been very little focus on quality control in public education. Students who are behind academically are typically placed in remedial programs, some of which are supported by Title I funds from the federal government, but it is rare for districts to ensure that the programs are effective and that there is evidence that students are actually being helped. These programs must be evaluated so that we can be sure that we have not relegated the neediest students to programs that cause them to be further behind and fail to address their academic needs.

Focus on the Problems Facing Low-Performance Schools

Low-performing schools tend to be racially segregated, and they generally serve the poorest children (Orfield & Eaton, 1996). Such schools also tend to have high turnover among staff, particularly among administrators. At many high-poverty schools in California, large numbers of teachers are uncredentialed and lack training in the subjects they teach (Darling-Hammond, 1997). Low-performing schools also tend to suffer from a dysfunctional culture where low expectations for students, lack of order and discipline, and poor professional norms are common.

These schools need help, not humiliation. They need policies that ensure they can attract and retain highly skilled professionals. State governments in partnership with colleges and universities should devise intervention strategies to assist struggling schools. There is much research available on high-performing, high-poverty schools (Jerald, 2001; Sizemore, 1988) and on programs that have proven successful for raising achievement (Traub, 2002). Drawing on this research, intervention teams should be deployed to work closely with teachers, administrators, and parents in failing schools to create conditions that lead to improvements in teaching and higher levels of achievement. Such an approach will not lead to immediate improvement in achievement measures but should begin the process of gradually turning low-performing schools around.

Make Schools More Responsive to the Parents and Families They Serve Through Systems of Mutual Accountability

One of the reasons schools in middle-class communities tend to perform well is that the parents they serve are empowered to insist on high-quality education. Middle-class parents tend to have a clear sense of what a good education is, and they generally have the wherewithal to make sure that their children get one, even if it means pulling their kids out of mediocre or failing schools as the last recourse (Nocera, 1991). NCLB contains provisions to allow parents to remove their children from failing schools, but no funds for transportation or access to information on superior alternatives. Poor parents are much more likely to defer to the decisions made by the professional educators who serve them, and they are more likely to accept the schools they are assigned to even if they are not happy with the education their children receive (Noguera, 2001b).

Poor parents constitute a captured market in public education; they typically have no option or choice but to accept what they are provided. When educators know that a constituency has no ability to challenge how it is being served, where does the incentive come from to serve it well?

The only way to ensure that poor parents are treated as valued consumers is for districts to devise strategies to ensure that the concerns and satisfaction of parents are taken into account in operations. Ideally this should take the form of systems of mutual accountability in which the responsibilities of schools, parents, and students are clearly spelled out so that all can be held accountable for their role in the educational process. Some schools have attempted to do this through the formation of site councils that involve parents in decision making (Noguera, 2001a) and through the formal contracts that establish norms and expectations for school officials, parents, and students and are signed by all parties.

Implement Diagnostic Assessment to Strengthen the Link Between Teaching and Learning

In most states, standardized tests are used for ranking purposes; test scores are used to make comparisons between students and schools, not to figure out how to help those in need. Typically state exams are given in the spring and the results are not available until the fall. By this time, students have been assigned to new teachers and, in some cases, new schools. Such an approach limits the possibility that data generated from the tests could be used to provide teachers with an accurate sense of the academic needs of students. It also makes it difficult to use data from the tests to make modifications in instruction.

Diagnostic assessments administered at the beginning of the school year can provide schools with a clearer sense of the strengths and weaknesses of students. Such an approach would make it possible for schools to monitor student performance over time and measure the performance of students in relation to established standards. Provided with a clearer and more accurate sense of the learning needs of students, schools would be in a better position to make informed decisions about curriculum and instruction and how best to use supplemental resources (such as Title I funds and grants). Schools should strive to ascertain how much academic growth occurs over a course of a year so that they can determine whether the approaches they use to support teaching and learning are effective. This requires treating assessment as an ongoing process of evaluating student knowledge and ability, not through the administration of more standardized tests but through meaningful analysis of student work.

It is common for teachers to assert that it is not fair to expect them to produce dramatic gains in achievement in a single year. Even the most gifted teachers cannot take students who start the year reading at the third-grade level and bring them to the ninth-grade level in a year. However, all teachers should be able to demonstrate that they add value to the knowledge and skills possessed by students, and that during the course of a school year their students experienced some form of academic growth.

This kind of accountability requires not only a change in assessment but, even more important, a change in the way we typically think about teaching. Too often, teachers see teaching and learning as disconnected activities. This is especially true in high schools where teachers are regarded as subject matter specialists and perceive themselves as hired to cover material within a set curriculum. They see their job as teaching the material and the students' job as learning it. Such an approach to teaching makes it unlikely that teachers will take responsibility for the learning that is supposed to take place in their classrooms. It also reduces the likelihood that significant gains in achievement will occur, because teachers see their work as only remotely related to student learning outcomes.

A substantial body of research shows that higher levels of learning and achievement are most likely to occur through improvements in the quality of teaching (Ferguson, 2000). When teachers are fully invested in learning and when they base their effectiveness on the academic growth of their students, they will routinely look for evidence that the instruction they provide is enabling their students to acquire the knowledge and skills deemed important. When teaching and learning are connected in these ways, the ultimate evidence of teacher effectiveness and student learning is the quality of work produced by students. Ideally, this should also be reflected in higher test scores and a variety of authentic indicators of learning and achievement.

Build Partnerships Between Schools, Parents, and the Communities They Serve

There is a vast body of research that has established the importance of parental involvement in raising levels of academic achievement (Epstein, 1991). Yet although the advantages of constructive partnerships between parents and schools are clear, it is often the case that such partnerships have been difficult to bring about in low-income areas. In poor communities, tensions and strains often characterize relations between parents and schools, and distrust and hostility tend to be more common than cooperation in pursuit of shared goals.

Given the importance of parental involvement, it is imperative that schools devise strategies to establish partnerships based on respect and recognition of mutual need. Several programs, such as the Comer school reform model (Comer, 1987), the local site councils in Chicago (Wong, Anagnstopoulos, Rutledge, Lynn, & Dreeben, 1999), and the use of formal contracts between parents and schools have proven effective as strategies for engaging parents in constructive partnerships with schools. Such approaches should be encouraged as a matter of policy, both to address the captured-market problem described previously and to develop the kinds of relationships between parents and schools that are essential for academic achievement and the welfare of students.

Beyond parents, schools serving poor children and communities will often need other sources of help in meeting their needs. In many communities, help could be provided by private businesses and corporations, community organizations and nonprofits, churches and local government—organizations that have a vested interest in the health and well-being of the communities in which they are located. Some of these organizations may have no prior experience working with schools, and they may need to be persuaded to play a role in supporting public education and to do more than simply make token donations. To address the lack of resources that is common to urban public schools, strategic partnerships with other organizations should be developed to provide schools with technical support, material resources, and personnel to assist schools in meeting student needs.

A partnership developed in Pomona, California, provides an excellent example of how this can be done. This district straddles two counties—Los Angeles and San Bernardino—and because of its shared jurisdiction, it had been neglected for years by both local governments. About ten years ago, the district decided to purchase a large shopping mall that had been abandoned and had become an eyesore. Using school bond money, the district purchased the property to generate revenue and to enhance its ability to help the families it serves. Serving as the anchor tenant, the district then began to lease property at the mall to private businesses and nonprofit organizations that provide child services. It also decided to locate the district personnel office at the mall to recruit new teachers. Today the mall is a vibrant youth services center. It generates revenue for the district, and the service organizations housed there provide services to youths and families in the district.

This kind of strategic partnership requires vision and imagination. It also requires creative use of resources and know-how to successfully manage relationships between public and private organizations. A recent publication of the National League of Cities (2002) encourages local governments, especially municipal leaders, to play a greater role in developing these kinds of partnerships. Similar calls have been made by researchers and policymakers who recognize that improving public schools will require a higher level of civic engagement than previously observed in most communities (McLaughlin, 2000; Stone, 2001).

Conclusion

The movement for standards-based reform has succeeded in getting educators and policymakers to focus their attention on the
need for schools to find ways to raise student achievement. There is
evidence that it is forcing schools that were previously complacent
to become more serious and coherent in how they approach teaching and learning; for the first time, many school districts are being
forced to prove that they can educate all of the children they serve.
These are not insignificant accomplishments. However, pressure
alone will not produce substantial improvements in public education, particularly in communities with the greatest concentration
of poverty. Schools serving poor children need help, and thus far,
the advocates for standards-based reform have not displayed a willingness to provide the help that is needed.

The six recommendations that I have outlined represent my
estimation of the type of policy initiatives and concrete assistance
that is needed by schools in poor communities. In putting these
recommendations forward, I have avoided the impulse to suggest
changes that are necessary but politically unviable. For example,
if we were serious about leaving no child behind, we would make
sure that all children in the United States are covered by health
insurance. As basic and important as this need might be, I recognize that at the moment at least, there is no political will to bring
this needed reform about. Given this unfortunate political reality,
I have tried to be pragmatic and I have limited my recommendations to initiatives that are politically feasible. That does not mean
that making them happen will be easy, but I do believe that it is
essential to bring these issues into policy debates about standards
and accountability.

Historically, when politicians contemplate how to "fix" public
schools, they seize on a fad or gimmick—a quick-fix solution that
they hope will miraculously change public education (Tyack and
Cuban, 1995). Among policymakers, the most popular reforms of

the day include charter schools, vouchers, and testing. Less well known but no less influential are more substantive reforms, such as small learning communities and phonics-based approaches to teaching reading, that schools have pursued to solve their problems. Although some of these strategies and others have merit and have shown promise in some schools, no reform measure is likely to produce the wholesale improvement that is desired. This is because the educational challenges faced by poor communities are not merely educational; these challenges cannot be addressed in a vacuum. What is needed is a more comprehensive and ambitious approach to address larger environmental and societal challenges related to inequality, poverty, and powerlessness.

It is not fair or reasonable for our society to expect schools to solve the problems facing young people, especially those from poor families, without help. Unfortunately, that is the situation at the moment. I believe we must respond to this challenge by calling attention to the great injustice of this situation while simultaneously doing all we can to improve our schools.

The future of our society will ultimately be determined by the quality of our public schools. This simple fact has been understood throughout our nation's history. Finding ways to fulfill the great promise and potential of American education is the task before us. For the sake of the country, the kids, and our future, I hope that we can rise to meet this challenge.

11

Racial Isolation, Poverty, and the Limits of Local Control as a Means for Holding Public Schools Accountable

There is perhaps no other sector that reflects the fractured nature of civil society in the United States more than public education. Despite a U.S. Supreme Court decision calling for schools to be racially integrated, public schools across the United States remain largely segregated with respect to the race and class makeup of their student populations (Orfield and Eaton 1996). Public schools are not only segregated, but in most American cities, poor children have been consigned to schools that show very little evidence of serving their educational needs. On every known measure of academic performance, the vast majority of students attending urban public schools in the United States (especially those who are African American and Latino) are deficient with respect to basic literacy and math skills (Miller 1995; James, Jurich, and Estes 2001).

In California, the state's Academic Performance Index (API) rankings reveal that poor academic performance is most common in school districts serving low-income populations, particularly in racially isolated urban areas where poverty tends to be concentrated (Ed Data 2002). This is true in large cities such as Los Angeles, Fresno, and Oakland, and it is also true in smaller cities such as Compton, Marin City, and East Palo Alto. The State of California holds local school districts accountable for the academic performance of students, but it does relatively little to ensure that schools meet the conditions that are necessary to provide adequate educational opportunities for all students. Although numerous studies have shown that poverty and racial isolation contribute significantly to school failure (Coleman 1988; Jencks 1972; Kozol 1991), the state does very little to mitigate the effects of these external conditions. Instead, responsibility for monitoring educational quality is delegated to educational leaders in school districts and elected school boards, in keeping with the long-standing practice of allowing local communities to manage and operate public schools (Blasi 2001).

There is a vast body of research and evidence that shows such an approach does not work. In most cases, poor communities lack the resources necessary to monitor the quality of education provided to students. Concentrated poverty and racial isolation limit the ability of parents to exert control over the schools that serve their children, and educational leaders in such communities often lack the resources to take on the task themselves. For a variety of reasons that shall be presented, conditions external to schools, such as poverty, crime, housing affordability, and health care access, exert considerable influence over conditions within schools (Coleman et al. 1966; Noguera 1996). Unless the state intervenes decisively to support schools in low-income communities, it is unlikely that such schools will ever improve.

Drawing on research and work carried out in schools and community organizations in Oakland, California, over a twenty-year period, this chapter presents an analysis of the ways in which poverty and racial isolation have contributed to the problems that have plagued schools in the district. The analysis presented draws on the concept of social capital, a concept that has been used by social scientists to study how social relationships and networks are related to the quality of civic life. Social capital has also been employed to understand a variety of issues and problems facing inner-city communities (Sampson 1998; Wacquant 1998). Through an analysis of the factors that hinder the development of social capital in low-income communities, I show why local control is inadequate as a mechanism for holding schools accountable in high-poverty areas. I also hope to use such an approach to draw attention to what it might take to transform inner-city schools into genuine assets for the communities that they serve.

Race, Class, and School Accountability

Although there is considerable variation among local school districts in the United States with respect to the demographic composition of the students and communities they serve, the policies used to regulate America's public schools are amazingly consistent. This is the case with respect to the application of federal statutes (for example, Special and Compensatory Education) that are used to regulate the provision of educational services to specially designated populations. It is also the case with respect to the strategies employed by states to hold school districts accountable. Since 1997, most state governments have implemented academic standards and assessments to monitor student achievement (Elmore 1996). With few exceptions, there is also a high level of consistency in the policies that provide the legal parameters for school governance through a practice commonly referred to as local control.

Throughout the United States, communities of all kinds elect individuals to school boards who have primary responsibility for managing the affairs of public schools.[1] Local control is a unique form of governance that is a product of the decentralized and largely unplanned historical process that gave birth to public education in the United States (Katznelson and Weir 1994). Unlike most other nations that have centrally planned and managed educational systems, the United States has a highly decentralized system in which primary responsibility for the affairs of schools is delegated to local school boards. Local control continues to be widely practiced even during periods of intense criticism over the quality of public education, largely because it is perceived as inherently more democratic than a centralized federal or state-managed system (Linn 2000).

Local governance of public schools ostensibly serves as a means to ensure that schools are responsive and accountable to the communities that they serve. Locally elected school board members are typically responsible for overseeing matters pertaining to financial management and personnel (such as collective bargaining agreements), while the education professionals they hire have primary responsibility for managing the provision of educational services. The system is designed so that those with a vested interest in the affairs of public schools—parents and the local community—are well positioned to monitor conditions in their schools.

Yet inequities among school districts and the communities they serve are rampant and extreme, and local control does not make it easier for schools to address the academic needs of poor students. Academic performance outcomes generally reflect broader patterns of inequality that are evident elsewhere in American society (Kozol 1991; Noguera and Akom 2000). Local control and financing of public education exacerbate educational inequality because there is wide variation in the ability of local communities to generate revenue and support for schools at the local level (Cibulka 2001). As a result of local control, affluent communities with a higher tax base are generally able to provide more funding for schools than poor communities are. Even in states such as California, where as a result of *Serano v. Priest*,[2] the formula used to finance schools is more equitable, there is wide variation in the ability of communities to generate supplemental resources.

Differences in per pupil spending often mirror differences in the abilities of school districts to generate and sustain civic engagement in various activities and affairs related to the management and operation of public schools. While affluent communities generally have little difficulty eliciting community participation in school board elections, site decision-making councils, and other avenues for civic involvement, low-income communities often encounter obstacles in enlisting and sustaining the involvement of parents and a diverse cross-section of community members in such activities (Epstein 1993).

Low levels of parental and community participation in public schools are frequently interpreted as an indication of disinterest in education. Yet these patterns follow trends that are common to other forms of civic engagement (for example, voting, participation within political parties and community organizations) in low-income communities (Putnam 1995). The reasons that have been suggested for lower involvement vary, ranging from lack of time and information (Gold 2001), to feelings of powerlessness and a low sense of individual and collective efficacy (Lareau 1989). Whatever the explanation, it is clear that in urban areas such as Oakland, where poverty is concentrated and poor people are socially isolated, the parents of the children who experience the greatest difficulty in school also tend to be the least involved.

Poverty, Racial Isolation, and Oakland's Failing Schools

As is true for most other school districts in the United States that cater to poor children and their families, on most measures of academic performance, the Oakland Unified School District demonstrates little evidence of success in educating its students. For example, data from the California Department of Education show that forty-three of Oakland's fifty-six elementary schools received a ranking of 5 or less on the API.[3] This means that according to the state's performance measure, two-thirds of Oakland's elementary schools are considered low performing. Under the 1999 Public School Accountability Act, "low-performing" schools are subject to various sanctions and possible state takeover if they show no improvement over three years.

The challenge confronting the district as a result of the policy is daunting. More than half of Oakland's elementary schools received an API rating of 1 or 2 (the lowest possible score) from the state. Prospects for change appear even more remote among secondary schools. All but one of the sixteen middle schools and all seven of the district's high schools received API ratings below 5. The API ratings for Oakland's schools are consistent with a broader set of academic indicators such as the dropout rate (25.2 percent),[4] the suspension and expulsion rate, student grade point averages, and college eligibility rates (19.6 percent).[5] All of these indicators serve to reinforce the widespread impression that Oakland public schools are failing and that enrollment in them should be avoided by those who can.

Yet despite the public embarrassment engendered by the publication of the school rankings, the threat of state takeover may actually do little to prod the district to improve. With hundreds of failing schools and districts across California, the ability of the state to intervene is likely to be limited.[6] Moreover, the state's own track record in managing failing districts indicates that it may be no more able to improve schools than local school districts.[7] Oakland has received more than its share of ridicule and blame for the failure of its schools. In 1996 national attention was focused on the district as a result of the controversy created by the district's adoption of a policy that called for Ebonics (also known as Black vernacular English) to be treated as a legitimate second language. As news and confusion spread about the school board's new language policy, Oakland was immediately subjected to ridicule and scorn for promoting what critics referred to as "bad English" and "slang" in the media (Perry and Delpitt 1997). Within a few weeks of the board's resolution, the California State Legislature and U.S. Congress moved quickly to prohibit the use of state or federal funds to support implementation of the policy. The district even came under attack from several prominent African American leaders who charged it with damaging the education of Black children through its poorly conceived policy.[8]

Responding to the Nonacademic Needs of Students and the "Captured Market" Problem

Interestingly, even as Oakland's schools were castigated over the Ebonics resolution, few of those who engaged in the attack offered any recommendations for actions the district might take to solve the problem it was attempting to address. The widely misunderstood policy had been adopted by the school board in response to a recommendation from a task force on African American student achievement. The task force had been formed for the purpose of devising a strategy to address widespread academic failure among African American students. (The grade point average for Black students in Oakland in 1996 was 1.8.) While it might be fair to question the district's emphasis on Ebonics as a strategy for raising student achievement, the absence of alternative suggestions served as the strongest indication that the critics had no idea themselves of what should be done to respond to the problem.

Yet as disturbing as the outlook for schools in Oakland might appear, a closer look at the characteristics of the students it serves reveals that the situation is more complex than it seems. According to the state's data, nearly two-thirds of students in the district qualify for free or reduced-price lunch based on household income (Education Data Partnership 2001), and over 40 percent of its students come from families served by the CalWORKS program (formerly Aid to Families with Dependent Children). The concentration of poverty is even more intense when one considers that all of the schools that received an API rating of 1 or 2 and have been designated "low performing" serve student populations where over 90 percent of the children qualify for free or reduced-price lunch. In addition, more than a third of the district's students are from families that recently migrated to the United States whose first language is not English (Education Data Partnership 2001). The school district is also responsible for providing adequate educational opportunities for these students, who speak over seventy different languages.

Oakland students also come to school with a wide array of unmet social, material, and emotional needs that affect their ability to learn. For example, because their families are often uninsured, many poor children lack access to adequate health and dental care (Alameda County Health Department 1998). This means that they are less likely to receive preventive treatment and more likely to rely on hospital emergency rooms when they become ill. As is true for poor children elsewhere in the country, Oakland students are more likely to suffer from asthma and tooth decay and less likely to receive eyeglasses when they need them (Alameda County Health Department 1998). As a result of poverty and the high cost of housing in the Bay Area, many Oakland students experience a high level of transience and are forced to change schools frequently when their families move into new housing. Finally, although data on these issues are less reliable, anecdotal evidence from teachers suggests that large numbers of Oakland's students come to school hungry, without adequate clothing, and suffering from stress as a result of domestic conflict in their families (Noguera 1996).

At Lowell Middle School in West Oakland where I conducted research in the early 1990s, over 40 percent of the students suffered from some form of chronic respiratory condition, and two-thirds of all students lived in a household with someone other than a biological parent (Noguera 1996). District officials applied considerable pressure on the school's leadership to raise test scores (which were among the lowest for middle schools in the district), but they did little to address the health and welfare needs of students at Lowell even though they were well aware of the obstacles these created. District administrators adopt a narrow focus on raising student achievement, not because they do not understand that a broad array of social and economic factors influence academic outcomes, but because they lack the resources to address the external conditions that have an impact on student learning.

District administrators are not the only ones who ignore the health and welfare needs of poor children as they press schools that serve them to improve. State and federal policymakers collect data on some of the needs of poor children, but do little to ensure that districts such as Oakland receive additional resources to address these needs.[9] Instead, although more affluent children in neighboring school districts such as Piedmont, Moraga, and Orinda arrive at school better prepared academically and generally have fewer unmet needs, significantly more money is spent on their education than is spent on children in Oakland (Ed Data 2001). Even as the state moves forward with its effort to hold all schools accountable for the academic performance of students, it continues to ignore the fact that poor and affluent students have vastly different needs and are generally educated under very different conditions. Moreover, the state's accountability policies, like the idea of local control, ignore the fact that low-income communities such as those served by public schools in Oakland lack the resources to hold schools accountable for the services they provide to students.

Despite the severity of the problems facing children in school districts like Oakland, such matters have generally not resulted in state or national intervention. Rather, under the pretense of local control, Oakland's educational problems are treated as local matters to be addressed by locally elected officials and the community itself. The state and federal governments allocate a variety of supplemental funds to serve the special needs of particular populations of students (such as special education, bilingual education, and compensatory education), and authority for managing the affairs of schools in Oakland is delegated to the locally elected school board. With seven elected and three appointed members,[10] the board of education has responsibility for managing a district of fifty-five thousand students with an annual operating budget of approximately $370 million. Although the per-pupil expenditure in Oakland is greater than the state average ($7,120 in Oakland; $6,334 is the state average), the funds available are largely insufficient to meet the health and welfare needs of Oakland's impoverished students.

Yet lack of financial resources is only one of the reasons that so many of the needs of Oakland's children are unaddressed. Despite the severity of the education and welfare challenges facing Oakland's schools, matters related to financial management have often taken precedent over these issues. The Oakland Unified School District (OUSD) is the largest employer in the city, and in a city with high levels of poverty and unemployment, economic considerations, such as the letting of contracts for construction, maintenance, and educational consulting, and collective bargaining issues generally, often take on greater importance and receive more attention than educational issues. Conflicts over how to allocate the resources controlled by the school district are of such great importance to the economy of the city that providing quality education to all students has often not been treated as a priority issue.

Finally, there is another important reason that educational issues have often been neglected in Oakland and in many other school districts that are located in impoverished communities throughout the country. Public schools in Oakland serve a captured market. The student population, which as I've pointed out is largely poor, immigrant, and non-White, is completely dependent on the school system. Private schools are not accessible to most poor families due to cost, and leaving the system is typically not possible even if one is dissatisfied with the quality of school services provided. With a majority of the students served by Oakland's schools trapped by economic circumstances, dependent and unable to leave, affairs of the district can be managed with little concern for whether those served are satisfied with the quality of education provided. With the exception of the superintendent and principals who are removed easily and frequently, employees in the district can be confident that their positions are secure even though the system they work for largely fails to fulfill the mission for which it was created.

Like other school districts in California, state funding to Oakland's public schools is determined by the average daily attendance of its students. As long as parents continue to enroll their children in the district's failing schools, the miserable status quo can be sustained indefinitely.

The Role of Social Capital in Improving the Quality of Public Schools

Several researchers have suggested that the quality of education children receive is directly related to the ability of parents to generate social capital (Coleman 1988; Lareau 1996; Noguera and Bliss 2001). Social capital is a concept that has been used by social scientists to describe benefits individuals derive from their association with and participation within social networks and organizations (Sampson 1998; Woolcock 1998; Putnam 1995). Like economic capital, social capital can provide concrete benefits to those who have access to it, such as jobs, loans, educational opportunities, and a variety of services. The more connected one is to groups or individuals who have access to resources, the greater the possibility is that one can obtain concrete material and social benefits.

However, becoming connected to influential social networks is not easy. Access to some networks may be based on family ties, income, religious affiliations, or association with powerful groups that have been cultivated over time. It is generally not possible to simply join an exclusive social network. In addition to having less economic capital, the poor often have less social capital than the affluent because the connections they have tend to be limited to other poor people or to organizations with fewer resources (Saegert, Thompson, and Warren, 2001).

In cities such as Oakland, poverty and racial isolation constitute significant barriers to acquiring social capital, particularly bridging and bonding forms of social capital that have been identified as most important for community development (Woolcock 1998). *Bridging social capital* refers to the connections that link poor people to institutions and individuals with access to money and power.

In Oakland, poor people of color generally lack bridging social capital because they are often excluded from influential social networks as a result of race and class barriers and social isolation. For example, although Oakland has several powerful and influential Black churches, their membership is more likely to be drawn from middle-class residents who reside in more affluent neighborhoods and the suburbs than from the lower-class communities in which the churches are located (Commission for Positive Change 1990). The same is true of many African American political clubs in Oakland such as the NAACP, the Niagara Democratic Club, and the East Oakland Democratic Club. Influential churches and civic associations play important roles in the political life of the city and often provide important services to the poor. But most poor people in Oakland do not participate in these organizations, and their absence further exacerbates their marginalization and social isolation.

Bonding social capital that provides connections among and between poor people (Woolcock 1998) and serves as a basis for solidarity and collective action is also in short supply in Oakland. Over the past fifteen years, Oakland has attracted large numbers of Mexican and Asian immigrants who have moved into neighborhoods in East and West Oakland that have been traditionally African American (Clark 1998). This demographic shift has had the effect of diminishing community cohesion as language and cultural differences have contributed to fragmentation and distrust between new and older residents. Aside from the fact that they reside on the same streets and even live in the same apartment buildings, these rapidly changing communities are made up of strangers who perceive themselves as having little, if anything, in common.[11] Rather than working together in pursuit of common community interests, growing diversity has increased the level of competition over community resources, which in turn has heightened tensions and fueled intergroup conflict. Tensions and occasionally violent outbursts related to demographic change have most frequently been manifest in Oakland's public schools, one of the few sites where different groups come into direct contact with each other (Noguera and Bliss 2001).

Finally, poor people in Oakland tend to be concentrated in neighborhoods that lack strong social institutions, public services, and businesses. The census tracts where poor people reside in greatest numbers also have the highest rates of crime and are therefore regarded as less desirable places to live by the middle class (City of Oakland 1994). In East and West Oakland, the poorest sections of the city, there are few banks, pharmacies, or grocery stores. Libraries, parks, and recreational centers are present in these neighborhoods, but residents frequently complain that drug trafficking and crime have rendered these potential community assets unusable (Office of Economic Development 1994). Sociologist Loïc Wacquant has argued that public institutions in inner-city neighborhoods may actually generate negative social capital (that is, undermine social cohesion) because their unresponsiveness to the needs of residents undermines and erodes the social well-being of the community (Wacquant 1998). Furthermore, in addition to possessing few social assets, the poorer neighborhoods of East and West Oakland have a disproportionate number of vacant, abandoned, and derelict sites. Undesirable land use facilities such as solid waste transfer stations, drug treatment centers, and industrial plants that emit toxic pollutants are also plentiful in these areas (Office of Economic Development 1994).

Throughout the United States, close examination of residential patterns reveals a high level of racial segregation and class isolation (Clark 1998; Massey and Denton 1993). This is also the case in Oakland, where since the 1960s, race and class boundaries have tended to correspond to fairly distinct geographical patterns and census tracts. Reflecting a pattern common to cities throughout the United States, Oakland's flatland neighborhoods disproportionately comprise lower-class racial minorities, while white middle-class and affluent residents of a variety of backgrounds reside in the hills and outer ring suburbs. Following a trend evident in other parts of the United States, formerly white suburbs to the south and east of Oakland are now more racially diverse, but data from the 2000 census suggest that race and class segregation remains firmly intact there as well (U.S. Census 2000). Unlike the pre–civil rights period when racial boundaries were enforced by legally sanctioned segregation, restrictive covenants, and occasionally violence, in the post–civil rights era property values and social networks play a similar role (Massey and Denton 1993).

Social Capital and Institutional Responsiveness

The prevalence of race and class isolation often has direct bearing on the quality of schools that children attend. In Oakland, children tend to enroll in schools located in neighborhoods where they live. As a result of this practice, the poorest children generally enroll in the lowest-performing schools, while middle-class children from more affluent neighborhoods attend better schools. As Table 11.1 reveals, differences between schools in different neighborhoods are striking. Although the district does not prevent low-income

Table 11.1.   Selection of Oakland Schools by Neighborhood and API Rating

	Neighborhood	API Rating
Schools in poor neighborhoods		
Golden Gate	West Oakland	1
ML King	West Oakland	2
Sobrante Park	East Oakland	1
Brookfield	East Oakland	1
Schools in affluent neighborhoods		
Chabot	Claremont	9
Hillcrest	Montclair	10
Joaquin Miller	Hills	10

parents from enrolling their children in higher-performing schools, lack of transportation and limited space make this an option that few can exercise.

The relationship between poverty and school quality requires further elaboration. Research shows that poor children are generally less prepared than middle-class children with respect to their academic skills at the time they enroll in school (Jencks and Phillips 1998). Rather than adopting measures that might reduce the effects of differences in prior academic preparation, schools often exacerbate preexisting differences in ability by providing poor children with an inferior education.

In this respect, Oakland is no exception. The schools where a majority of poor children are enrolled not only have lower test scores, they also tend to have inferior facilities and are generally more disorganized. They also have fewer certified teachers and higher turnover among principals. Some of the schools, such as Lowell Middle and McClymonds High School in West Oakland, tend to have lower enrollment because they have difficulty attracting students, while several of the schools in the San Antonio and Fruitvale sections of East Oakland are overcrowded and literally bursting at the seams.

Despite the consistency of this pattern, there is no evidence that shows that the condition of schools in low-income neighborhoods in Oakland is a product of intentional policy or a conspiracy aimed at depriving poor children of quality of education. At least part of the problem lies with the lack of social capital in Oakland's low-income communities created by poverty and social isolation, and the disproportionate social capital possessed by others. The leadership of Oakland's public schools is more likely to be pressured with demands from its unions and the small but influential number of middle-class parents it serves than by advocates and parents of poor children. The first two constituencies are well organized and politically savvy, and they have access to financial and legal resources. Occasionally poor parents also organize themselves to apply pressure on the school district, but their efforts are rarely sustained. Even when they are, the demands of poor parents can be more easily ignored because they typically lack the ability to exert leverage on school officials.

Yet differences in political influence explain only part of the reason that the needs of poor children receive less attention. Research on social capital in schools shows that poor children of color and their parents also tend to be treated differently in schools (Lareau 1996; Ada 1988; Noguera 2001). While middle-class parents often have access to resources (education, time, transportation, and so forth) and networks (contacts with elected officials, Parent Teacher Associations, and, if necessary, attorneys) that enable them to exert influence over schools that serve their children, poor parents typically have no such resources (Epstein 1993; Noguera 2001). Even if they lack these sources of support, middle-class parents possess the ultimate tool for exercising leverage on schools: they generally can withdraw their children if they are not satisfied with the schools they attend. As I've pointed out already, poor parents typically lack this option, and for this reason how satisfied they feel about the schools their children attend has little bearing on the quality of education that is provided.

Coleman has argued that social capital can produce a mutual sense of accountability between parents and school personnel, or what he terms "social closure." This is particularly likely to be the case when association with a particular school is based on shared beliefs and values that reinforce the goals of schooling (Coleman 1988). When schools are concerned about satisfying the needs of those they serve, they tend to pay closer attention to the quality of services they provide (Fantini, Gittell, and Magat, 1970). Coleman has suggested that parochial schools are more likely to exhibit a greater degree of social closure and to be more responsive to the needs of the parents they serve than public schools because shared religious beliefs and values serve as the basis for generating a sense of community and affinity (Coleman 1988). As a result of race, class, and cultural differences, poor parents in cities like Oakland generally have less in common with school personnel than do middle-class parents. Lack of social closure created by these differences results in poor parents' having limited ability to exert constructive influence on schools if they are dissatisfied with the quality of education provided to their children.

For all of these reasons, poor parents are less able to hold the schools their children attend accountable for the quality of education they provide. They have less time to attend meetings related to school governance, fewer personal resources to contribute to schools financially, and fewer options to exercise if they are dissatisfied with the treatment they or their children receive. As a captured market, they are a group of consumers who are compelled to accept the quality of educational services provided to them, whether they like it or not.

A Dream Deferred: Racial Politics and the Unfulfilled Promise of Black Power in Oakland

With academic failure so persistent and widespread, one might wonder why a community with a reputation and history for political activism would not have acted long ago to radically reform its schools. Oakland was, after all, the birthplace of the Black Panther Party, an organization that took on another public institution that was perceived as failing to serve community needs, namely the police department, which it accused of engaging in rampant harassment and brutality. Oakland's history of Black leadership and political activism goes back to the 1930s when it served as the national headquarters of the powerful Sleeping Car Porters Union (Franklin and Moss 1988). In the 1920s Oakland had one of the most active chapters of UNIA (Universal Negro Improvement Association, the largest Black political organization in U.S. history, headed by Marcus Garvey) on the West Coast. In the 1970s, Oakland voters transformed the city from a company town dominated by Kaiser

Aluminum and controlled by White Republicans into a city where all of the major public officials (mayor, city manager, superintendent of schools, police chief, state assemblyman, and congressman) were African American (Bush 1984).

However, political activism and racial succession in politics have not made it possible for those served by the Oakland public schools to exert influence and control over them. Unlike unions and political organizations that have typically been composed of individuals from middle-class and stable working-class backgrounds, since the advent of school desegregation, public schools in Oakland have catered primarily to children from lower-class families. Poor people in Oakland have not had the power or resources to effectively exercise influence over their public schools. Middle-class residents have been less likely to take on this challenge because their children are less likely to be enrolled in failing schools with poor children or in the district at all. Poor parents and community activists have organized at various times to call for reform and improvement in the city's schools. For the most part, such efforts have not resulted in significant or sustained improvements. Moreover, the fact that Black middle-class administrators have held important positions throughout the district for over thirty years has done little to bring about greater accountability and responsiveness to the needs and aspirations of those who rely on the public schools.

For the past ten years, there have been renewed attempts to mobilize grassroots pressure for school improvement. The Oakland Community Organization (OCO), a broad multiracial, faith-based coalition, has mounted considerable pressure on the district for meaningful improvement and reform. At large public gatherings it has organized, OCO has pressured public officials to pledge their support for changes in the operation and management of the schools. Yet although their efforts have led to the adoption of significant policy changes such as site-based decision making and an initiative to create several new, smaller schools (Thompson 2001), general academic improvement remains unattained.

The election of Jerry Brown as mayor of Oakland in 1999 also brought increased pressure and attention on the schools. Brown raised the need to reform Oakland's public schools prominently in his mayoral campaign, and he pledged to use his office to bring about a complete overhaul of the school district. Brown's efforts to improve Oakland's schools consisted primarily of attempts to obtain greater control over the leadership of the district. He attempted to do this by getting the school board to appoint his ally, George Musgrove, as interim superintendent. He was also successful in getting voters to amend the city charter so that he could appoint three members to the board. However, after a year in office, Musgrove was not selected to serve as the permanent superintendent by the board. By all accounts, the mayor's relationship with the new superintendent, Dennis Chaconas, was not good, and the only concrete change that can be attributed to the mayor's influence was the opening of a new military academy charter school (Brown 2001).[12]

Part of the problem with the approach that was taken by OCO, Mayor Jerry Brown, and the State of California was that more than just pressure was needed for Oakland's schools to improve. While a great deal needs to be done to increase the administrative efficiency of the district and to generally improve the quality of teaching, the simple fact was that the schools cannot serve the needs of Oakland's poorest children without greater support. Other public agencies must provide additional resources and services to address the health, welfare, and safety needs of students so that the schools can concentrate their attention on serving their educational needs.

Dennis Chaconas, the superintendent of Oakland's public schools, made concerted efforts to address the problems plaguing the school district. He shook up the central administration by replacing several long-term managers with younger professionals recruited from outside the district. He also applied greater pressure on the principals of low-performing schools and removed several principals from schools where there was little evidence of progress in raising achievement. Experience suggests that placing greater demands on the district administration, the school board, or the schools themselves is unlikely to lead change. Unless increased pressure is accompanied by systemic changes in the way schools respond to the needs of students and parents and genuine assistance is provided to the schools serving the neediest children, it is unlikely that lasting, significant change will be made.

Changing Schools from the Outside In: The Potential Role of Social Capital and Civic Capacity-Building Efforts

Given the failure of past reform efforts in Oakland and in the other large urban school districts, there is a growing consensus that alternative strategies to improve the quality of public education must be considered. Although by no means popular among policymakers and reform advocates, strategies that attempt to develop the social capital of parents and to cultivate the civic capacity of communities may be the most important steps that can be taken to further educational reform in cities like Oakland. If carried out in a coordinated manner, the two strategies could bring about several significant changes in the way public schools in Oakland have functioned and produce lasting changes in school systems.

There are several reasons to be optimistic about the potential of such an approach. First, developing the social capital of parents may be the only way to address the captured market problem. It is generally true that any organization that is able to function as a monopoly over a segment of a market can afford to operate without regard for the quality of service it provides to its clientele (Gormley 1991). It is often difficult to improve such organizations because there is no incentive for good service or penalty for poor service. This is true whether the organization in question is a public hospital, an airline, or a police department. If the quality of service provided has no bearing on the ability of an organization to continue to operate and if those who receive the service have no way to effectively register their concerns, self-initiated change is less likely.

Unlike many defenders of public education, proponents of vouchers and various school-choice-schemes have understood the importance of addressing the captured market problem. Voucher advocates have argued that the solution to the problem lies in allowing parents to change schools by voting with their feet—allow them to leave a school when they are not satisfied with the quality of education offered to their children. They argue that such a strategy will force bad schools to close when they lose students and that competition is the best way to promote reform (Chubb and Moe 1990; Gormley 1991). Not surprisingly, polling data show high levels of support for vouchers among low-income, minority voters in urban areas where the worst schools tend to be located (Wilgoren 1997).

Despite the understandable appeal of vouchers, advocates generally ignore the fact that schools rather than parents retain the ultimate choice over who will be admitted to a school, and the supply of good schools is limited. Vouchers will not provide parents with access to selective private schools both because of the prohibitive cost of tuition and because the selectivity of such schools is designed to favor an elite and privileged population of students. Moreover, the few high-performing public schools in Oakland have limited space and enrollment and cannot easily accommodate increased demand for access. Finally, research on voucher programs shows that there is no clear evidence that private schools are better at educating low-income students than public schools (Rouce 1999). There is even less evidence that other private and parochial schools are clamoring for an opportunity to educate poor children if and when they flee from failing public schools.

Efforts aimed at developing the social capital of parents can address the captured market problem when combined with policies that empower parents and make schools accountable to those they serve. In Chicago, this has been done through the development of elected local site councils (LCSs) that are composed of parents and community representatives (Hess 1999). The LCS has responsibility for hiring and monitoring the performance of the school principal, reviewing and approving the school's budget, and receiving reports on its academic plans. Under such an arrangement, how parents feel about the education their children receive is more likely to be taken into consideration because parents are empowered as decision makers at school sites (Fine 1993).

To be effective, such a strategy must also be combined with ongoing efforts to organize and keep parents informed about their rights and responsibilities so that the LCS does not come under the control of a small number of well-organized people or become manipulated by a savvy administrator. For this to happen, efforts to develop the social capital of parents must be accompanied by technical assistance, translation services, child care, and active support from community-based organizations. Churches and community groups that possess strong ties with poor communities, especially recent immigrants, are often well positioned to provide training and to facilitate contact and communication between parents and schools.

Many new charter schools have been designed with these goals in mind. At several new charter schools, parents are required to serve on the site council or to provide services to their school voluntarily (Clinchy 2000). In some of these new schools, such an approach creates conditions for a genuine partnership between parents and educators. Unlike many public schools that do not actively encourage parents to be involved in the education of their children, many new charters require active participation and have a clearly enunciated approach for promoting their rights and responsibilities.

Strategies such as these represent significant investments in the social capital of parents because they fundamentally change the relationship between parents and schools. Unlike traditional schools where parents most often interact with school personnel as individuals, the approach used in Chicago and several charter schools provides a basis for collective empowerment. Acting on their common interest in quality education, organized parents are better positioned to demand good service from schools and to hold them accountable when their expectations are not met.

Developing Civic Capacity

Like social capital, civic capacity building also occurs outside schools but can have a direct impact on what happens within them. Civic capacity building requires organizations and institutions that may not have any direct relationship to education to play an active role in supporting schools in their efforts to provide services to students (Stone 2001). It compels the leaders of public and private organizations to think creatively about how to bring the resources they control to bear on the goal of educating students. Most important, civic capacity building forces the members of a community to cease blaming schools for their failures and to focus instead on how to help them improve.

In a city like Oakland, civic capacity building could involve at least four different kinds of activities. First, it could entail the use of community volunteers in roles as tutors and mentors for students. Several school districts have been very successful at getting public and private organizations to provide release time to their employees so that they can provide services in schools. In San Francisco, a private nonprofit corporation coordinates the recruiting and training of volunteers who provide a variety of services in schools. Several other school districts have taken advantage of the AmeriCorps program to get university students to provide college counseling, tutoring, and other services to students. Strategies such as these enable schools to reduce the adult-to-student ratio and make it possible to address the needs of students who have fallen behind academically.

Second, civic capacity can also involve the formation of school-community partnerships to provide work-related internships and to support the development of career academies. Research on high schools has shown that career academies are possibly the most successful means for increasing student engagement in school (Conchas 2001). Several Oakland high schools already have career academies, some of which perform quite well; however, involvement by community-based organizations and businesses has been minimal. To obtain the maximum benefit from these partnerships, on-site learning opportunities through internships need to be created so that the partnerships can produce genuine career opportunities for students. The Biotech Academy established by the Bayer Corporation at Berkeley High School and now in place at five other high schools in the Bay Area is a model of what can be accomplished. Students in the program receive advanced training in science and math, and through the participation of local community colleges and California State University at Hayward, students have the opportunity to pursue related studies in biotechnology so that they do not get stuck in entry-level jobs. When done successfully, school-community partnerships can provide students with meaningful learning opportunities outside school, enhance the relevance of what they learn in school, and in the process transform education from an activity that is strictly school based to one that is embraced by the entire community.

Third, school-community partnerships that lead to enhanced civic capacity can also focus on the provision of professional development services to school personnel. Given the high turnover among teachers and administrators in a district like Oakland, there is an ongoing need for professional development and training. Partnerships with local universities may be the most effective way to provide support to teachers in pedagogy and curriculum content. However, public and private organizations can also play a role in supporting administrators, particularly school principals, who increasingly are required to take responsibility for a broad array of activities beyond traditional school management. Given the work demands that school personnel must contend with, most professional development activities need to be site based. It is also important for those who provide the training and support to have a genuine knowledge of the work performed by educators.

Finally and most important, the area where civic capacity development is most urgently needed is in the provision of health and welfare services to students and their families. Throughout the country, there are several effective models for providing a range of services to students at schools. In all cases, the best programs are based on a partnership between schools and community agencies. For example, the Children's Aid Society in New York City operates eight community schools that offer health, dental, recreational, and employment training services to students and their families (Dryfoos 1997). A number of Beacon and Full Service schools operate throughout the country, and they often remain open twelve hours per day by drawing on a second shift of community professionals to run after-school programs. While many of these programs are exceptional, the number of students served by them is minuscule. Most of the best programs operate at individual school sites, and not a single one operates throughout an entire school district.

Given the high levels of poverty among school children in Oakland, a comprehensive, citywide strategy for providing social services at school sites is needed. For the sake of cost efficiency, this will necessarily involve improved cooperation between the school district, city government (which funds recreational and youth services), and county government (which funds health and social services). Private organizations (such as the YMCA and Girls and Boys Clubs), as well as churches and nonprofits, can also play important roles in developing systems of support for students, but the large public agencies will undoubtedly have to take the lead since they control the bulk of resources for social services.

Given that all three of these public agencies provide services to the same population of families, improved coordination in service delivery could actually reduce redundancy and increase cost efficiency. However, interagency cooperation is difficult to accomplish on a large scale because the individuals staffing these organizations generally have no prior history of cooperating, and bureaucratic narrow-mindedness is not a small hurdle to overcome. For this reason, leadership and support from the mayor, superintendent, school board, and county board of supervisors will be needed so that those who carry out coordination activities have the backing to overcome the obstacles they will inevitably encounter.

Conclusion

In contrast to many analyses of urban school systems in the United States (Kozol 1991; Maeroff 1989), it is my hope that the one presented here is relatively optimistic. I genuinely believe that it should be possible for Oakland public schools to effectively serve the educational needs of its students. Furthermore, by creating conditions that enable schools to be held accountable by those they serve and drawing on the active support and participation of the numerous assets and resources present in the city, Oakland should be able to significantly improve its schools. This is not to suggest that the obstacles to bringing this transformation about are not formidable, but clearly the conditions and possibility for change do exist.

The same may not be true for other poor communities that have less money and fewer community assets. Strategies that develop the social capital of parents and civic capacity of communities in socially isolated areas where poverty is concentrated are less likely to produce lasting improvements in public schools. Small cities like East Palo Alto or Compton, California; North Chicago, Illinois; and Poughkeepsie, New York, simply cannot be expected to elevate the quality of their schools on their own. In such places, the array of social and economic hardships besetting the community is so vast, and the availability of resources so limited, that outside assistance will be needed if change is to be made. In such places, the limitations of local control of schools and the inequities it tends to reinforce are most evident.

Rather than presuming that all schools can be treated the same, state and federal officials must recognize that socioeconomic conditions within the local context can act as significant constraints limiting possibilities for local control of schools. Put more simply, without the power and resources to exert control over schools, low-income communities cannot be expected to hold their schools accountable. Nor is it reasonable to expect that schools in such communities will be able to solve the vast array of problems confronting students and their families on their own. Unless states enact measures to militate against the effects of poverty and racial isolation, local control will remain little more than a guise through which the state can shirk its responsibility for ensuring that all students have access to quality education.

The fractured nature of civil society in the United States may make it unlikely that policymakers will enact the kinds of far-reaching changes in social policy that are needed. Ideology, racism, and divisions related to class, national origin, and even geography have historically prevented politicians and vast segments of the general public from considering problems affecting the poor as a matter of national concern. The No Child Left Behind Act, which will significantly increase the federal government's role in failing local school districts, is unlikely to provide the help that is needed. The measure does nothing to address the horrid conditions present in many failing schools, and it does not even begin to attempt to ameliorate the social inequities that have an impact on schooling.

For African Americans, the government's continued neglect of public education represents a significant problem. Although reforming public schools will not eliminate poverty or racial discrimination, education continues to be the only legitimate source of opportunity available to the poor. Beyond the skills and job opportunities that education can make possible, it can also serve as a means for the poor and oppressed to imagine a more just social order (Frèire 1970). Having the ability to imagine alternative pos-sibilities is often how social movements that lead to greater societal change are born (Horton and Frèire 1990). For communities strug-gling to meet basic needs, improvements in education can be an effective means to obtain tangible benefits even without other more far-reaching social reforms.

Public education has historically occupied a special place within American civil society because it has often been the birthplace of democratic reform (Tyack 1980). For African Americans, educa-tion has long been recognized as vital to collective improvement because "it is the one thing they can never take away" (Anderson 1988). Education is also the only social entitlement available to all children in the United States regardless of race, class, or national origin (Carnoy and Levin 1986). In the past ten years, support for improving public education has also been the only domestic issue that has generated broad bipartisan consensus among policymakers. Given its unique status, it makes sense for those interested in find-ing ways to reduce poverty and racial inequality to focus at least some of their energies on efforts to improve the quality and charac-ter of public education in the United States.

12

Transforming Urban Schools
Through Investments in Social Capital

I spend a great deal of time in urban public schools. As a researcher and educator, I am frequently called on to speak to students and teachers, to organize workshops for parents, and to use my skills to assist in addressing some of the many problems facing urban schools. I work on projects with parents, teachers, and students in an attempt to improve conditions in schools through the use of action-oriented research. In some cases, I develop working relationships with schools based on a collaborative project that is carried out over an extended period of time, sometimes over the course of several years. Despite the intractability of the problems and issues we take on—student achievement, teacher effectiveness, discipline and safety, support services for children and families, race relations, bilingual education—I enjoy engaging in the work because it provides me with a sense that I am doing something concrete about issues that affect people's lives in important ways. I feel this way even though there are relatively few schools that I can point to that have found ways to successfully respond to the broad array of complex challenges that are out there. This is because the problems and issues confronting urban schools are typically manifestations of larger societal problems related to social inequality, racism, and the deterioration of urban areas. Still, I derive a degree of satisfaction from the experience of being connected in a concrete way to the struggles and aspirations of those I've worked with and from knowing that through such connections, I am able to develop a perspective on the challenges facing urban schools that is situated in a real-life context and linked organically to the experiences of those most directly affected.

Because I spend a lot of time in urban schools, I've become fairly adept at discerning how the aesthetic of the physical surroundings and the subtleties of interactions between adults and children relate to the character of a particular school and the cultural norms that operate within. The lighting of hallways, the cleanliness of restrooms, the positioning and demeanor of secretaries in the front office, the absence or prevalence of greenery on the playground: these are just some of the signs I take note of to obtain insights into the culture and atmosphere of a particular school. For sure, I learn more from my conversations with teachers, administrators, and students and from my visits to classrooms or the school cafeteria, but the initial observations are often the most telling and informative.

Two recent visits to urban schools—one a large high school, the other a small elementary school—provide examples of how significant first impressions can be. These examples also provide insights into the role of social capital in relationships between parents and school personnel and between urban schools and the communities that they serve.

Who Counts, Who Doesn't: Social Capital and the Uneven Relationship Between Parent and Principal at Urban Schools

I had been contacted by the principal of a large urban high school in the San Francisco Bay Area who wanted to discuss her strategic plan for reforming the school, which she planned on submitting to the school board for review that evening. I arrived at the high school in the late afternoon just as school was letting out. As I parked and walked toward the front office, I noticed groups of students casually milling around the front of the building. It was one of the few sunny and warm days we had had in the month of January, and it felt good to be outdoors. Some kids dressed in athletic gear moved across the parking lot quickly, with a clear sense of direction, and appeared to be on their way to practice. Most of the students appeared to be hanging out in small groups throughout the campus. Most seemed engaged in light conversation, and the occasional burst of laughter suggested to me that for the moment at least, things were calm on this Thursday afternoon.

About five minutes into my conversation with the school principal, an African American woman in her early forties, we were interrupted by one of her assistant principals, a Caucasian man in his mid- to late fifties. His furrowed brow conveyed a look of deep concern on his weathered face. Interrupting our conversation, he informed the principal that a large group was in his office demanding to see her immediately. They were there to protest the decision she had made earlier in the day to suspend a student who had been fighting with another student. He explained that they sought an audience with the principal to explain their daughter's side of the conflict.

The principal responded by saying, "Tell them I can't see them now, but that if the girl hit the other student, she's out for three days. Period." By the troubled look on the assistant principal's face, it was evident that the principal's response was of little help to him. He informed her that the student claimed she had been attacked and only struck back at her assailants in self-defense. Again, the principal was dismissive. "It doesn't matter. If you hit another person, you're outta here. If they need to talk to me about it, tell them they can wait, but it's gonna be at least an hour."

As she turned to me to resume our conversation about her plan, I asked her what students were expected to do if they found themselves in a situation where they felt compelled to defend themselves. I confessed to her that as a parent, I instructed my own children to defend themselves if they were attacked and no adults were present to intervene. With the assistant gone, she smiled and confided, "I met with these folks earlier today, and let me tell you, the momma is worse than the daughter. She probably wants to beat them girls up herself. If I see her, she'll just get in my face and start to hollering. I really don't need that. Sure, I think that self-defense is legitimate at times, but I know when I'm dealing with problem people, and this girl and her momma have serious problems."

The second incident occurred at an urban elementary school where I had been invited by the principal to speak to her teachers about expectations for African American children. The principal, a White woman in her mid-fifties, contacted me because she was under pressure from central administration in the school district to raise reading test scores. She wanted me to speak to the faculty about their expectations toward African American children because she believed "these teachers don't think these kids can learn."

I arrived at the school at about 8:30 A.M., parked in the lot out front, and walked to the main office. As I entered the building I was greeted by the principal, who was standing with a broad smile on her face in the main entrance. She extended her hand and told me how glad she was that I had taken the time to visit her school. Just as she was about to launch into the issues that had prompted my visit, three girls—Latinas who appeared to be ten or eleven years of age—entered the building laughing playfully with each other. At the moment of their arrival, the principal stopped midsentence to confront the girls. "Young ladies! Is that the way we carry ourselves in the halls when class is in session? I do believe you're tardy, aren't you?" The girls nodded sheepishly, and as one attempted to speak to explain her tardiness to the principal, she was immediately cut off: "I don't want to hear why you are late. I want to see you walk quietly into the office to get a late pass. Your parents can send me a note explaining why you are late."

Just as she finished her sentence, a well-dressed woman in her mid-forties entered the front door. From the look on her face it was evident that she was accompanying the three girls. It was also immediately clear that she was not at all happy about the scolding that was in progress as she entered, and her face revealed her displeasure toward the principal. Upon noticing the woman and immediately recognizing her as a parent of one of the girls, the principal abruptly changed her tone of voice and facial expression. Her frown melted into a smile, and the sternness in her voice transformed into a warm, though phony, greeting. "Good morning. I was just telling the girls that they have to use their inside voices when they enter the school building because classes are in session." Then, turning to the girls with the same warm and friendly tone of voice, the principal continued, "Girls, since your mother is here, you won't need a late pass. So hurry off to class; you don't want to be too late." The parent did not return the smile. Instead, she nodded her head with a false smile that seemed to connote her displeasure and spoke directly to the girls. "Come on, I don't want you to be late for your class either, and I've got to get to work." The parent then shot a quick glance of disgust at the principal, shaking her head as if the very sight of her was distasteful. As the group left, the principal turned to me, and said, "That's just some of what I deal with all day, every day, around here. I'm the authority figure, and not everyone's comfortable with the rules, but we have to have 'em." She then led me to the teachers' lounge for our first meeting of the day.

These two vignettes provide profound insights into the ways in which cultural capital (Bourdieu 1985) influences the character of interactions between school officials and the parents they serve, a phenomenon that has been well documented by scholars such as Annette Lareau (1990), Ann Ferguson (1995), and Michelle Fine (1993). These interactions also illustrate how urban public schools have the potential to serve as sources of either negative or positive social capital (Wacquant 1998). In the first case, a school rule—prohibition against assaulting another student—is applied with rigidity and without regard to mitigating circumstances based on the principal's belief that the student and her mother have "serious problems." The vague reference to problems in this instance seems to mean that they possess a hostile attitude, that their behavior is aggressive, and irrational. According to the principal, who has the power to determine how this situation will be handled, such people have serious problems, and consequently, both child and parent are in need of discipline by the rules.

The character of this interaction also reveals the degree of social distance between school official and parent—a separation that may be based on differences in class and social status, as well as differences in roles. As an outsider in this situation who had not met the girl, her mother, or her family, I immediately assumed that the principal would behave in such a perfunctory manner only if the parent and child were poor. Given what I know about the school—the racial and socioeconomic composition of its students—and given that the matter in contention concerns a fight between two students, I assume the parent is not only low income but also probably African American. I draw this conclusion because in my many visits to urban schools, I have witnessed numerous occasions in which parents, especially African Americans and recent immigrants, have been treated with disregard and disrespect by school officials. This pattern of treatment is also well documented in the research on relations between parents and urban schools (Comer 1981; Epstein 1991; Fine 1993). Sometimes the affront is blatant: a dismissive explanation of a rule or policy or even a direct insult. More often the disrespect is less obvious and more nuanced, taking the form of a condescending bit of advice or less-than-prompt response to a request for help.

My assumption about the parent is confirmed when I encounter the group (parent, child, and relatives) as I leave the principal's office. Agitated by the long wait and the sense that they have been wronged by the school rules, the family sits impatiently, waiting for the principal in the adjoining office until our meeting is over. Without knowing their net worth or income, their clothing and appearance, speech and demeanor convey the habitus (Bourdieu 1988) that I typically associate with lower-class, inner-city African

Americans. The fact that the principal walks past the group without acknowledging their presence as she walks me to the door is further evidence that in her eyes, these people don't count in an important way; they have "problems," and the principal feels completely justified in her resolve to deal sternly with both student and parent.

Cheryl Harris (1993) has argued that physical attributes that signify membership to a particular race and class interact in significant ways with rights and interests related to property and material assessments of individual worth. In a society that has historically been characterized by rigid racial stratification (Omi and Wanant 1986; Fredrickson 1981) and in which whiteness has served as a primary signifier of privilege because it has been used to limit access to economic and political capital (Roediger 1991; Ignatiev 1995), blackness and "coloredness" have historically served as negative social referents and been accorded negative value. When blackness is combined with membership in the lower class, the value of an individual or group is even further diminished.[1] It is not immediately clear how these factors may have influenced the principal's perception of this parent and child; however, it cannot be presumed that because both parties are Black, such racially informed judgments are not being made (Frazier, 1957; Rist, 1973; Hall, 1990).

This interaction between the principals and the parents at these two schools also exemplifies how urban public schools can operate as a source of either "negative" or "positive" social capital (Wacquant 1998; Gargiulo and Benassi 2000; Bourdieu and Wacquant, 1992). Drawing on Bourdieu's concept of social capital (1986), which he defines as "the sum total of the resources, actual or virtual, that accrue to an individual (or a group) by virtue of being enmeshed in a durable network of more or less institutionalized relationships of mutual acquaintance and recognition" (p. 248), it is possible to conceive of schools as public institutions and social resources that have the potential of generating and developing social capital for a community. The forms of social capital produced at urban schools can be either negative—because they serve to maintain and reproduce the marginality of inner-city residents—or positive—because they provide the forms of cultural capital valued in the broader society and economy and support the formation of social networks that promote the interests of inner-city residents.

A key factor determining which form of social capital will be produced is the nature of the relationship that exists between the school—and the individuals who work there—and the community—including, but not limited to, the parents of the children enrolled. Where connections between school and community are weak, urban public schools are more likely to operate as negative social capital. This is because it is typically the case that the personnel at most urban public schools do not reside within the communities they serve, and social barriers related to differences in race, culture, and class can create a tremendous gulf between school and community (Noguera 1996; Haymes 1995). This separation between school and community can reinforce or contribute to the development of biases among the outsider professionals who come to see the poor children, their families, and the communities that they serve as deficient, dysfunctional, and even hopeless. Evidence that this has occurred may be seen in the extent to which low academic performance is normalized, the extent to which teachers are evaluated in relation to the academic outcomes of their students, or the degree to which violence within the school is perceived as a "natural" environmental condition. Given that such characteristics are common to many urban public schools (Anyon 1996; Payne 1986; Maeroff 1988), Wacquant's contention that urban schools, like other public services in the inner city, are a symptomatic feature of "America's racialized urban core where there is a dearth of core organizations necessary to contribute to the community's functioning and well-being" (1998, p. 28) helps to explain why many urban public schools operate as negative social capital.

Furthermore, such schools generate negative social capital because they contribute to the problems of the community by deepening the marginalization of the children and families they serve. Various authors have argued that certain norms, customs, and traits that may have efficacy and value in one context actually prove to be detrimental and counterproductive in another context. According to Wacquant, "The same property may take on a different value and have divergent effects, depending on the arena of action in which it is invested" (Wacquant 1998, p. 27). A frequently cited example is the use of Black English, or Ebonics, a form of speech commonly used in primarily black social settings, but one that is negatively sanctioned and often denigrated in school and business settings (Kochman 1973; Foster 1997). Ideally, schools should serve as mediating institutions where individuals can be taught to code-switch—master standard English and learn where and when its use is required—while still affirming the culture and aspirations of its students. If such skills are not taught, or if Black English and those who use it are negatively sanctioned and denigrated, then the school is more likely to produce oppositional behaviors (Ogbu 1987; Fordham 1996), which are likely to hurt the long-term prospects for the social mobility of the children served (Kochman 1969; Dillard 1972).

However, in the cases described here, more is at work than a simple judgment based on speech, style, or status. In the first scene, the act of disciplining is delegated to the assistant because the principal is unwilling to speak to the protesting parent. It may be that the principal and the parent had met previously and the principal formulated her opinion of the parent based on an earlier interaction. However, as Coleman (1988) has pointed out, maintaining social distance is one of the ways in which groups and individuals sanction and constrain the actions of others. Inviting the parent into her office, listening to her concerns, engaging in an equal exchange over the particular incident and the relevant rules that may have been broken would not only connote respect but also convey in a profound way that this individual and her concerns were important. That such treatment was not extended demonstrates powerfully how perceptions of cultural capital can influence the nature of relationships between urban schools and the families they serve.

In the second case, the perceived value of the student's cultural capital is made evident as I observe the principal's reaction to the sudden arrival of her middle-class parent. Instead of mere wards of the school who can be scolded without retort and dispatched quickly to class, the appearance of their presumed-to-be White middle-class mom elicits a sudden and dramatic change in treatment. In her presence, the girls are no longer treated as loud and disruptive rule breakers. Under the watchful eye of a White, middle-class parent, the students are spontaneously transformed into welcomed members of the school community, and the fact that they might have a legitimate reason for being late is suddenly taken into consideration. As members of the community, they are spoken to with kindness, and their middle-class mother is accorded the respect and deference typically extended to consumers whose business is valued and sought.

In this case, the parent is perceived as possessing positive cultural capital derived from education, income, class, and perhaps race. Race remains an unknown factor in both interactions for it is never mentioned or named. The degree to which the perceived whiteness of the parent prompts cordial treatment from the principal is not discussed but may be relevant given how differently the principal treats the Latin-looking girls. That interaction (principal to student) may be explained by differences in age and position, but again that too is unknown. What does seem evident is that as children related to such an individual, the students immediately reap the benefits of derivative association and experience a significant improvement in treatment as a result. I believe it is likely that the principal's change in tone and behavior is based on her understanding that a White, middle-class parent has a keen sense of her individual rights and a powerful sense of entitlement with regard to how she expects to be treated by teachers or administrators in a public school (Nocera 1990). Unlike the parent in the first scenario, the middle-class parent also possesses a powerful weapon that is typically inaccessible to the poor: the power of choice. I will explore this point in further detail later, but for now, let it suffice to point out that an essential difference between the two parents in these examples, and between poor and middle-class parents generally, is that one has the resources and wherewithal to abandon a school and choose another if she does not like the treatment that she and her children receive. In contrast, the other parent is more likely to feel that the school her daughter attends is the only one available to her, and as such, the principal holds all of the power when the two meet because she has the ability to unilaterally exercise power by suspending the student should she deem it necessary or desirable.

Problematizing Failure: The Role of Urban Schools in the Reproduction of Social Inequality

Particular incidents such as those described at the beginning of this chapter help in understanding the ways in which urban schools interact with the communities they serve at a microlevel; however, it is also important to understand how broader patterns of interaction operative at the macrolevel influence the formation of social capital. As has been demonstrated in numerous studies, public schools in the United States serve as great sorting machines through which inequality and privilege are reproduced (Bowles and Gintis 1976; Carnoy and Levin 1985; Katznelson and Weir 1985). They are not alone in carrying out this function, but they more than any other social institution reproduce existing social and economic inequities with an air of legitimacy that makes the process seem almost natural (Apple 1982; Giroux 1988). This is because the production of workers and professionals, future leaders and future criminals, conforms to prevailing ideological conceptions of merit and mobility. That is, those we expect to succeed—such as children from affluent families—tend to be more likely to succeed, while those we expect to fail—poor children, especially those from the inner city and whose primary language is not English—tend to be more likely to fail. The conventional wisdom is that the winners and losers earn what they receive in the end and that the process of sorting is fair and based largely on achievement (Bowles and Gintis 1976). It is also assumed that school failure is the by-product of individual actions—a failure to study and do homework, to behave in class, to attend school regularly—while the collective and cultural dimensions of school failure are ignored (Apple 1982).

The fact that the production of winners and losers corresponds so closely with larger societal patterns of race and class privilege has not generated much public concern in recent years beyond those most directly affected. This is due in large part to hegemonic forces that condition popular attitudes and expectations such that the persistence of these patterns seems "normal" or even "natural" (MacLeod 1987). For this reason, even in a period in which more public attention and resources are being channeled into education than at any other time in this nation's history (Tyack and Cuban 1995), little, if any, of the public discourse focuses on the issues and questions related to social reproduction. Certainly policymakers speak out with indignation about the "crisis in public education" and decry the failure of urban schools in particular. But individual outcome measures (such as grades, test scores, or graduation rates) are used to gauge progress, while more nebulous indicators—school climate and perceptions of safety, the morale and collegiality of teachers, the quality of relations between a school and the parents it serves—are ignored. Amid all the outpouring of concern about the state of public education, too often the factors that those most directly involved regard as important—access to resources and materials, the state of facilities, availability of trained professionals—receive little attention while instead, resources are directed to preparation for the newest test and the latest curriculum innovation. So far, there is no renewed interest in equalizing funding between schools (Anyon 1996), interest and funding for desegregation is waning (Orfield and Eaton 1996), and there is no urgent effort afoot to address the acute lack of resources in personnel, materials, and services for schools in the most economically and socially marginal communities (Kozol 1991).

If there is a crisis in public education,[2] few commentators would disagree that it is most acute in America's urban areas. The inner city, especially those areas now referred to by some city planners as "no-zones"—no banks, no grocery stores, no community services, no hospitals (Greenberg and Schneider 1994)—possesses more than its share of failing schools. At schools in these areas, dropout rates hover at around 50 percent, test scores are generally well below national averages, and metal detectors are as ubiquitous as swings and slides on the playground (Maeroff 1988). To the extent that the media carry any news of success at such schools, it is most likely that it will appear in some human interest story about a single student, teacher, or coach who managed to overcome tremendous odds to accomplish something noteworthy that normally isn't possible or expected for children living in the ghetto or barrio.[3]

Urban schools in the United States are the backwater of public education, and their continued failure blends in easily with the panorama of pathologies afflicting the inner city and its residents. This fact is so well known and so taken for granted that like inner-city crime, the issue is often not even deemed newsworthy. Following the random shootings in Jonesboro, Arkansas, in 1998, the refrain repeated most often was that "this wasn't supposed to happen in a community like this" (Perlstein 1992). White middle-class boys in a White middle-class community aren't supposed to shoot their teachers and classmates. Such a scenario is presumed to be limited to schools in the impoverished inner city. As such, its occurrence in suburbia is to be explained, at least in part, by "urban influences" that creep into wholesome neighborhoods like an infectious disease via the media or through children from "broken families."[4]

For all of these reasons, the failure of urban schools and the children they serve is not problematized; rather it is expected. New programs and policies are adopted with some regularity, but there is little willingness to address the fact that urban schools are inextricably linked to and affected by the economic and social forces present within the urban environment. However, they are not merely creatures of their environment. They have the potential to either contribute to the further decline of the quality of life in urban areas, or to serve as a viable social asset that can further the development of positive social capital. My own experience working with urban schools leads me to believe that any serious policy for improving urban public schools must address the educational issues in concert with other issues, such as poverty, joblessness, and the lack of public services. Such an approach has not been attempted since the Great Society programs of the 1960s (Pinkney 1984; Wilson 1981), and under the current paradigm of neoconservatism, there is little likelihood that such a comprehensive effort will be launched again in the near future.

Absent the political will to support the re-creation of massive social welfare programs and investments that would spur development in economically depressed urban areas, it may still be possible that social reforms can be initiated that can bring gradual and concrete improvement to conditions in the inner city. I believe such an approach must focus centrally on the development of social capital through the improvement of urban public schools. Specifically, the goal must be to transform urban schools into sources of social stability and support for families and children by developing their potential to (1) serve as sources of intracommunity integration and (2) provide resources for extracommunity linkages. These forms of social capital have been identified by Coleman (1988), Woolcock (1998), Putnam (1995), and others as key elements of strategies for addressing the needs of poor communities. I believe the urban public schools are uniquely and strategically situated to contribute significantly in both of these areas and that the benefits that will derive from such developments will extend beyond the confines of school to the broader community.

Before explicating the elements of such a strategy, two points must be made regarding why it is needed:

- Urban schools are increasingly the most reliable source of stability and social support for poor children. This is largely because unlike other public and private institutions, public schools are required to provide access to all children regardless of their status (Noguera 1996; Comer 1981). Children who are homeless, undocumented, sick or disabled, hungry or abused, all have a right to access public education. Given the harsh realities confronting the poorest people in this country, schools are often the only place where children can be guaranteed at least one meal, a warm building, and relative safety under adult supervision; public schools are, in effect, the most significant remnant of the social safety net available to poor people in the United States (Fischer et al. 1996) . The fact that they generally have stable funding and therefore follow fairly predictable operating procedures means that for many poor children, their attendance at school is the most consistent and stable aspect of their lives.

- At an ideological level, the notion of equal opportunity through education continues to have broad appeal in American society.[5] The first public schools were created in part because of broad popular support for the ideal that public schools were needed to ensure some degree of equal opportunity (Katznelson and Weir 1985). Legal precedent continues to favor universal

access to public education even though the right to an
education is not guaranteed in the U.S. Constitution
(Kirp 1982). Although there is little evidence of public
support for radically equalizing funding between and
among schools, there is considerable public support for
using education to extend opportunities to the lower
class for social mobility through education.

The implication of both of these points is that it may be possible
to generate significant investments in urban public schools (and
charter schools) as a strategy for addressing poverty, social isolation, and economic marginalization in the inner city. A key element to achieving such a possibility necessarily involves directing
resources and adopting policies that promote the development of
social capital among inner-city residents. Specifically, strategies
that encourage the development of social organizations and social
networks that can exert influence over local schools are needed.
As will be shown in the pages ahead, the cultivation of these forms
of social capital can facilitate a greater degree of empowerment,
accountability, and control by parents and community residents
over the schools that serve them. I will argue that to the extent
that such outcomes can be realized, urban schools can become a
powerful resource for community development and facilitate other
forms of political and economic empowerment that can ultimately
transform the character and quality of life of urban areas through
bottom-up, grassroots initiatives.

Empowering a Captured Population

While structural factors related to the political economy of urban
areas, and more specifically related to deindustrialization, globalization of the world economy, suburbanization, and middle-class flight,
have had a profound effect on the character of urban areas (Wilson
1981; Massey and Denton 1993) and urban schools (Maeroff 1988;

Payne, 1986), social capital can also be employed as a theoretical construct to help explain the persistent failure of urban schools and to promote efforts aimed at improvement and change.

As I pointed out in the two vignettes, a major difference distinguishing the middle-class parent from the lower-class parent is the power of choice. By virtue of the human capital (education and information) and economic capital they possess, middle-class parents have the ability to leave a school if they do not like the way their children are treated or if they perceive the quality of education offered as inadequate. Leaving may mean enrolling a child in another public school or opting out of the system altogether by sending their child to a private school. However, leaving is not the only option available because middle-class parents also have other resources at their disposal to fight for what they want. Politically savvy middle-class parents can petition higher authorities such as the superintendent or school board; they can use organizations such as the Parent Teachers Association, churches, or the National Association for the Advancement of Colored People to exert influence on school officials; or they can draw on external contacts, such as lawyers or the media, to press for what they want or believe they are entitled to.

In contrast, lower-class parents typically lack the ability to choose the school their children attend, both because the cost of private school is prohibitive and because they may lack transportation to gain access to better schools in more affluent neighborhoods (Fuller and Elmore 1996). Furthermore, unlike middle-class parents, the ability of poor parents to fight for what they want is often constrained because they tend not to receive the same kind of respect and responsiveness from school authorities when they seek recourse for change. Like the parent in the first vignette, lower-class parents, even when angry or passionate about their concerns, are more likely to be disregarded and not taken seriously by school officials (Lareau 1990; Kozol 1995; Comer 1981). Most writers on this problem have argued that poor parents and children need to acquire the cultural capital (speech, style, customs, and others) valued by the middle class in order to enhance their ability to obtain the services needed for their children (Ogbu 1978; Solomon 1992). However, such a transformation is extremely difficult to bring about and may even be impossible for most. Abandoning forms of behavior that one has acquired over the course of a lifetime, and that continue to have value in particular communities and settings, in exchange for those of another group or class, requires a high degree of motivation and self-conscious acquisition. Even if cultural assimilation occurs actively and willingly, there may be no guarantee of acceptance by members of the dominant group if discriminatory attitudes related to race and class are operative. There is considerable evidence that even middle-class minorities, especially blacks, are subject to forms of racial bias and discrimination (Cose 1995; Hacker 1992; Barrett 1999), and the acquisition of the requisite cultural capital by itself may not be enough to counter the effects of such practices.

Moreover, such a formulation places the onus for change on the less powerful actors, thereby absolving those with more power of responsibility for modifying their own dismissive actions. It may be that it is as unrealistic to expect middle-class school officials in positions of authority to change their attitudes toward the poor as it is to expect the poor to adopt a new set of cultural norms. For this reason, I believe greater emphasis must be placed on the development of a different kind of social capital—that which is derived from organization and association. Putnam (1995) suggests that we ask ourselves, "What types of organizations and networks most effectively embody—or generate—social capital, in the sense of mutual reciprocity, the resolution of dilemmas of collective action, and the broadening of social identities?" (p. 26). Within the context of economically depressed urban areas, I believe that to the extent parents and concerned community allies are able to marshal resources, organizational and legal, and expand their social networks in ways that enable them to increase the support they receive from churches, businesses, nonprofit organizations, and established civic groups, urban schools can be transformed into community assets that more effectively respond to the needs of those they serve.

As a way of illustrating how such a change can be brought about, I will use the case of a public hospital that recently was forced to change the way in which it provides health services to its patients. For the sake of protecting the identities of those who work there, I will call this particular hospital the Wellness Medical Center. It is administered by a county government in the State of California and is widely regarded by the public as the hospital of last resort. By that, I mean with the exception of trauma care, for which it is well known and respected (largely because it serves more burn victims and individuals with gunshot wounds than any other hospital west of the Mississippi), few patients with private health insurance patronize this hospital. The wait for medical service is typically quite long—even for emergencies—waiting rooms are generally crowded and dirty, and service from hospital personnel, including physicians, tends to be rushed and impersonal. For years, the patient base for Wellness Medical Center has been drawn largely from two sources: indigent care for poor people lacking health insurance and senior citizens and others receiving some form of public assistance who are covered by MediCal.[6] Individuals from these two constituencies have constituted a captured market, meaning they had no other options for health services, and until recently, no other health facility was interested in providing services to them.

In 1999, the status of MediCal patients was significantly elevated as compensation for health services to recipients was significantly increased. Suddenly patients whose access to health care had been limited largely to public health facilities were being actively courted by private hospitals. In effect, through a simple change in the law, their social capital, at least within the field of public health, increased markedly, and they were transformed from being seen as an undesirable drain on resources into valued prospective customers.

The change in law had a profound effect on Wellness Medical Center. Until that time, MediCal patients were the only customers capable of generating revenue, meager as it might be, for the hospital. If this population abandoned Wellness to seek health services at private facilities, Wellness would be left with indigent care alone, a patient base that would lead to the ultimate financial collapse of the hospital because services to this population generate no income for the hospital at all. Faced with the prospect of losing their only paying customers, hospital administrators at Wellness became very concerned about finding ways to improve the quality of customer service. In response to what they perceived as a looming crisis, consultants were hired who could assist in bringing about what they described as "a change in the culture of the institution."[7]

I was one of the consultants who was hired to work with the clerks in admissions and registration. These are the frontline employees who are responsible for admitting patients and scheduling appointments. Throughout the hospital, they were widely regarded as unfriendly, unresponsive, and often rude toward patients. Changing their attitude and conduct toward patients was seen by the hospital administration as essential to improving the quality of service.

As I conducted interviews and observations with the clerks over the next six weeks, I came to see that their attitudes and behavior toward patients were directly related to the conditions under which they worked and a by-product of their treatment by management. Working in cramped quarters with equipment that often malfunctioned and unable to assist sick and injured patients who became angry and frustrated while waiting to be seen by a physician, the clerks frequently became angry and irritable themselves. Their own sense of hopelessness about their working conditions produced indifference and frustration, and when confronted by sick patients who had become angry over the long wait to see a doctor, they often returned the hostility directed at them or responded with what appeared to be callous disregard toward their health needs. When I produced my final report to management with a list of recommendations on how to improve patient service in admissions and registration, I explained how service was linked to working conditions and that it would not be possible to address the former without responding to the latter.

Though they had a genuine interest in improving customer service, hospital administrators had difficulty responding to the concerns of the workers. Even though most of my recommendations seemed fairly simple and obvious (provide clerks with functioning equipment, redesign the registration work area, employ fair and consistent rules for all employees, and so forth), the administration had trouble responding because they claimed they were hampered by cumbersome bureaucratic procedures and intractable union regulations. Nonetheless, because they understood that the survival of the hospital, and by extension, protection of their jobs, was at stake, they found ways to respond positively to the clerks, who in turn gradually began to improve the quality of patient service. They did so because they understood that a failure to respond would prevent them from retaining the patient population they valued.

Wellness Medical Center is a lot like many urban public schools. Like this public hospital, they too provide services to a captured market, have a guaranteed source of revenue (average daily attendance in the case of public schools, state and county subsidies in the care of Wellness), and very little regard for the quality of service provided. Like the employees at Wellness who informed me that they go to private hospitals for their own health needs, the ultimate indication of the quality of service provided at urban public schools is the fact that the vast majority of teachers would not educate their own children in the schools where they work (Noguera 1995). Urban schools with a long track record of failure often develop norms that normalize student failure and insulate professional educators from any sense of responsibility over student outcomes (Payne 1986). What is important about a case like this one is that it shows that when patients, and by extension parents, have the power and means to choose who will provide a particular service (health or education), service suppliers have greater incentive to treat their clients with dignity and respect. That is, even without changing the race, class, or status of the clientele—the key ingredients of their perceived social capital—service providers can be compelled to improve the quality of service if their clients have access to alternative suppliers; otherwise they run the risk of being put out of business.

This is not the same as the arguments that are typically used by proponents of school vouchers or school choice. Proponents of these policies (Chubb and Moe 1988; Cobb 1992) typically overlook the fact that vouchers don't ensure access to good schools. Under voucher systems, choice remains in the hands of private schools, which are not obliged to accept students simply because they apply and have vouchers. Unlike educational facilities, hospitals and clinics generally have the capacity to expand their client base quite easily. In contrast, the ability of schools to expand is limited by capacity based on size and space, and even more important, the status of schools is directly related to their selectivity. Hence, while private hospitals might jump at the prospect of serving greater numbers of paying MediCal patients, private schools are less likely to open their doors to poor minority parents and their children even if they have vouchers.[8] For this reason, vouchers are more likely to benefit middle-class parents who can use the voucher as a subsidy for private school tuition payments and draw from their own resources to make up the difference.[9] Finally, numerous studies have shown that choice without access to transportation and adequate information about schools is a farce. Where they have been implemented, choice systems tend to favor those with the most social capital (the middle class, the well connected, the highly motivated), while those with the least are left behind at the least desirable schools (Wells and Crain 1992).

What this case suggests is that by empowering patients with the means to exercise choice, the service supplier has greater incentive to improve the quality of service and satisfy customer needs. Significantly, the benefits of this empowerment accrued not only to those covered by MediCal, but to the uninsured as well, since any improvement in conditions at the Wellness Medical Center would be available to all who patronized the hospital. A similar approach is needed to change the relationship between supplier and con-sumer at urban public schools such that they are compelled to become more responsive to those they serve. Given the limitations of choice and vouchers already pointed out, I believe the answer can be found only through the adoption of strategies that give greater power in site decision making to parents, and thereby pro-vide them with the means to hold schools more accountable.

Transforming Urban Schools by Increasing Community Control

In 1968, public education in New York City screeched to a halt as over one million children were kept out of school as a result of a strike by the United Federation of Teachers (UFT). The strike was called in response to a conflict between the union and parents at one of New York City's three demonstration school districts located in the Ocean Hill–Brownsville section of Brooklyn (Fantini, Gittell, and Magat 1970). As part of an experiment referred to as community control, district governance had been turned over to a locally elected board made up of parents, church leaders, and com-munity residents. The board was empowered to make decisions related to the governance of schools (three elementary, one inter-mediate, and one middle school) in the district. This included the hiring and firing of administrators, the allocation of resources, and general oversight of educational performance. The experi-ment began in the fall of 1968 with the hope that increased local involvement in school governance would lead to an improve-ment in the quality of schools in this low-income neighborhood (Fantini et al. 1970).

Shortly after the experiment commenced, conflict between the union and the board erupted when the board, acting under the recommendation of Superintendent Rhody McCoy, called for the involuntary transfer of eighteen teachers. These teachers were accused of undermining the goals of the experiment in community control, and the board used their dismissal as a signal to the union that it was indeed in control. More than just an issue of who had power and who could exercise control, the conflict between the community board and the union also exposed profound differences related to the racial implications of the experiment. To a large degree, the concept of community control was embraced because it satisfied two distinct needs: (1) a desire to improve schools in this low-income neighborhood that had long been perceived as dysfunctional and of low quality and (2) a desire for a concrete, local manifestation of Black and Puerto Rican nationalism, which at the time called for self-reliance and racial empowerment. Through community control, parents and activists, religious leaders and politicians, united in wresting control of neighborhood schools out of the hands of predominantly White educators who were perceived as indifferent and unsympathetic to the needs of the community and its children. In their place, educators who shared the racial and cultural background of residents, and the ideological aspirations of the board, were invited to help implement this larger agenda of political empowerment. To begin to fulfill these larger aspirations, community control of local schools would also entail transforming the curriculum such that it reflected and embraced the cultural and historical ideals and images valued by the community and its representatives on the board.

Despite the controversy associated with what was being done in Ocean Hill–Brownsville, the call for greater community control of schools and other public services was a strategy that had been popular in antipoverty programs for some time. Beginning in 1964 with the passage of the Equal Opportunity Act, community-action programs serving low-income communities were encouraged to "develop, conduct and administer programs with the maximum feasible participation of residents of the area and members of the groups served."[10] Similar proposals for greater community control over public services had been made with regard to the management of public housing and police departments, where citizens' review boards were called for as a way of improving relations between community and police and reducing charges or police brutality (Skolnick and Currie 1994). While such proposals in housing and law enforcement have represented a significant departure from past practice, community control at an urban public school in New York City was not unlike the kind of relationship that existed between schools and the communities they serve in many parts of the country. In fact, the logic of the idea was completely consistent with the principle of local control—an idea central to the character of American public schools since their creation in the mid-nineteenth century (Cremin 1988; Katznelson and Weir 1985; Tyack 1980). Kenneth Clark, the psychologist who championed racial integration of schools, articulated the fundamental logic of the proposal in this way:

> If an epidemic of low academic achievement swept over suburban schools drastic measures would be imposed. Administrators and school boards would topple, and teachers would be trained or dismissed. If students were regularly demeaned or dehumanized in those schools, cries of outrage in the PTA would be heard—and listened to—and action would be taken immediately. Accountability at schools in small towns and suburbs is so implicitly a given that the term "community control" never is used by those who have it [Fantini et al. 1970].

While a certain degree of control might be taken for granted in middle-class suburban schools, within the context of the economically and socially marginal communities of the inner city, the notion that community residents had the ability to elect representatives to govern local schools was seen as a radical and risky experiment. Critics of the idea, such as Daniel P. Moynihan, argued that placing poor people in control of neighborhood schools "simply weighs them down with yet another burden with which they are not competent to deal."[11] Similar, arguments were made by UFT President Albert Shanker, who argued that community control would turn the schools over to vigilantes and racists, and others who condemned the Ocean Hill-Brownsville experiment as too political (Alsop 1968; Schrag 1967), and overly ambitious.

Ultimately, it was the UFT strike and the Mayor John Lindsay's (who initially supported the plan) capitulation to the teachers' union that brought an end to community control in Ocean Hill-Brownsville. Yet despite the fact that the community control experiment was aborted long before its impact on the educational performance of children could be assessed, as is often true with other policy innovations, the idea of improving urban schools through various forms of decentralized management and parental empowerment has resurfaced in recent years and gained new credibility. Community control is no longer the title affixed to these initiatives, but throughout the country, reforms aimed at increasing parent involvement in school on decision-making bodies (Comer 1981), increasing site-based management, and transferring decision-making authority to locally elected boards are being carried out. Ironically, the logic underlying these new initiatives is almost identical to that which gave birth to the community control movement in New York in 1968: by increasing school accountability to the parents they serve and by providing parents with the organizational capacity to exert control over schools, they can be forced to improve and become more responsive toward those they serve.

Lessons from Existing Models of Parental Empowerment

In the final pages, I describe how investments in social capital can be used to facilitate school improvement in urban areas. These examples are drawn from two cases that I have worked closely with: Berkeley High School and the San Francisco Unified School District. There are undoubtedly other examples of schools and school districts in other cities that have employed similar strategies. However, I've chosen to present these two cases because my intimate involvement with the process of parental involvement provides me with greater insight into how such policies have produced change. In my own experience, on matters pertaining to the empowerment of poor people, firsthand knowledge derived from direct observation and participation are more valuable and perhaps even more reliable than objective reports. I have found that it is too easy for researchers to exaggerate, distort, or fail to comprehend whether participation is genuine and authentic, or whether those said to be empowered actually feel that way.

Putnam (1995) has argued that the most important forms of social capital consist of "features of social organizations, such as networks, norms and trust, that facilitate action and cooperation for mutual benefit" (pp. 35–36). Coleman applies the concept of closure to his analysis of social capital to argue that norms and sanctions on behavior that support group goals and aspirations develop only when "the trustworthiness of social structures allows for the proliferation of obligations and expectations" (p. 107). Particularly in relationships that exist between parents and schools, Coleman argues that student performance is enhanced by the degree of closure in parent-school relationships. In the arguments he makes to support this point, Coleman suggests that a major reason for the lower dropout rate at Catholic schools than public schools is that "it is the religiously based high schools that are surrounded by a community based on the religious organization. These families have intergenerational closure: whatever other relations they have, the adults are members of the same religious body and parents of children in the same school" (p. 114).

Congruity in values leads to a reinforcement of social norms that promote regular school attendance, conformity to school rules, and concern for academic achievement. In contrast, Coleman argues that public schools tend to have relatively low social closure with the families they serve, and consequently children often get lost in the discontinuity between the values and norms promoted at school (which may be nebulous and difficult to discern) and those that are supported by families.

Building on Coleman's point, I argue that public schools can more effectively serve the needs of the children who attend them when efforts aimed at producing greater closure are pursued. There are several ways in which this can be accomplished. For example, public schools can work toward developing a clear sense of mission and purpose so that it is clear to parents and students what they can and should expect from a particular school. Another way to create a greater degree of closure is to provide parents with organizational resources that enable them to serve as more effective advocates for their children. This may also include providing parent representatives with a role in decision making at the school and district levels.

The latter approach has been actively pursued in the San Francisco Unified School District, where a concerted effort to invest in parents has been in place for the past six years (Noguera 1996). As part of Superintendent Waldemar Rojas's strategy for raising student achievement, the following policies and actions have been taken: (1) an office of parent relations has been established for the purpose of coordinating communication between the district and parents; (2) parent centers aimed specifically at Latino, Asian, and African American parents have been funded and developed; (3) a variety of community-based mobilizations, including marches, conferences, and rallies, have been organized for the purpose of generating active parental participation in school and districtwide affairs; and (4) parents have been delegated a greater role in the governance of the district and particular schools. A representative of the districtwide PTA sits on the superintendent's cabinet, and parents have decision-making authority at schools that have been reconstituted schools,[12] particularly in the selection of new teachers and administrators.

Documenting the impact of these strategies is difficult. Test scores and other key indicators of student performance (grades, graduation rates, admission to college, and others) for all ethnic groups have risen steadily for each of the six years that the plan has been in place, but there is no way of knowing how much credit should be assigned to the district's strategy of investing in parents for this change in student outcomes. Undoubtedly the measure of the plan's effectiveness cannot be based on student achievement measures. Instead, indications of enhanced social capital among the most marginal parents are more important. If Coleman is right, and the development of social capital and closure are key factors in improving the quality of education, then what we need is some evidence that this is in fact occurring.

As a consultant to the district over the past five years,[13] I have witnessed firsthand how the district's emphasis on parental empowerment has influenced the character of discussion of educational issues at the site and district levels. For the past three years, the district has organized a citywide parent empowerment conference that attracted over eight hundred parents in each of the three years it has been held. Most significant for me was the fact that the district provided transportation and child care, and parents from the poorest parts of the city attended. Beyond providing workshops on what is commonly referred to as parent education (for example, how to help your child with homework, how to be an advocate for your child, things you should know about college), the sessions also addressed some of the controversial policy issues facing the district. Sessions on the impact of Propositions 187, 209, and 227 have been held,[14] as well as policy-oriented discussions on issues such as social promotion. All three of the parent centers previously mentioned were created as a result of the conferences, and each of the centers currently reports active involvement at workshops and other events for parents that they sponsor at schools in the community.[15]

Finally, and perhaps most significant, in the raucous and bitter hearings over reconstitution, which pitted angry members of the teachers' union against an adamant district administration, parents have played an unpredictable role. Both sides have courted parents heavily to support their dichotomous positions on the issue—for the union, that reconstitution is too heavy-handed and disruptive; for the administration, that drastic measures are needed to improve conditions in schools. However, instead of being manipulated by one side or the other, parents have frequently staked out independent positions, favoring reconstitution in some cases, opposing it in others. Their presence at meetings has influenced board decisions, because unlike the two combatants—the union and the administration—the parents live in San Francisco and vote in elections.

The other sign that the district's emphasis on parental empowerment is having an impact on schools comes from visiting the schools themselves. I have had firsthand experiences at only a handful of schools, so I do not claim that my impressions are at all generalizable, but at those I've visited, I have been struck by the extent to which parents work with faculty and feel a sense of ownership toward their school. For example, I was asked to speak at E. R. Taylor Elementary School at a meeting of parents and teachers that was set up to determine how funds from a newly won Healthy Start grant would be used. The school was located in a predominantly black, low-income neighborhood known as Bayview, and most of the parents attending the meeting came from housing projects in the area. Before my speech, I met with a small group of parents and teachers who explained how much work they had put into writing the grant. One of the parents, a Samoan woman in her mid-forties, who appeared to be a leader in the group, explained to me how the use of the funds would be prioritized:

> We have a lot of children at this school who don't eat breakfast in the mornings. Some of them haven't seen an eye doctor or dentist. The people from the State Department said that this grant is a Healthy Start grant, which means it should be for the health of the children. Nothing else can come before that. We believe that healthy children will do better in school.

As the woman spoke, the rest of the group looked on, smiling and nodding with approval. It was clear to me that this woman, regardless of her lack of education or income, was the recognized leader in the group, and not merely a token representative. After my speech, the same parent, and not the principal who had originally contacted me, took it on herself to invite me back to the school in three months to see what kind of progress they had made toward achieving their goals.

What is most striking to me about this experience is how significantly it contrasts with my visits to most other urban schools. More often than not, in my conversations with teachers and administrators at urban public schools, parents are described as uncaring, dysfunctional, unsupportive, and part of the problem. Rather than being seen as partners capable of making meaningful contributions to the education of children, they are more likely to be seen as obstacles in the way of progress and problems to be overcome.

This was the case at Berkeley High School (BHS), where for the longest time, the poor academic performance of Black and Latino students was explained as a by-product of parent disinterest in education. BHS is a relatively large school with approximately three thousand students and over 150 teachers, counselors, and administrators. According to the school district's data, approximately 40 percent of the students are White, 40 percent are

African American, 10 percent are Latino, and 10 percent are Asian American. Racial differences generally correspond to class differences in that the vast majority of White students are from middle-class and affluent backgrounds, while the majority of African American and Latino students come from low-income families.

To an outsider, the school seems amazingly diverse, but from within, racial fragmentation is apparent in almost every aspect of the school. On the basis of almost every significant indicator, BHS is a school that does not serve its Black and Latino students well. Nearly 50 percent of Black and Latino students who enter BHS in the ninth grade fail to graduate from the school, and among those who do graduate, few complete the course requirements necessary for admission to the University of California or the state college system (Berkeley Alliance 1999). These students also comprise the overwhelming majority of students who are suspended or expelled for disciplinary reasons. Moreover, the adjunct continuation high school, which was established to serve students with poor attendance and behavioral problems, is almost entirely composed of African American and Latino students.

As might be expected, not only are African American students disadvantaged and marginal within the school community, but so are their parents. At most school activities that call for parental involvement and participation, African American and Latino parents are vastly underrepresented. This is also true of decision-making bodies where parents have a voice in how resources are allocated, and it is most dramatically evident on back-to-school nights, when parents are invited to meet their children's teachers. Historically, the auditorium where several hundred parents gather prior to visiting the classrooms of their kids' teachers is nearly entirely White, with little more than a handful of Black and Latino parents sprinkled throughout the crowd.

In 1996 a group that I helped to establish known as the Diversity Project began searching for ways to increase the involvement of parents who previously had been most marginal to school. We did this because we believed that if we were going to be successful in our efforts to address disparities in academic achievement within the school, we would have to take on this issue because we would have to find ways to empower those who were most disenfranchised. As we approached this work, we recognized that those who benefited under the present circumstances might perceive themselves as having a vested interest in preserving the status quo and might resist efforts to support change that produces greater equity. As we carried out our work, we positioned ourselves as facilitators of discussion rather than as advocates for a particular agenda because we sought to prevent ourselves from becoming trapped in a polarized conflict over change at the school. It was our hope that organizing African American and Latino parents would provide us with a means to ensure that the change effort would not be dependent on our advocacy alone and also serve to counterbalance the influence that would be exerted by the opponents of change.

Research in the form of a series of focus group discussions served as our entrée into organizing. Focus group discussions were set up for Latino and African American parents to elicit their views on the state of the school. Specifically, we wanted to know what concerns they had about the education their children were receiving, what kinds of obstacles they encountered when interacting with school officials on behalf of their children, and what kinds of changes they felt would help make BHS more receptive to their concerns.

Over the course of six months, over seventy-five focus groups were conducted with over four hundred parents. To ensure that maximum opportunity was provided for open communication, all of the sessions with Spanish-speaking parents were conducted in Spanish. Food and child care were also provided as an added incentive to attract high levels of participation. Finally, the focus groups were tape-recorded, the sessions were transcribed, and a report summarizing the issues raised was presented to a newly formed strategic planning committee for inclusion in their report to the school.

The parent outreach committee of the Diversity Project also recruited parents to join them in conducting the focus groups and carrying out the research. This was important because the active core group of the committee is now taking leadership at the school in devising strategies aimed at institutionalizing parental involvement. The group has already gotten the BHS administration to designate a surplus classroom that will be used as a parent center, and they have written grants to foundations for the purpose of hiring two part-time parent organizers.

Aside from these accomplishments, there is other evidence that the organization of Black and Latino parents is already beginning to have an impact on the school. At a community forum in May 1998 that was held for the purpose of soliciting responses to the plan as it was being drafted, nearly half of the parents present were African American and Latino. Most of these were parents who had become active in the leadership of the parent outreach group. During the meeting, several spoke out openly about their criticisms of the plan and freely offered suggestions on what they would like to see included in it. After the meeting, several teachers commented that it was the first meeting that they had attended in which the composition of the parents present matched that of the student body. The Diversity Project hopes to build on this accomplishment in the future so that the ongoing effort to undermine racial inequality within the school is led and actively supported by the parents of the children who have the most to gain.

When parents are respected as partners in the education of their children and when they are provided with organizational support that enables them to channel their interest to the benefit of the school, the entire culture of the organization can be transformed. Parents have knowledge of children's lives outside school, which teachers typically do not have, and that knowledge can prove helpful in developing effective pedagogical strategies (Ladson-Billings 1992; Spindler and Spindler 1987). More important, the familiarity between school and parent that develops as a result of such partnerships can also begin to generate social closure and transform urban schools from alien and hostile organizations into genuine community assets.

Notes and References

Introduction

Notes

1. I have trouble writing about Black men in the third person since I am a Black man and I have experienced many of the challenges I describe here.

2. To illustrate how academic trends in elementary and secondary schools carry over into adulthood, recent data from the U.S. Department of Education reveal that Black women are nearly twice as likely as Black men to earn a bachelor's degree and two-thirds more likely to earn a medical degree.

3. On several occasions the U.S. Supreme Court has upheld the right of undocumented children to attend our nation's public schools.

4. The Development, Relief and Education for Alien Minors Act (also referred to as the DREAM Act) has been proposed by members of the U.S. Congress to make it possible for undocumented students to enroll at public colleges and universities. However, the bill has never been voted on and remains trapped in committee while its sponsors wait for a sign that the current backlash against immigrants has subsided.

References

Apel, D. (2004). *Imagery of Lynching: Black Men, White Women, and the Mob.* New Brunswick, N.J.: Rutgers University Press.

Baker, L. D. (1998). *From Savage to Negro: Anthropology and the Construction of Race, 1896–1954*. Berkeley: University of California Press.

Belk, A. (2006). *A New Generation of Native Sons: Men of Color and the Prison-Industrial Complex*. Washington, D.C.: Joint Center for Political and Economic Studies Health Policy Institute.

Bell, C., and Jenkins E. J. (1990). "Preventing Black Homicide." In J. Dewart (ed.), *The State of Black America*. New York: National Urban League.

Bhabha, H. (1994). *On the Location of Culture*. London: Routledge.

Children's Defense Fund. (2006). *Annual Report*. Washington, D.C.: Children's Defense Fund.

Cosby, W., and Poussaint, A. (2007). *Come On People: On the Path from Victims to Victors*. Nashville, Tenn.: Nelson Publishing.

Earls, F. (1994). "Violence and Today's Youth." *Critical Health Issues for Children and Youth*, 4(3), 4–23.

Ellison, R. (1947). *Invisible Man*. New York: Random House.

Guinier, L., and Torres, G. (2002). *The Miner's Canary*. Cambridge, Mass.: Harvard University Press.

Jencks, C. (1972). *Inequality: A Reassessment of the Effect of Family and Schooling in America*. New York: Basic Books.

Littles, M., Bowers, R., and Gilmer, M. (2007). *Why We Can't Wait: A Case for Philanthropic Action: Opportunities for Improving Life Outcomes for African American Males*. New York: Ford Foundation.

Oakes, J. (1985). *Keeping Track: How Schools Structure Inequality*. New Haven, Conn.: Yale University Press.

Obidah, J. (1995). "Life After Death: Critical Pedagogy in an Urban Classroom." In I. Hall, C. H. Campbell, and E. J. Miech (eds.), *Class Act: Teachers Reflect on Their Own Classroom Practice*. Cambridge, Mass.: Harvard Educational Review.

Pierce, C. (1995). "Stress Analogs of Racism and Sexism: Terrorism, Torture, and Disaster." In C. V. Willie, P. P. Rieker, B. M. Kramer, and B. S. Brown (eds.), *Mental Health, Racism, and Sexism*. London: Taylor & Francis.

Ridgeway, G. (2007). *Analysis of Disparities in the New York Police Department's Stop, Question, and Frisk Practices*. San Francisco: Rand Corporation

Schott Foundation. (2004). *Public Education and Black Male Students*. Cambridge, Mass.: Schott Foundation.

Tyack, D. (1974). *The One Best System*. Cambridge, Mass.: Harvard University Press.

Chapter One: Joaquin's Dilemma

1. Tatum, B. (1992). "Talking About Race, Learning About Racism: The Application of Racial Identity Development Theory in the Classroom." *Harvard Educational Review*, 62(1). Cross, W., Parnham, T., and Helms, J. (1991). *Shades of Black: Diversity in African American Identity*. Philadelphia: Temple University Press. Phinney, J. (1990). "Ethnic Identity in Adolescents and Adults: Review of Research." *Psychological Bulletin, 108*, 499–514.

2. Troyna, B., and Carrington, B. (1990). *Education, Racism and Reform*. London: Routledge

3. Noguera, P., and Bliss, M. (2001). *A Four Year Evaluation Study of Youth Together*. Oakland, CA: Arts, Resources and Curriculum.

4. Erikson, E. (1968). *Identity, Youth and Crisis*. New York: Norton.

5. Troyna, B., and Carrington, B. (1990). *Education, Racism and Reform*. London: Routledge.

6. Noguera, P. (2001). "The Role of Social Capital in the Transformation of Urban Schools." In S. Saegert, P. Thompson, and M. Warren (eds.), *Social Capital and Poor Communities*. New York: Russell Sage Foundation.

7. Orfield, G., and Eaton, S. (1996). *Dismantling Desegregation*. New York: New Press.

8. Williams, B. (ed.). (1996). *Closing the Achievement Gap*. Alexandria, VA: Association for Supervision and Curriculum Development. Noguera, P., and Akom, A. (2000, June 5). "Disparities Demystified." *Nation*.

9. Ogbu, J. (1987). "Opportunity Structure, Cultural Boundaries, and Literacy." In J. Langer (ed.), *Language, Literacy and Culture: Issues of Society and Schooling*. Norwood, NJ: Ablex. Fordham, S. (1996). *Blacked Out: Dilemmas of Race, Identity, and Success at Capital High*. Chicago: University of Chicago Press. Fordham, S., and Ogbu, J. (1986). "Black Students and School Success: Coping with the Burden of Acting White." *Urban Review, 18*, 176–206.

10. Other researchers have argued that recent immigrant students of color are largely immune to the insidious association between race and achievement that traps students from domestic minority backgrounds. For so-called voluntary minorities, whether they be Mexican, Asian, African, or West Indian, schooling is more likely to be perceived as a pathway to social mobility, and for this reason, they are also more likely to adopt behaviors that increase the likelihood of academic success. Having been raised in societies where people of their race or ethnic group are in the majority, they typically have not been subjected to the kinds of socialization processes that lead them to see themselves as members of subordinate or inferior groups. With none of America's racial baggage to encumber them, many are able to excel if provided the opportunity to receive a quality education.

11. Steele, C. (1997, June). "A Threat in the Air: How Stereotypes Shape Intellectual Identity and Performance." *American Psychologist, 52*, 613–629.

12. Steele (1997), p. 614.

13. Lee, S. (1996). *Unraveling the Model Minority Stereotype*. New York: Teachers College Press.

14. McWhorter, J. (2000). *Losing the Race*. New York: New Press. Meier, D. (1995). *The Power of Their Ideas*. Boston: Beacon Press.

15. Steinberg, L. (1996). *Beyond the Classroom*. New York: Simon and Schuster.

16. Phelan, P. A., Davidson, H., and Cao, Y. (1998). *Adolescent Worlds*. Albany, NY: SUNY Press. McPartland, J., and Nettles, S. (1991). "Using Community Adults as Advocates or Mentors for At-Risk Middle School Students: A Two-Year Evaluation of Project RAISE." *American Journal of Education*, 99, 568–586.

17. Omi, M., and Winant, H. (1986). *Racial Formation in the United States*. New York: Routledge. Horseman, R. (1981). *Race and Manifest Destiny*. Cambridge, MA: Harvard University Press.

Chapter Two: The Trouble with Black Boys

Notes

1. Skolnick and Currie 1994, pp. 422–424; Earls 1994, p. 6.

2. National Research Council 1989, pp. 416–420; Poussaint and Alexander 2000, p. 22.

3. Kaplan et al. 1987, p. 141; Centers for Disease Control 1988, p. 17; Auerbach et al. 2000, p. 2.

4. Roper 1991, p. 12; Skolnick and Currie 1994, p. 416.

5. Auerbach et al. 2000, p. 3; National Research Council 1989, p. 417.

6. Spivak et al. 1988, p. 12.

7. Wilson 1987, p. 31; Massey and Denton 1993, pp. 17–41; Moss and Tilly 1993, p. 27; Hacker 1992, pp. 26–29; Feagin and Sikes 1994, pp. 33–42.

8. Meier, Stewart, and England 1989, pp. 40–57.

9. National Research Council 1989, p. 339; Carnoy 1994, p. 61.

10. Milofsky 1974, p. 63.

11. Oakes 1985, p. 74; Pollard 1993, pp. 341–356.

12. Pollard 1993, p. 345.

13. Jencks and Phillips 1998, pp. 45–62.

14. Coleman et al. 1966, pp. 16–33.

15. Brookover and Erickson 1969; Morrow and Torres 1995.

16. Brookover and Erickson 1969; Meier et al. 1998, p. 23.

17. Lee 2000, pp. 43–48.

18. Edmonds 1979, p. 4.

19. Frèire 1972, p. 88.

20. Carnoy 1994, pp. 105–111.

21. Taylor-Gibbs 1988, p. 212.

22. Jackson 1998, p. 14.

23. Garbarino 1999, p. 67.

24. Harry et al. 2000, p. 14.

25. Harry et al. 2000, p. 7.

26. Harry et al. 2000, p. 23.

27. Meier et al. 1989, p. 47.

28. Hilliard 1976, pp. 23–34.

29. Sandler 2000, p. 16.

30. Oakes 1985, p. 53.

31. Earls 1991, p. 14; Garbarino 1999, p. 26.

32. Ogbu 1987, p. 23.

33. Hoberman 1997, pp. 48, 49.

34. Ogbu 1990, p. 29; Fordham 1996, p. 12.

35. Wilson 1978, pp. 22–46; Wilson 1987, pp. 12–35; Massey and Denton, 1993, pp. 7–24; Tabb 1970, pp. 11–36.

36. Anderson 1990, p. 34.

37. Lewis 1966 pp. 74–88; Glazer and Moynihan 1963, pp. 221–267.

38. Murray 1984, pp. 147–254.

39. Ryan 1976, pp. 32–46.

40. McLeod 1987, p. 25.

41. Morrow and Torres 1994, pp. 112–134.

42. Willis 1977, pp. 62–81; Levinson et al., 1996, pp. 21–26.

43. Luker 1996, pp. 223–236.

44. Skolnick and Currie 1994, p. 429.

45. Erickson 1968, p. 32; Cross et al. 1991, pp. 13–19.

46. Goffman 1959, pp. 23–34.

47. Taylor-Gibbs 1988, pp. 113–124; Kunjufu 1985, p. 23; Anderson 1990, pp. 23–36.

48. Giroux 1983, pp. 23–36.

49. Levinson et al., 1996, p. 12.

50. Spring 1994, p. 34; Apple 1982, p. 47.

51. Thorne 1993, p. 22.

52. Spring 1994, p. 16; Loewen 1995, pp. 43–51.

53. Apple 1982, p. 64.

54. Dyson 1994, p. 21.

55. Troyna and Carrington 1990, p. 18.

56. Miles 1989, pp. 32–47.

57. Troyna and Carrington 1990, p. 73.

58. Dyson 1994, p. 34; Thorne 1993, p. 45.

59. Peshkin 1991, p. 65.

60. Erikson 1968, p. 18.

61. Tatum 1992, p. 39; Cross et al. 1991, pp. 34–49.

62. Metz 1978, p. 221; Peshkin 1991, p. 46.

63. Phelan et al. 1998, pp. 10–18.

64. Steinberg 1996.

65. Peshkin 1991.

66. Fordham 1996, p. 47; Ogbu 1987, p. 87; Solomon 1992, p. 22; Steinberg 1996, p. 185.

67. Ferguson 1999, p. 134.

68. Fordham 1996, p. 46; Ogbu 1987, p. 34.

69. Kao and Tienda 1998, p. 36; Anderson 1990, p. 249.

70. Sizemore 1988, p. 45; Edmonds 1979, p. 11.

71. Noguera 2000.

72. Mickelson 1989, pp. 42–49.

73. Metropolitan Life Survey 2000, p. 184.

74. Weinstein et al. 1995, pp. 124, 125.

75. Ladson-Billings 1994, p. 36; Foster 1997, p. 122; Lee 2000, p. 57.

76. University of California Report of Black Student Achievement, unpublished manuscript by Michelle Foster, February 2001.

77. Sizemore 1988; Murphy and Hallinger 1985.

78. Sizemore 1988.

79. Edmonds 1979, p. 20.

80. McPartland and Nettles 1991.

81. Watson and Smitherman 1996.

82. Ampim 1993; Myers 1988.

83. Boykin 1983.

84. Noguera 1995.

85. Smitherman 1977, p. 234.

86. Kunjufu 1985, p. 16; Madhubuti 1993, p. 88; Majors and Billson 1992, p. 92; West 1993, p. 47.

87. Anderson 1990, p. 38.

88. Kunjufu 1985, p. 18; Hilliard 1991, p. 113.

89. Ferguson 2000, p. 23.

References

Ampim, M. (1993). *Towards an Understanding of Black Community Development*. Oakland, CA: Advancing the Research.

Anderson, E. (1990). *Street Wise: Race, Class and Change in an Urban Community*. Chicago: University of Chicago Press.

Anderson, J. (1988). *The Education of Blacks in the South, 1860–1935*. Chapel Hill: University of North Carolina Press.

Apple, M. (1982). *Education and Power*. Boston: ARK.

Auerbach, J. A., Krimgold, B. K., and Lefkowitz, B. (2000). *Improving Health: It Doesn't Take a Revolution*. Washington, DC: Kellogg Foundation.

Baker, D. (1983). *Race, Ethnicity and Power*. London: Routledge.

Boykin, W. (1983). "On the Academic Task Performance and African American Children." In J. Spencer (ed.), *Achievement and Achievement Motives*. New York: Freeman.

Brookover, W., and Erickson, E. (1969). *Society, Schools and Learning*. East Lansing, MI: Michigan State University Press.

Carnoy, M. (1994). *Faded Dreams: The Politics and Economics of Race in America*. Cambridge: Cambridge University Press.

Centers for Disease Control. (1988). "Distribution of AIDS Cases by Racial/Ethnic Group and Exposure Category: United States, June 1, 1981–July 4, 1988." *Morbidity and Mortality Weekly Report, 55*(3), 1–10.

Coleman, J., Campbell, E., Hobson, C., McPartland, J., Mood, A., Weinfeld, F., and York, R. (1966). *Equality of Educational Opportunity*. Washington, DC: Government Printing Office.

Cross, W., Parnham, T., and Helms, J. (1991). *Shades of Black: Diversity in African American Identity*. Philadelphia: Temple University Press.

Dyson, A. (1994). "The Ninjas, the X-Men, and the Ladies: Playing with Power and Identity in an Urban Primary School." *Teachers College Record, 96*(2), 219–239.

Earls, F. (1991). "Not Fear, nor Quarantine, But Science: Preparation for a Decade of Research to Advance Knowledge About Causes and Control of Violence in Youths." *Journal of Adolescent Health, 12*, 619–629.

Earls, F. (1994). "Violence and Today's Youth." *Critical Health Issues for Children and Youth, 4*(3).

Edmonds, R. (1979). "Effective Schools for the Urban Poor." *Educational Leadership, 37*(1), 15–27.

Erikson, E. (1968). *Identity, Youth and Crisis*. New York: Norton.

Feagin J. R., and Sikes, M. P. (1994). *Living with Racism: The Black Middle-Class Experience*. Boston: Beacon Press.

Ferguson, R. (2000). *A Diagnostic Analysis of Black-White GPA Disparities in Shaker Heights, Ohio*. Washington, DC: Brookings Institute.

Fordham, S. (1996). *Blacked Out: Dilemmas of Race, Identity, and Success at Capital High*. Chicago: University of Chicago Press.

Foster, M. (1997). *Black Teachers on Teaching*. New York: New Press.

Frèire, P. (1972). *The Pedagogy of the Oppressed*. New York: Continuum Publishing.

Garbarino, J. (1999). *Lost Boys: Why Our Sons Turn to Violence and How to Save Them*. New York: Free Press.

Girabaldi, A. (1992). "Educating and Motivating African American Males to Succeed." *Journal of Negro Education, 61*(1), 4–11.

Giroux, H. (1983). *Theory and Resistance in Education*. Westport, CT: Bergin and Harvey.

Glassgow, D. (1980). *The Black Underclass: Poverty, Unemployment and Entrapment of Ghetto Youth*. New York: Vintage Books

Glazer, N., and Moynihan, D. (1963). *Beyond the Melting Pot*. Cambridge, MA: MIT Press.

Goffman, E. (1959). *The Presentation of Self in Everyday Life*. New York: Doubleday Anchor.

Greenberg, M., and Schneider, D. (1994). "Young Black Males Is the Answer, But What Was the Question?" *Social Science Medicine, 39*(2), 179–187.

Hacker, A. (1992). *Two Nations: Black and White, Separate, Hostile, Unequal*. New York: Scribner.

Hale, J. (1982). *Black Children: Their Roots, Culture and Learning Styles*. Provo, UT: Brigham Young Press.

Harry, B., Klingner, J., and Moore, R. (2000, November 17). "Of Rocks and Soft Places: Using Qualitative Methods to Investigate the Processes That Result in

Disproportionality." Paper presented at the Minority Issues in Special Education conference, Harvard University.

Hauser, R., and Anderson, D. (1991). "Post High School Plans and Aspirations of Black and White High School Seniors: 1976–1986." *Sociology of Education*, 64, 140–165.

Hilliard, A. (1991). "Do We Have the Will to Educate All Children?" *Educational Leadership*, 49(1), 31–36.

Hoberman, J. (1997). *Darwin's Athletes*. Boston: Houghton Mifflin.

Jackson, J. (1998, Sept.–Oct.). "The Myth of the Crack Baby." *Family Watch Library*.

Jencks, C., and Phillips, M. (1998). *The Black-White Test Scores Gap*. Washington, DC: Brookings Institute.

Kao, G., and Tienda, M. (1998). "Educational Aspirations Among Minority Youth." *American Journal of Education*, 106, 349–384.

Kaplan, H., Johnson, R., Bailey, C., and Simon, W. (1987). "The Sociological Study of AIDS: A Critical Review of the Literature and Suggested Research Agenda." *Journal of Health and Social Behavior*, 28, 140–157.

Kunjufu, J. (1985). *Countering the Conspiracy to Destroy Black Boys*. Chicago: African American Images.

Ladson-Billings, G. (1994). *The Dreamkeepers*. San Francisco: Jossey-Bass.

Leake, D., and Leake, B. (1992). "Islands of Hope: Milwaukee's African American Immersion Schools." *Journal of Negro Education*, 61(1), 24–29.

Lee, C. (2000). *The State of Knowledge About the Education of African Americans*. Washington, DC: Commission on Black Education, American Educational Research Association.

Levinson, B., Foley, D., and Holland, D. (1996). *The Cultural Production of the Educated Person*. Albany, NY: SUNY Press.

Lewis, O. (1966). *La Vida: A Puerto Rican Family in the Culture of Poverty—San Juan and New York*. New York: Random House.

Loewen, J. (1995). *Lies My Teacher Told Me*. New York: New Press.

Luker, K. (1996). *Dubious Conceptions: The Politics of Teenage Pregnancy*. Cambridge, MA: Harvard University Press.

MacLeod, J. (1987). *Ain't No Makin' It*. Boulder, CO: Westview Press.

Madhubuti, H. (1990). *Black Men: Obsolete, Single, Dangerous?* Chicago: Third World Press.

Majors, R., and Billson, M. (1992). *Cool Pose: The Dilemmas of Black Manhood in America*. New York: Simon & Schuster.

Massey, D., and Denton, N. (1993). *American Apartheid*. Cambridge, MA: Harvard University Press.

McPartland, J., and Nettles, S. (1991, August). "Using Community Adults as Advocates or Mentors for At-Risk Middle School Students: A Two-Year Evaluation of Project RAISE." *American Journal of Education*.

Meier, K., Stewart, J., and England, R. (1989). *Race, Class and Education: The Politics of Second Generation Discrimination*. Madison: University of Wisconsin Press.

Metropolitan Life. (2000). *The American Teacher, 2000*. Washington, DC: Metropolitan Life Insurance Company.

Metz, M. (1978). *Classrooms and Corridors*. Berkeley: University of California Press.

Mickelson, R. (1990). "The Attitude Achievement Paradox Among Black Adolescents." *Sociology of Education, 63*(1), 44–61.

Miles, R. (1989). *Racism*. London: Routledge.

Milofsky, C. (1974). "Why Special Education Isn't Special." *Harvard Educational Review, 44*(2).

Morrow, R., and Torres, C. (1995). *Social Theory and Education*. Albany, NY: SUNY Press.

Moss, P., and Tilly, C. (1993). "Raised Hurdles for Black Men: Evidence from Interviews with Employers." Working paper, Department of Policy and Planning, University of Massachusetts–Lowell.

Murphy, J., and Hallinger, P. (1985). "Effective High Schools: What Are the Common Characteristics?" *NASP Bulletin, 69,* 18–22.

Murray, C. (1984). *Losing Ground*. New York: Basic Books.

Myers, L. J. (1988). *Understanding an Afrocentric World View: Introduction to an Optimal Psychology*. Dubuque, IA: Kendall-Hunt Publishers.

National Research Council. (1989). *A Common Destiny: Blacks and American Society*. Washington, DC: National Academy Press.

Noguera, P. (1995). "Reducing and Preventing Youth Violence: An Analysis of Causes and an Assessment of Successful Programs." In *1995 Wellness Lectures*. Oakland, CA: University of California Office of the President.

Phelan, P., Davidson, A., and Cao Ya, H. (1998). *Adolescent Worlds*. Albany, NY: SUNY Press.

Oakes, J. (1985). *Keeping Track*. New Haven, CT: Yale University Press.

Ogbu, J. (1987). "Opportunity Structure, Cultural Boundaries, and Literacy." In J. Langer (ed.), *Language, Literacy and Culture: Issues of Society and Schooling*. Norwood, NJ: Ablex Press.

Ogbu, J. (1990). "Literacy and Schooling in Subordinate Cultures: The Case of Black Americans." In K. Lomotey (ed.), *Going to School*. Albany, NY: SUNY Press.

Peshkin, A. (1991). *The Color of Strangers, the Color of Friends*. Chicago: University of Chicago Press.

Pollard, D. S. (1993). "Gender, Achievement and African American Students' Perceptions of Their School Experience." *Education Psychologist, 28*(4).

Poussaint, A., and Alexander, A. (2000). *Lay My Burden Down: Unraveling Suicide and the Mental Health Crisis Among African Americans*. Boston: Beacon Press.

Roper, W. (1991). "The Prevention of Minority Youth Violence Must Begin Despite Risks and Imperfect Understanding." *Public Health Reports, 106*(3).

Ryan, W. (1976). *Blaming the Victim*. New York: Vintage Books.

Sandler, D. P., Wilcox, A. J., and Everson, R. B. (1985). "Cumulative Effects of Lifetime Passive Smoking on Cancer Risks." *Lancet, 1,* 312.

Sandler, S. (2000). *Turning to Each Other, Not on Each Other: How School Communities Prevent Racial Bias in School Discipline*. San Francisco: Justice Matters.

Sizemore, B. (1988). "The Madison Elementary School: A Turnaround Case." *Journal of Negro Education, 57*(3).

Skolnick, J., and Currie, E. (1994). *Crisis in American Institutions*. New York: HarperCollins.

Smitherman, G. (1977). *Talkin' and Testifyin': The Language of Black America*. Boston: Houghton Mifflin.

Solomon, P. (1992). *Black Resistance in High School*. Albany, NY: SUNY Press.

Spivak, H., Prothrow-Stith, D., and Hausman, A. (1988). "Dying Is No Accident." *Pediatric Clinics of North America, 35*(6), 1339–1346.

Spring, J. (1994). *American Education*. New York: McGraw-Hill.

Steinberg, L. (1996). *Beyond the Classroom*. New York: Simon & Schuster.

Tabb, W. (1970) *The Political Economy of the Black Ghetto*. New York: Norton.

Tatum, B. (1992). "Talking About Race, Learning About Racism: The Application of Racial Identity Development Theory in the Classroom." *Harvard Educational Review, 62*(1).

Taylor-Gibbs, J. (1988). *The Black Male as an Endangered Species*. New York: Auburn House.

Thorne, B. (1993). *Gender Play*. New Brunswick, NJ: Rutgers University Press.

Troyna, B., and Carrington, B. (1990). *Education, Racism and Reform*. London: Routledge.

Watson, C., and Smitherman, G. (1996). *Educating African American Males: Detroit's Malcolm X Academy*. Chicago: Third World Press.

Weinstein, R., Madison, S., and Kuklinski, K. (1995). "Raising Expectations in Schooling: Obstacles and Opportunities for Change." *American Educational Research Journal, 32*(1).

West, C. (1993). *Race Matters*. Boston: Beacon Press.

Willis, P. (1977). *Learning to Labor*. New York: Columbia University Press.

Wilson, W. (1978). *The Declining Significance of Race*. Chicago: University of Chicago Press.

Wilson, W. (1987). *The Truly Disadvantaged*. Chicago: University of Chicago Press.

Chapter Three: And What Will Become of Children Like Miguel Fernández?

Notes

1. During the 2003–04 academic year, I worked as a consultant to Region I, one of the ten school districts that comprise the New York City Public Schools. I was asked to assist Walton High School, which was being broken down from one large, comprehensive high school into several smaller, autonomous learning communities. I spent much of the year assisting administrators of the school as they carried out this task.

2. As a researcher and the director of the Metro Center at New York University, I work with many schools throughout the United States. For a description of my research, see Noguera (2003).

3. In much of the sociological literature on immigration, it has been held that assimilation would lead to social mobility for immigrants. Second- and third-generation immigrants have generally fared better than new arrivals. For Latinos, available research suggests the opposite may be true. See Jiobu (1988).

4. For an analysis of these propositions and their impact on Latinos in California, see Chavez (2001).

References

Chavez, L. (2001). *Covering Immigration*. Berkeley: University of California Press.

Clark, W. (1998). *The California Cauldron*. New York: Guilford Press.

Cornelius, W. (2002). "Ambivalent Reception: Mass Public Responses to the New Latino Immigration to the United States." In M. Suarez-Orozco and M. M. Paez (eds.), *Latinos: Remaking America*. Berkeley: University of California Press.

Garcia, E. (2001). *Hispanic Education in the United States*. Lanham, MD: Rowan and Littlefield.

Gonzalez, E. D. (2004). *The Bronx*. New York: Columbia University Press.

Haney, W. (2003). "Attrition of Students from New York Schools." Invited testimony at a public hearing before the New York Senate Committee on Education, September 23.

Hayes-Bautista, D. (2002). "The Latino Health Research Agenda for the Twenty-First Century." In M. Suarez-Orozco and M. M. Paez (eds.), *Latinos: Remaking America*. Berkeley: University of California Press.

Hondagneu-Stoleto, P. (2001). *Domestica: Immigrant Workers Cleaning and Caring in the Shadows of Affluence*. Berkeley: University of California Press.

Jiobu, R. (1988). *Ethnicity and Assimilation*. Albany, NY: SUNY Press.

Jonnes, J. (1986). *We're Still Here: The Rise, Fall, and Resurrection of the South Bronx*. Boston: Atlantic Monthly Press.

Jonnes, J., and Jonnes, J. (2002). *South Bronx Rising: The Rise, Fall, and Resurrection of an American City* (2nd ed.). New York: Fordham University Press.

Kozol, J. (1995). *Amazing Grace: The Lives of Children and the Conscience of a Nation*. New York: Crown.

Meier, K., and Stewart, J. (1991). *The Politics of Hispanic Education*. Albany, NY: SUNY Press.

Noguera, P. A. (2003). *City Schools and the American Dream*. New York: Teachers College Press.

Noguera, P. A. (2004a). "Transforming High Schools." *Education Leadership*, *61*(8).

Noguera, P. A. (2004b). "Social Capital and the Education of Immigrant Students: Categories and Generalizations." *Sociology of Education*, *77*(2).

Oakes, J. (2002). "Adequate and Equitable Access to Education's Basic Tools in a Standards Based Educational System." *Teachers College Record*, special issue.

Ogbu, J. (1987). "Variability in Minority Student Performance: A Problem in Search of an Explanation." *Anthropology and Education Quarterly*, *18*(4), 312–334.

Orfield, G., and Eaton, S. (1996). *Dismantling Desegregation*. New York: New Press.

Portes, A., and Rumbaut, R. (2001). *Legacies: The Story of the Immigrant Second Generation*. Berkeley: University of California Press.

Rawls, J. (1999). *A Theory of Justice*. Harvard University Press.

Rooney, J. (1995). *Organizing the South Bronx*. Albany, NY: SUNY Press.

Smith, R. (2002). "Gender, Ethnicity, and Race in School and Work Outcomes of Second Generation Mexican Americans." In M. Suarez-Orozco and M. M. Paez (eds.), *Latinos: Remaking America*. Berkeley: University of California Press.

Suarez-Orozco, M., and Qin-Hilliard, D. (2004). *Globalization, Culture and Education in the New Millennium*. Berkeley: University of California Press.

Suarez-Orozco M., and Suarez-Orozco, C. (2001). *Children of Immigration*. Cambridge, MA: Harvard University Press.

Sugrue, T. J. (1996). *The Origins of the Urban Crisis: Race and Inequality in Postwar Detroit*. Princeton, NJ: Princeton University Press.

Tobier, E. (1998). "The Bronx in the Twentieth Century: Dynamics of Population and Economic Change." *Bronx County Historical Society Journal, 35*(2), 69–102.

Wallace, D., and Wallace, R. (1998). *A Plague on Your Houses: How New York Was Burned Down and National Public Health Crumbled*. London, New York: Verso.

Wunsch, J. L. (2001). "From Burning to Building: The Revival of the South Bronx 1970–1999." *Bronx County Historical Society Journal, 38*(1), 4–22.

Zentella, A. C. (2002). "Latin@ Languages and Identities." In M. Suarez-Orozco and M. M. Paez (eds.), *Latinos: Remaking America*. Berkeley: University of California Press.

Chapter Four: How Listening to Students Can Help Schools to Improve

Clinchy, E. (Ed.). (2000). *The new small schools*. New York: Teachers College Press.

Cohen, M. (Ed.). (2001). *Transforming the American high school*. Washington, DC: Aspen Institute.

Cotton, K. (1996). *School size, school climate, and student performance*. Retrieved June 16, 2006, from http://www.nwrel.org/scpd/sirs/10/c020.html.

Harvard Civil Rights Project. (2000). *Implications for high stakes testing in grades K–12*. Cambridge, MA: Harvard University.

Jencks, C., & Phillips, M. (1998). *The Black-White test score gap*. Washington, DC: Brookings Institute.

Lugg, C. C. (2005, Spring). A second term for the Bush administration. *Politics of Education Association Bulletin, 29,* 6–8.

Manpower Research Development Corporation. (2002). *Foundations for success: Case studies of how urban school systems improve student achievement*. New York: Manpower Research Development Corporation.

Mickelson, R. (1990). The attitude achievement paradox among Black adolescents. *Sociology of Education, 63*, 44–61.

Newman, F. (Ed.). (1992). *Student engagement and achievement in American secondary schools*. New York: Teachers College Press.

Newman, K., Fox, C., Harding, D., Mehta, J., & Roth, W. (2004). *Rampage: The social roots of school shootings*. New York: Basic Books.

Noguera, P. A., & Bliss, M. (2001). *Youth leadership and inter-group violence*. Oakland, CA: Youth Together.

Page, L. (2002). *National evaluation of smaller learning communities: Literature review*. Cambridge, MA: Abbott.

Siskin, L. (1993). *Realms of knowledge: Academic departments in secondary schools*. Boston: Falmer.

Steinberg, L. (1996). *Beyond the classroom*. New York: Simon & Schuster.

Stiefel, L., Berne, R., Iatarola, P., & Fruchter, N. (2000). High school size: Effects on budgets and performance in New York City. *Educational Evaluation and Policy Analysis, 22*, 27–39.

Valenzuela, A. (1999). *Subtractive schooling*. Albany, NY: SUNY Press.

Wasley, P. M., Fine, M., Gladden, M., Holland, N., King, S., Mosak, E., et al. (2000). *Small schools, great strides: A study of new small schools in Chicago*. New York: Bank Street.

Chapter Five: Latino Youth

Note

1. Much of the sociological literature on immigration holds that assimilation would lead to social mobility for immigrants.

Second- and third-generation immigrants have generally fared better than new arrivals. For Latinos, available research suggests the opposite may be true.

References

Ada, F.A.F. (1988). The Pajaro Valley experience: Working with Spanish speaking parents to develop children's reading and writing skills through the use of children's literature. In T. Skutnabb-Kangas and J. Cummins (eds.), *Minority Education*. London: Multilingual Matters.

Brodkin, Karen. (1999). *How Jews Became White Folk and What That Says About Race in America*. New Brunswick, NJ: Rutgers University Press.

Fass, Paula S. (1989). *Outside In: Minorities and the Transformation of American Education*. New York: Oxford University Press.

Gans, Herbert. (1967). *The Levittowners*. New York: Pantheon Books.

Garcia, Eugene E. (2001). *Hispanic Education in the United States*. Lanham, MD: Rowan and Littlefield.

Glazer, Nathan, and Moynihan, Daniel. (1963). *Beyond the Melting Pot*. Cambridge, MA: MIT Press.

Hayes-Bautista, David E. (2002). The Latino health research agenda for the twenty-first century. In Marcelo Suarez Orozco and Mariela M. Paez (eds.), *Latinos: Remaking America* (pp. 215–235). Berkeley: University of California Press.

Jiobu, Robert M. (1988). *Ethnicity and Assimilation*. Albany, NY: SUNY Press.

Kao, Grace, and Tienda, Marta. (1998). Educational aspirations among minority youth. *American Journal of Education, 106*(3), 349–384.

Katznelson, Ira, and Weir, Margaret. (1994). *Schooling for All: Class, Race, and the Decline of the Democratic Ideal*. Berkeley: University of California Press.

Meier, K., Stewart, J., and England, R. (1989). *Race, Class and Education: The Politics of Second Generation Discrimination*. Madison: University of Wisconsin Press.

Noguera, Pedro A. (2003). *City Schools and the American Dream*. New York: Teachers College Press.

Noguera, Pedro A. (2004). Social capital and the education of immigrant students: Categories and generalizations. *Sociology of Education, 77*(2).

Noguera, Pedro. A., and Wing, Jean. (2006). *Unfinished Business: Closing the Racial Achievement Gap in Our Nation's Schools*. San Francisco: Jossey-Bass.

Oakes, Jeannie. (2002). Adequate and equitable access to education's basic tools in a standards-based educational system. *Teachers College Record*.

Ogbu, John. (1988). Variability in minority student performance: A problem in search of an explanation. *Anthropology and Education Quarterly, 18*(4), 312–334.

Olsen, Laurie. (2000). *Made in America: Immigrant Students in Our Public Schools*. New York: New Press.

Orfield, Gary, and Eaton, Susan. (1996). *Dismantling Desegregation: The Quiet Reversal of Brown v. Board of Education*. New York: New Press.

Portes, Alejandro, and Rumbaut, Ruben. (2002). *Legacies: The Story of the Immigrant Second Generation*. Berkeley: University of California Press.

Roediger, David. (1991). *The Wages of Whiteness*. New York: Verso Press.

Smith, Roger. (2002). Gender, ethnicity, and race in school and work outcomes of second generation Mexican Americans. In Marcelo Suarez-Orozco and Mariela M. Paez (eds.), *Latinos: Remaking America* (pp. 110–125). Berkeley: University of California Press.

Suarez-Orozco, Marcelo, and Suarez-Orozco, Carola. (2001). *Children of Immigration: The Developing Child*. Cambridge, MA: Harvard University Press.

Valdez, Guadalupe. (1999). *Con Respeto: Bridging the Distances Between Culturally Diverse Families and Schools: An Ethnographic Portrait*. Stanford, CA: Stanford University Press.

Zentella, Ana Celia. (2002). Latino languages and identities. In Marcelo Suarez-Orozco and Mariela M. Paez (eds.), *Latinos: Remaking America* (pp. 321–338). Berkeley: University of California Press.

Chapter Six: Preventing and Producing Violence

1. Several educational organizations have designated violence prevention their highest priority. For example, the Association of California School Administrators made efforts to reduce violence in schools their top priority for the 1993–94 school year. For a discussion of national education priorities since 1980, see Beatrice Gross and Ronald Gross, eds., *The Great School Debate* (New York: Touchstone Books, 1985).

2. Evidence that there has been an escalation in the number of violent incidents occurring in schools is provided in an analysis of trends in Jackson Toby, "Everyday School Violence: How Disorder Fuels It," *American Educator,* 1993–94 (Winter), 4–6.

3. Numerous bills for curtailing violent crimes are presently under consideration in the Senate and House of Representatives. For a critical discussion of the Clinton administration's crime bill, see Elliott Currie, "What's Wrong with the Crime Bill?" *Nation,* January 31, 1994, pp. 4–5.

4. In New York City, over $28 million was spent on metal detectors during the 1980s. See Pat Kemper, "Disarming Youth," *California School Boards Journal,* 1993 (Fall), 25–33.

5. Kemper, "Disarming Youth," p. 27.

6. An example of such an approach can be seen in Denver, where assistant principal Ruben Perez at the Horace Mann Middle School suspended ninety-seven students in a three-day period for a variety of nonviolent infractions. In defense of his action, Perez argues that "the troublemakers weren't doing us any good. They were just interrupting the educational process for good students who come to school every day." See Florangela Davila, "Denver Debates School Ousters," *Washington Post,* January 20, 1995, p. 18. There is also the case of Dejundra Caldwell, who was sentenced to three years in prison for stealing twenty dollars worth of ice cream from the school

cafeteria at a high school in Birmingham, Alabama. See Kenneth Freed, "Youth Receives Three Years for Stealing Ice Cream," *Los Angeles Times*, September 30, 1994, p. 23. See also Harold Foster, *Ribbin' Jivin' and Playin' the Dozens: The Unrecognized Dilemma of Innercity Schools* (Cambridge, MA: Ballinger, 1974). Foster hypothesizes that Black males are suspended and expelled more often than Whites because they exhibit certain "cool" behaviors that teachers and administrators perceive as rude, arrogant, intimidating, sexually provocative, and threatening.

7. For a discussion of the success of mentoring in accessing the needs of "at-risk" students, see James McPartland and Saundra Murray Nettles, "Using Community Adults as Advocates or Mentors for At-Risk Middle School Students: A Two-Year Evaluation of Project RAISE," *American Journal of Education*, 99(4), 1991, 568–586.

8. For a discussion on how to address violence through the curriculum, see Tim Daux, "Fostering Self-Discipline," *Rethinking Schools*, 4(3), 1990, 6–7.

9. For a discussion of this approach and others being used by urban school districts to improve the delivery of social services to students and their families, see Jeannie Oakes, *Improving Inner-City Schools: Current Direction in Urban District Reform* (Madison, WI: Center for Policy Research in Education, 1987).

10. See Erin Hallisey, "Gang Activity in State's Prisons on the Increase," *San Francisco Chronicle*, May 17, 1994, p. 14.

11. For example, during 1992, in the city of Oakland, California, the number of violent crimes committed by juveniles while on school property was substantially fewer than the number of violent crimes committed away from school property. See Oakland Police Department, "Oakland Police Department Report on Crime in the City of Oakland," September 1992.

12. According to a recent national poll on attitudes toward public education conducted by Public Agenda, a national organization that conducts research on educational issues, the need for safety in schools was identified as the most important issue of public concern. For a summary and discussion of the survey, see Jean Johnson

and John Immerwahr, "What Americans Expect from the Public Schools," *American Educator*, Winter 1994–1995, 4–13.

13. A 1989 survey by the Justice Department reported that incidents of violence in urban schools occurred with twice the frequency as such incidents in suburban schools and nearly four times the frequency of incidents in rural schools. See Sara Rimer, "Violence Isn't Just in Cities, Suburban and Rural Schools Fine," *New York Times*, April 21, 1993, p. A16.

14. An example of the get-tough approach can be seen in the policies advocated by the American Federation of Teachers (AFT). Citing figures that indicate a dramatic rise in violence in public schools throughout the country, the AFT compiled a list of the tough actions being taken by school districts and new policies adopted by state legislatures to curtail the problem. The AFT also recommended that its local affiliates include violence reduction strategies in collective bargaining agreements. See Priscilla Nemeth, "Caught in the Crossfire," *American Teacher*, 77(2), 1992, 607. Also see an editorial by AFT president Albert Shanker, "Privileging Violence: Too Much Focus on the Needs and Rights of Disruptive Students," *American Educator*, Winter 1994–1995, 8.

15. During a visit to an urban high school, I commented to a school administrator that I was impressed by the lack of graffiti on school walls. The administrator laughed and told me, "This is a lockdown facility. They can't even get out of their classrooms while class is in session without being picked up. We run this place like San Quentin."

16. Such an approach has been advocated in a number of newspaper editorials (see, for example, "Time to Get Tough on School Violence," *Oakland Tribune*, November 21, 1991, p. 13, and "Cracking Down on Violence in Schools," *San Francisco Chronicle*, November 21, 1991, p. 24), and in several school districts. See Celeste Hunter, "Jail Threat Effective in Truancy Program," *Los Angeles Times*, January 9, 1994, p. 16.

17. A clear example of how traditional approaches to fighting school violence have failed can be seen in Richmond, California. Despite

making a substantial increase in funding for metal detectors and other security measures, several schools in the district have reported an increase in violence. In fact, two students were shot at Richmond High School after metal detectors were installed at the school entrances. See Rob Shea, "High School Kids Want Security Program Junked," *West County Times*, April 21, 1994, p. 14.

18. Statistics frequently cited as evidence of the problem include the number of students who report bringing weapons to school (13 percent); the number of teachers (one in ten) and students (one in four) who report that they have been victims of violence at school (Associated Press report on a Metropolitan Life Survey sponsored by *American Teacher*, December 17, 1993); and the perception of students, teachers, and administrators regarding the degree to which violence is a problem. See John McDermot, *Violent Schools—Safe Schools* (Washington, DC: National Institute of Education, 1978).

19. In Richmond, California, although the school district was still in the process of repaying a $30 million loan to the state after declaring bankruptcy in 1989, it set aside $50,000 in 1993 to pay for the installation of metal detectors. One teacher remarked: "They're spending money on this and we still need paper in our classrooms." In defense of the expenditure, a school administrator responded, "The overall program of the district is to provide a safe environment regardless of the cost. It's something we have to do." Ikimulisa Sockwell, "Detecting Weapon-Free Schools," *West Contra Costa Times*, December 8, 1993, p. 13.

20. One opinion poll conducted by the *Los Angeles Times* found that concerns about safety remain high, despite a 12 percent decrease in the number of violent crimes committed in the state. See Belinda Lawson, "Fear of Crime Remains High Despite Reduction in Crime Rate," *Los Angeles Times*, October 22, 1994, p. 17.

21. According to the American Federation of Teachers (AFT), several school districts do not accurately report the number of violent incidents that occur in the schools because they fear negative publicity. See Nemeth, "Caught in the Crossfire," pp. 6–7. The *New York Times* claimed that similar attempts are made to downplay the frequency of

violent incidents in New York City schools, in "Controlling School Violence," *New York Times*, May 3, 1993, p. A24.

22. For a discussion on how the conception of the asylum influenced the design and operation of public schools, see David Rothman, *Discovery of the Asylum* (Boston: Little, Brown, 1971), pp. 83–84. Also see David Tyack, *The One Best System* (Cambridge, MA: Harvard University Press, 1974), pp. 51–58.

23. Rothman, *Discovery*, p. 15.

24. Rothman, *Discovery*, p. 235.

25. Rothman, *Discovery*, pp. 137–139.

26. Lawrence Cremin, *American Education: The Metropolitan Experience, 1876–1980* (New York: HarperCollins, 1988), p. 118.

27. The progressive intentions of educators and social reformers is documented in Cremin, *American Education*, pp. 164–179.

28. Michael Katz, *Reconstructing American Education* (Cambridge, MA: Harvard University Press, 1987), p. 17.

29. G. Stanley Hall, *Adolescence: Its Psychology and Its Relations to Physiology, Sex, Crime, Religion, and Education*, 2 vols. (New York: D. Appleton, 1904).

30. Cremin, *American Education*, p. 195.

31. Cremin, *American Education*, p. 295.

32. Jeannie Oakes, *Keeping Track: How Schools Structure Inequality* (New Haven, CT: Yale University Press, 1985), p. 28; Martin Carnoy and Henry Levin, *Schooling and Work in the Democratic State* (Stanford, CA: Stanford University Press, 1985), p. 95.

33. Cremin, *American Education*, p. 21.

34. Tyack, *The One Best*, p. 82.

35. Tyack, *The One Best*, pp. 91–97.

36. The observer was Edward Joseph Rice, a pediatrician who visited thirty-six schools in 1892 to prepare a series of articles on the condition of urban schools. Focusing again on the body, Rice observed one teacher scold her students by asking, "How can you learn

anything with your knees and toes out of order?" From Edward
J. Rice, *The Public School System of the United States* (New York:
Century Press, 1893), p. 98.

37. Tyack, *The One Best*, p. 74.

38. Norton Grubb, "The Old Problem of 'New Students': Purpose,
Content, and Pedagogy," in Irwin Flexnard and Harry Passo (eds.),
Changing Populations, Changing Schools (New York: Teachers College
Press, 1995), pp. 3–5.

39. Lawrence Cremin, *The Transformation of the School* (New York:
Vintage Books, 1961), p. 68.

40. Oakes, *Keeping Track*, pp. 32–33.

41. Writing about disciplinary practices used in the military and in
prisons in eighteenth-century France, Michel Foucault describes
a preoccupation with the production of "docile bodies" in which
"power is dissociated from the body, and aptitude is turned into a
capacity which it seeks to increase. . . . If economic exploitation
separates the force and the product of labour, let us say that disciplinary coercion established in the body the constricting link between an
increased aptitude and an increased domination." Michel Foucault,
Discipline and Punish (New York: Vintage Books, 1979) p. 138.

42. For a discussion of how changes brought about by migration and
immigration changed the character of eastern U.S. cities, see
Daniel P. Moynihan and Nathan Glazer, *Beyond the Melting Pot*
(Cambridge, MA: Joint Center for Urban Studies, 1963),
pp. vii–xxi.

43. The factors leading to the deterioration of urban areas are well
described in William Julius Wilson, *The Truly Disadvantaged*
(Chicago: University of Chicago Press, 1987).

44. James Conant, *Slums and Suburbs* (New York: McGraw-Hill, 1961).

45. Conant, *Slums and Suburbs*, p. 22.

46. Describing the loss of school control as a "crisis in authority,"
Mary Haywood Metz analyzes how school districts attempted to
respond to this situation in *Classrooms and Corridors: The Crisis of*

Authority in Desegregated Secondary Schools (Berkeley: University of California Press, 1978).

47. Allen Ornstein, "Discipline: A Major Function in Teaching the Disadvantaged," in Richard Heidenreich (ed.), *Urban Education* (Arlington, VA: College Readings, 1972).

48. Ornstein, "Discipline," p. 2.

49. In a study on the changes in school culture that accompanied desegregation, Metz describes how many schools experienced a crisis of authority, much of which she attributes to fundamental miscommunications between White teachers and Black students. See Metz, *Classrooms and Corridors*.

50. Tyack, *The One Best*, p. 54.

51. In response to the rise in attacks on teachers, the American Federation of Teachers has developed a victim support program. For a discussion of the program and the problems responsible for its creation, see Nemeth, "Caught in the Crossfire," pp. 6–7.

52. Foucault, *Discipline*, p. 54.

53. During the hearing, the father mentioned that he had recently lost his job and that the financial problems created by his unemployment had added to the problems he was having with his wife.

54. In describing how power-knowledge relations constrain the ability of those designated to exercise authority to use their own judgment, Foucault writes, "Power-knowledge relations are to be analyzed not on the basis of a subject of knowledge who is or is not free in relation to the power system, but on the contrary the subject who knows, the objects to be known and the modalities of knowledge must be regarded as so many effects of these fundamental implications of power-knowledge and their historical transformation." Foucault, *Discipline*, pp. 27–28.

55. A national study carried out by the U.S. Office of Civil Rights reports that Black students are 74 to 86 percent more likely than White students to receive corporal punishment, 54 to 88 percent more likely to be suspended, and three to eight times as likely to be expelled. See Kenneth Meier, Joseph Stewart, and Robert

England, *Race, Class and Education: The Politics of Second Generation Discrimination* (Madison: University of Wisconsin Press, 1989), pp. 84–86.

56. In 1991, Assembly Bill 2140 was proposed by Barbara Lee, Dem.-Oakland, to ensure that the removal of students from school was viewed as a last resort and "not to eliminate from the classroom students who are difficult to teach." See "Assembly Bill Would Alter School Suspension Policy," *Oakland Tribune,* November 27, 1991, p. B1.

57. Black parents and community members in Cincinnati also worked to defeat the approval of a school facilities bond measure that would have raised $348 million to finance repairs to deteriorating schools because of their anger over the treatment of Black students. See Adrian King, "Student Rights vs. School Safety: School Districts Grapple with the Racial Implications of New Security Measures," *Education Week,* January 19, 1994, p. 8.

58. A study conducted by Xavier University and cited by the *New York Times* supports the idea that violence is not solely an urban issue. The study found that 54 percent of the 294 suburban schools and 43 percent of the 344 small-town schools surveyed reported an increase in the number of violent incidents. See Daniel Goldman, "Hope Seen for Curbing Youth Violence," *New York Times,* April 21, 1993, p. A12.

59. For a discussion of how the equation of Blacks with crime has become central to public discourse about violence and crime, see Amos Wilson, *Black-on-Black Violence* (New York: Afrikan World Infosystems, 1990), p. 1–34. Also see Richard Majors and Janet Billson, *Cool Pose* (New York: Touchstone, 1992), pp. 33–35, for a discussion on perceptions of Black male violence.

60. This argument is made in Jackson Toby, "Everyday School Violence: How Disorder Fuels It," *American Educator,* Winter 1993/1994, pp. 4–13, and in Daniel Patrick Moynihan, "Defining Deviancy Down," *American Educator,* Winter 1993/1994, p. 16.

61. Meier et al., *Race, Class, and Education,* pp. 81–84.

62. Meier et al., *Race, Class, and Education,* p. 89.

63. Wilbur Brookover and Edsel Erickson, *The Sociology of Education* (Homewood, IL: Dorsey Press, 1975); Nancy St. John, *School Desegregation Outcomes for Children* (Hoboken, NJ: Wiley, 1975); Thomas Good and Harris Cooper, *Pygmalion Grows Up* (New York: Longman, 1983); Jerome Dusek and Gail Joseph, "The Bases of Teacher Expectancies: A Meta-Analysis," *Journal of Educational Psychology*, 75, 1983, 327–346; Rhona Weinstein and Charles Soule, "Expectations and High School Change: Teacher Researcher Collaboration to Prevent School Failure," *American Journal of Community Psychology*, 19(3), 1991.

64. For a discussion on the various forms of multicultural education and the discourses associated with it, see Christine Sleeter, *Empowerment Through Multicultural Education* (Albany, NY: SUNY Press, 1991), pp. 1–23.

65. "Border crossing" is a phrase coined by Henry Giroux to describe the personal transformation experienced by teachers and students engaged in critical discourse and pedagogy. He writes: "Critical educators take up culture as a vital source for developing a politics of identity, community and pedagogy. Culture is not monolithic or unchanging, but is a site of multiple and heterogeneous borders where different histories, languages, experiences, and voices intermingle amidst diverse relations of power and privilege. Within this pedagogical borderland known as school, subordinate cultures push against and permeate the alleged unproblematic and homogeneous borders of the dominant cultural forms and practices. . . . Radical educators must provide conditions for students to speak so that their narratives can be affirmed." Henry Giroux, *Border Crossings* (New York: Rutledge, 1992), p. 169.

66. These interviews were part of a survey that I conducted with 125 students at an urban continuation high school in Northern California in 1990 and 1991.

67. My impression of the attitudes and intentions of many urban teachers is supported by Carl Grant, who cites research on teacher attitudes in his "Urban Teachers: Their New Colleagues and Curriculum," in J. Kretovics and E. J. Nussel (eds.), *Transforming Urban Education* (Boston: Allyn & Bacon, 1994), pp. 315–321, and by

Pamela Boltin Joseph and Gale E. Burnaford, whose study on teachers' self-images challenges many of the prevailing notions about teachers' incompetence and indifference. See Pamela Boltin Joseph and Gale E. Burnaford (eds.), *Images of Schoolteachers in Twentieth Century America* (New York: St. Martin's Press, 1994).

68. Several exceptionally good high schools are described and analyzed in detail in Sara Lawrence Lightfoot, *The Good High School* (New York: Basic Books, 1983).

69. This school was also the only junior high school in the district where no weapons were confiscated from students. See "Selected School Characteristics," Office of the Superintendent, Oakland Unified School District, December 1993.

70. Continuation high schools are set up for students who have either been forced or have volunteered to leave a regular high school. Many students at continuation schools have a record of poor attendance or poor behavior in school, or both. Some students are required to attend continuation school as a condition of juvenile probation.

71. Efforts to close a campus for security reasons have often met with resistance from students. In Richmond, California, the district's attempt to close high school campuses at lunchtime led to protests and walkouts from school. See Sockwell, "Detecting Weapon-Free Schools," p. 13.

Chapter Seven: Schools, Prisons, and Social Implications of Punishment

Apple, M. (1982). *Education and power*. Boston: Ark Paperbacks.

Ayers, W., Dorhn, B., & Ayers, R. (Eds.). (2001). *Zero tolerance: Resisting the drive for punishment in our schools*. New York: New Press.

Bowles, H., & Ginits, S. (1976). *Schooling in capitalist America*. New York: Basic Books.

Brookover, W., & Erickson, E. (1969). *Society, schools and learning*. East Lansing: Michigan State University Press.

Casella, R. (2001). *"Being down": Challenging violence in urban schools*. New York: Teachers College Press.

Cremin, L. (1988). *American education*. New York: HarperCollins.

Devine, J. (1996). *Maximum security: The culture of violence in inner-city schools*. Chicago: University of Chicago Press.

Durkheim, E. (1961). The first element of morality: The spirit of discipline (E. K. Wilson & H. Schnurer, Trans.). In E. K. Wilson (Ed.), *Moral education*. New York: Free Press.

Fishman, J., & McCarty, L. P. (1998). *John Dewey and the challenge of classroom practice*. New York: Teachers College Press.

Gottfredson, D. (2001). *Schools and delinquency*. Cambridge: Cambridge University Press.

Hirschi, T. (1969). *Causes of delinquency*. Berkeley: University of California Press.

Johnson, J. (1995). Life after death: Critical pedagogy in an urban classroom. *Harvard Educational Review, 65*(2), 213–228.

Johnson, T., Boyden, J. E., & Pittz, W. (Eds.). (2001). *Racial profiling and punishment in U.S. public schools: How zero tolerance policies and high stakes testing subvert academic excellence and racial equity*. Oakland, CA: Applied Research Center.

Katznelson, I., & Weir, M. (1985). *Schooling for all*. Berkeley: University of California Press.

McWhorter, J. (2000). *Losing the race: Self-sabotage in Black America*. New York: The Free Press.

Meier, K., Stewart, J., & England, R. (1989). *Race, class and education*. Madison: University of Wisconsin Press.

Metropolitan Life. (2001). *The American teacher*. Washington, DC: Author.

Newmann, F. (1992). *Student engagement and achievement in American secondary schools*. New York: Teachers College Press.

Noguera, P. (2001a). Finding safety where we least expected it: The role of social capital in making schools safe. In W. Ayers, B. Dorhn, & R. Ayers (Eds.), *Zero tolerance: Resisting the drive for punishment in our schools*. New York: New Press.

Noguera, P. (2001b). Racial politics and the elusive quest for excellence and equity in education. *Education and Urban Society, 34*(1), 18–41.

Oakes, J. (1985). *Keeping track: How schools structure inequality*. New Haven, CT: Yale University Press.

Pollack, M. (1999, August 18). Changing student attitudes about violence. *New York Times*, p. 37.

Rawls, J. (1971). *A theory of justice*. Cambridge, MA: Harvard University Press.

Rousseau, J. (1974). *The essential Rousseau* (L. Bair, Trans.). New York: New American Library.

Shores, K. (2003, January 20). Academy instills values, discipline and structure. *South Florida Sun-Sentinel*.

Singer, S. (1996). *Recriminalizing delinquency*. Cambridge: Cambridge University Press.

Skiba, R. J. (2000a). *Zero tolerance, zero evidence: An analysis of school disciplinary practice*. Bloomington: Indiana University Education Policy Center.

Skiba, R. J. (2000b). When is disproportionality discrimination? The overrepresentation of Black students in school suspension. In W. Ayers, B. Dorhn, & R. Ayers (Eds.), *Zero tolerance: Resisting the drive for punishment in our schools*. New York: New Press.

Steinberg, L. (1996). *Beyond the classroom: The failure of school reform*. New York: Simon & Schuster.

Wacquant, L. (2000). Deadly symbiosis: When ghetto and prison meet and mesh. *Punishment and Society, 3*(1), 95–134.

Willis, P. (1977). *Learning to labor*. New York: Columbia University Press.

Chapter Eight: Racial Politics and the Quest for Excellence and Equity in Education

Notes

1. For reactions to the arguments and evidence cited in *The Bell Curve* (Herrnstein and Murray, 1994), see Fraser (1995) and Fischer et al. (1996).

2. To provide support from researchers to the work of MSAN, the College Board convened a research advisory board chaired by Edmond Gordon of Teachers College.

3. Several of the districts in MSAN are located in states where high-stakes testing has been adopted. For a discussion of these policies and their impact on schools and students, see Heubert and Hauser (1999).

4. To review articles that have appeared in the news media on MSAN, go to www.eths.k12.us/MSA/msanetwork.html.

5. For an analysis of how affluent parents can exercise their power to oppose and resist educational reforms aimed at producing equity in schools, see Oakes (2000).

6. Educational researchers have long recognized that cultural and class differences among students often require that different educational strategies be employed to meet the needs of different students. For a discussion on this topic, see Villegas (1988) and Erickson (1987).

7. Research by Suarez-Orzoco and Suarez-Orzoco (2001) indicates that immigrant students are more likely to be overrepresented among both high achievers and low achievers.

8. The lack of data on the performance of students at Berkeley High Alternative School prompted the Diversity Project to undertake an extensive study of the school. See Diversity Project (2000) for an analysis of the school.

9. An indication of how many former private school students enter BHS is provided from the Diversity Project survey on the Class of 2000. Nearly 25 percent of the ninth grade students responding to the survey reported that they had attended private school prior to entering BHS. Also, whereas the percentage of White students in

elementary and middle school in Berkeley is approximately 30 percent, the White student population at BHS is over 40 percent.

10. I have heard this sentiment expressed to me on numerous occasions by White parents in Berkeley. One Berkeley professor who was aggravated that her son entering kindergarten had not been assigned to the school she preferred informed me that "I would think that the district should be happy to have White middle-class kids like my son. For heaven's sake, I want to do all I can to support the public schools myself, but they've got to be more flexible in how they apply their rules" (interview April 16, 1998).

11. For a discussion on the history of these separate schools and the reasons for their eventual demise, see Kirp (1982).

12. The Diversity Project was established in the fall of 1996 as a collaboration between researchers from the Graduate School of Education at the University of California at Berkeley, and parents, teachers, and students from Berkeley High School. The focus of the project was to use research to understand and address the factors that contributed to racial disparities in the academic performance of students. See Diversity Project (1999) for a detailed discussion of the goals and findings of this research.

References

Berkeley Alliance. (1999). Comprehensive Report on Student Achievement. Unpublished manuscript.

Delpitt, L. (1988). The Silenced Dialogue: Power and Pedagogy in Educating Other People's Children. *Harvard Educational Review, 58*(3), 280–298.

Diversity Project. (1999). *Progress Report.* Berkeley, CA: Simon Graphics.

Diversity Project. (2000). Final Report: Recommendations and Findings. Unpublished manuscript. Berkeley: Graduate School of Education, University of California, Berkeley.

Erickson, F. (1987). Transformation and School Success: The Politics and Culture of Educational Achievement. *Anthropology and Education Quarterly, 18*(4).

Ferguson, R. (2001). "A Diagnostic Analysis of Black-White GPA Dispari-ties in Shaker Heights, Ohio." *Brookings Papers on Education Policy—2001*, pp. 347–414.

Fine, M., L. Weis, L. Powell, and L. Mun Wong. (1997). *Off White: Readings in Race, Power, and Society*. New York: Routledge.

Fischer, C., M. Hout, M. S. Jankowski, S. Lucas, A. Swidler, and K. Voss. (1996). *Inequality by Design: Cracking the Bell Curve Myth*. Princeton, NJ: Princeton University Press.

Fordham, S. (1988). Racelessness as a Factor in Black Student Success: Prag-matic Strategy or Pyrrhic Victory? *Harvard Educational Review*, 58(1), 54–84.

Fordham, S. (1996). *Blacked Out: Dilemmas of Race, Identity and Success at Capital High*. Chicago: University of Chicago Press.

Fraser, S. (1995). *The Bell Curve Wars*. New York: Basic Books.

Gibson, M. (1988). *Accommodation Without Assimilation*. Ithaca, NY: Cornell University Press.

Herrnstein, R., and C. Murray. (1994). *The Bell Curve: Intelligence and Class Structure in American Life*. New York: Free Press.

Heubert, J., and R. Hauser. (1999). *High Stakes: Testing for Tracking, Promotion and Graduation*. Washington, DC: National Academy Press.

Jencks, C. (1972). *Inequality*. New York: HarperCollins.

Jencks, C., and M. Phillips. (1998). *The Black-White Test Score Gap*. Washington, DC: Brookings Institute.

Kirp, D. (1982). *Just Schools*. Berkeley: University of California Press.

Kozol, J. (1991). *Savage Inequalities*. New York: Crown Books.

Maeroff, G. (1988). "Withered Hopes, Stillborn Dreams: The Dismal Panorama of Urban Schools." *Phi Delta Kappan*, 69, 632–638.

Matute-Bianchi, M. (1986). Ethnic Identities and Patterns of School Success and Failure Among Mexican Descent and Japanese American Students in a California High School: An Ethnographic Analysis. *American Educational Research Journal, 95*(1), 233–255.

McCarthy, C., and W. Crichlow. (1993). *Race, Identity and Representation in Education*. New York: Routledge.

McWhorter, J. (2000). *Losing the Race*. New York: New Press.

Meier, D. (1995). *The Power of Their Ideas*. Boston: Beacon Press.

Minority Student Achievement Network. (1999). Background Report. Unpublished manuscript. Evanston, IL: Evanston Township School District.

Newman, F. (1992). *Student Engagement and Achievement in American Secondary Schools*. New York: Teachers College Press.

Nocera, J. (1990). How the Middle Class Helped Ruin the Public Schools. *Utne Reader*, September-October.

Noguera, P. (1995). Ties That Bind, Forces That Divide: Berkeley High School and the Challenge of Integration. *University of San Francisco Law Review, 29*(3).

Noguera, P. (2001). The Trouble with Black Boys: The Impact of Cultural and Environmental Factors on the Academic Performance of African American Males. *Harvard Journal of African Americans and Public Policy, 3*, 45–73.

Oakes, J. (1999). Outreach: Struggling Against Culture and Power. *Outlook*. www.ucop.edu/outreach/outlook.

Ogbu, J. (1978). *Minority Education and Caste: The American System in Cross-Cultural Perspective*. Orlando, FL: Academic Press.

Ogbu, J. (1987). Variability in Minority Student Performance: A Problem in Search of an Explanation. *Anthropology and Education Quarterly, 18*, 312–334.

Olsen, L. (1997). *Made in America: Immigrant Students in Our Public Schools*. New York: New Press.

Olszewski, L. (1998). An Integrated High School in Search of Equality: Diverse Berkeley High Grapples with Low Achivement by Poor, Minorities. *San Francisco Chronicle*, January 13, p. 1.

Orfield, G., and S. Eaton. (1996). *Dismantling Desegregation*. New York: New Press.

Phelan, P., A. Locke Davidson, and H. Cao Yu. (1996). *Adolescents' Worlds*. New York: Teachers College Press.

Portilla, M. (1999). *Black Picket Fences: Privilege and Peril Among the Black Middle Class*. Chicago: University of Chicago Press.

Report on College Admissions for the Class of 1996. Unpublished Manuscript Berkeley High School College Advisor.

Spencer, M. (2000). African American Males' Academic Achievement Experiences: Assumptions About Opportunities and Facts About Normative Developmental Needs and Inopportune Structural Conditions. Paper presented at the U.S. Department of Education Symposium on African American Male Achievement, Washington, DC, December 4.

Spring, J. (1988). *American Education*. New York: McGraw-Hill.

Steele, C. (1992). Race and the Schooling of Black Americans. *Atlantic Monthly*, April.

Steele, C. (1997). A Threat in the Air: How Stereotypes Shape Intellectual Identity and Performance. *American Psychologist*, June.

Steinberg, L. (1996). *Beyond the Classroom*. New York: Simon & Schuster.

Stepick, A., and M. Castro. (1991). *Changing Relations Between Newcomers and Established Residents: The Case of Miami*. New York: Ford Foundation, Changing Relations Project.

Suarez-Orozco, M., and C. Suarez-Orozco. (2001). *Children of Immigration*. Cambridge, MA: Harvard University Press.

Villegas, M. (1988). School Failure and Cultural Mismatch: Another View. *Urban Review, 20*, 253–265.

Wells, A., and I. Serna. (1996). The Politics of Culture: Understanding Local Political Resistance to Detracking in Racially Mixed Schools. *Harvard Educational Review*, 66(1), 93–118.

Williams, B. (1996). *Closing the Achievement Gap*. Alexandria, VA: Association for Supervision and Curriculum Development.

Chapter Ten: Standards for What? Accountability for Whom?

Barton, P., Coley, R. J., & Goertz, M. E. (1991). *The state of inequality*. Princeton, NJ: Educational Testing Service, Policy Information Center.

Comer, J. (1987). New Haven's school-community connection. *Educational Leadership, 44*(6), 13–16.

Cremin, L. (1961). *The transformation of the school*. New York: Vintage Books.

Cremin, L. (1988). *American education: The metropolitan experience, 1876–1980*. New York: HarperCollins.

Darling-Hammond, L. (1997). *The right to learn: A blueprint for creating schools that work*. San Francisco: Jossey-Bass.

Dryfoos, J. (2001). *Evaluation of community schools: An early look*. Available from http://www.communityschools.org/evaluation/evalbrieffinal.html.

Eccles, J., & Gootman, J. A. (eds.). (2002). *Community programs to promote youth development*. Washington, DC: National Academy Press.

Elmore, R. (2003). *Doing the right thing, knowing the right thing to do: The problem of failing schools and performance-based accountability*. Unpublished manuscript, Harvard Graduate School of Education, Cambridge, MA.

Epstein, J. (1991). School and family connections: Theory, research, and implications for integrating societies of education and family. In D. G. Unger and M. B. Sussman (eds.), *Families in community settings: Interdisciplinary perspectives* (pp. 289–305). New York: Hayworth Press.

Feddeman, S., & Perlman, H. (2003, March 3). Romney announces MCAS retest results: 90 percent of class of 2003 have now passed. *Boston Globe*, p. 13.

Ferguson, R. (2000). *A diagnostic analysis of Black-White GPA disparities in Shaker Heights, Ohio*. Washington, DC: Brookings Institution.

Haney, W., Madaus, G., & Wheelock, A. (2003, March). *DOE report inflates MCAS pass rates for the Class of 2003*. Retrieved April 4, 2003, from http://www.massparents.org/news/2003/inflated_scores.htm.

Hubert, J., & Hauser, R. (eds.). (1999). *High stakes: Testing for tracking, promotion and graduation*. Washington, DC: National Academy Press.

Jerald, C. D. (2001). *Dispelling the myth revisited*. Washington, DC: Education trust.

Katznelson, L., & Weir, M. (1985). *Schooling for all*. Berkeley: University of California Press.

Kohn, A. (2000, September 27). Standardized testing and its victims. *Education Week*, pp. 46–47, 60.

Maeroff, G. (1988). Withered hopes and stillborn dreams: The dismal panorama of urban schools. *Phi Delta Kappan*, 69(9), 632–638.

McLaughlin, M. (2000). *Community counts: How youth organizations matter for youth development*. Washington, DC: Public Education Network.

Miller, L. S. (1995). *An American imperative*. New Haven, CT: Yale University Press.

National League of Cities. (2002). *Municipal leadership in education*. Washington, DC: Carnegie Corporation.

Nocera, J. (1991, September–October). How the middle class has helped ruin the public schools. *Utne Reader*, 66–72.

Noguera, P. A. (2001a). Radical politics and the elusive quest for equity and excellence. *Education and Urban Society*, 34(1), 18–41.

Noguera, P. A. (2001b). The role of social capital in the transformation of urban schools in social capital and low income communities. In S. Saegert,

P. Thompson, & M. Warren (eds.), *Social capital and poor communities* (pp. 189–212). New York: Russell Sage Foundation.

Noguera, P. A., & Akom, A. (2000). Disparities demystified. *Nation, 270*(22).

Noguera, P. A., & Brown, E. (2002, September 24). Educating the new majority. *Boston Globe,* 21.

Orfield, G., & Eaton, S. (1996). *Dismantling desegregation.* New York: New Press.

Schwartz, R., & Gandal, M. (2000, January 19). Higher standards, stronger tests: Don't shoot the messenger. *Education Week,* 40–41.

Schwartz, R., & Robinson, M. (2000). Goals 2000 and the standards movement. In D. Ravitch (ed.), *Brookings Paper on Education Policy* (pp. 3–24). Washington, DC: Brookings Institution Press.

Sizemore, B. (1988). The Madison elementary school: A turnaround case. *Journal of Negro Education, 57*(3), 37–62.

Stone, C. (2001). *Building civic capacity.* Lawrence: University of Kansas Press.

Traub, J. (2002, November 10). Does it work? *New York Times,* 8–15.

Tyack, D., & Cuban, L. (1995). *Tinkering toward utopia.* Cambridge, MA: Harvard University Press.

Wong, K., Anagnstopoulos, D., Rutledge, S., Lynn, L., & Dreeben, R. (1999). *Implementation of an educational accountability agenda: Integrated governance in the Chicago Public Schools enters its fourth year.* Chicago: Department of Education.

Chapter Eleven: Racial Isolation, Poverty, and the Limits of Local Control as a Means for Holding Public Schools Accountable

Notes

1. There are cities such as Boston and Chicago and jurisdictions where school board members are appointed by the mayor or some other elected official.

2. Serano *v.* Priest, 5 Cal.3d 584 (1971).

3. The academic performance index is a rating system that assesses the performance of schools based on the average scores received by its students on the Stanford 9 achievement tests. For information on Public Schools Accountability Act (PSAA), see http://www.cde. ca.gov/iiusp/.

4. Most researchers regard official dropout rates as inaccurate because they fail to capture students who drop out before entering high school.

5. College eligibility rates are determined by the number of high school graduates who have successfully taken the courses and obtained the test scores necessary for admission to either the University of California or the California State University system.

6. For a detailed description of conditions in California's public schools and the number of schools that may be subject to reconstitution as result of PSAA, see "Who Is Accountable to Our Children: Conditions in California Public Schools at the Beginning of the Millennium," available at http://www.law.ucla.edu/ reports517003.htm.

7. In the past, the State of California has intervened in school districts only when they were fiscally insolvent. In 1995, the State took over management of Compton public schools and turned control back to the locally elected school board in 2001. However, there is little evidence that conditions in Compton's schools have improved. See "Accountability Won't Rescue Disadvantaged Students," *California Educator*, 5 (June 2001).

8. In addition to the attacks from the media and politicians, critics of Oakland's language policy included individuals such as the Reverend Jesse Jackson and poet Maya Angelou. However, once these individuals learned that the district had no intention of teaching children Ebonics, as had been reported in the press, but rather sought to train teachers on how to work with students who speak Ebonics so that they can be taught standard English, their positions were reversed.

9. Evidence that the state and federal governments are aware of the additional needs of poor children can be seen in policies such as Compensatory Education and Economic Impact Aid, both of which provide additional funds to the schools attended by poor children.

10. As a result of a charter amendment proposed by former Oakland Mayor Jerry Brown (currently attorney general of California), the mayor has the power to appoint three members to the school board. Brown called for this measure to be instituted so that "genuine" reforms could be made in the system. Most observers agree that while this additional support will be helpful, it will not be sufficient to address the wide disparities in funding among school districts. For an analysis of the new education bill, see *New York Times*, January 8, 2002.

11. Efforts to address the lack of community organization in Oakland have recently been supported by the Koshland Committee of the San Francisco Foundation. For the past five years, the committee has developed an initiative in the San Antonio District, an area of Latinos, Southeast Asians, older African Americans, Native Americans, and White small business owners.

12. Even with his three appointees on the school board, (former) Mayor Brown was unable to gain the board's approval for the creation of the military academy. After several unsuccessful attempts to obtain approval from other authorizing bodies, Brown was granted approval from the governor's office, and the academy was opened to students in the fall of 2001.

References

Ada, A. F. (1988). "The Pajaro Valley experience: Working with Spanish speaking parents to develop children's reading and writing skills through the use of children's literature." In Tove Skutnabb-Kangas and Jim Cummins (eds.), *Minority Education*. London: Multilingual Matters, Ltd.

Alameda County Health Department. (1998). "By the numbers: A public health data view of Oakland."

Anderson, J. (1988). *The Education of Blacks in the South, 1860–1935*. Chapel Hill: University of North Carolina Press.

Blasi, G. (2001). "Reforming educational accountability." Unpublished conference paper.

Brown, P. (2001). "Oakland's schools military bearing rankles some." *New York Times*, August 24.

Bush, R. (1984). *The New Black Vote*. San Francisco: Synthesis Publications.

Carnoy, M., and H. Levin. (1986). *School and Work in a Democratic State*. Palo Alto, CA: Stanford University Press.

Chubb, J., and T. Moe. (1990). *Politics, Markets and America's Schools*. Washington, DC: Brookings Institute.

Cibulka, J. (2001). "Old Wine, New Bottles." *Education Next*, Winter. www.educationnext.org.

City of Oakland. (1994). *West Oakland Community—Existing Conditions*. Office of Economic Development.

Clark, W. (1998). *The California Cauldron*. New York: Guilford Press.

Clinchy, E. (ed.). (2000). *The New Small Schools*. New York: Teachers College Press.

College Board. (1999). *Reaching the Top: Report of the National Task Force on Minority High Achievement*. New York: College Board.

Coleman, J. S., et al. (1966). *Equality of Educational Opportunity*. Washington, DC: U.S. Government Printing Office.

Coleman, J. (1988). "Social capital in the creation of human capital." *American Journal of Sociology*, 94(suppl.), S95–120.

Comer, J. (1980). *School Power*. New York: Free Press.

Commission for Positive Change. (1990). *Good Education in Oakland*. Oakland, CA: The Commission.

Conchas, G. (2001). "Structuring success and failure: Understanding variability in Latino school engagement." *Harvard Educational Review, 70*(3), 475–504.

Dryfoos, J. (2001). "Evaluation of community schools: An early look." http://www.communityschools.org/evaluation/evalbrieffinal.html.

Ed Data. (2002). *District Financial Statements*. http://www.eddata. k12.ca.us/fiscal/fundingsummary.asp.

Education Data Partnership. (2001). *Fiscal, Demographic, and Performance Data on California's K–12 Schools*. http://www.ed-data.k12.ca.us.

Elmore, R. (1996). "The new accountability in state educational policy." In H. Ladd (ed.), *Holding Schools Accountable. Performance-Based Reform in Education*. Washington, DC: The Brookings Institute.

Epstein, J. (1993) "A response." *Teachers College Record, 94*(4), 710–717.

Fantini, M., M. Gittell, and R. Magat. (1970). *Community Control and the Urban School*. New York: Praeger.

Fine, M. (1993). "(Ap)parent involvement: Reflections on parents, power and urban schools." *Teachers College Record, 94*(4), 26–43.

Franklin, J., and A. Moss. (1988). *From Slavery to Freedom*. New York: Knopf.

Frèire, P. (1970). *Education for Critical Consciousness*. New York: Continuum Press.

Gold, E. (2001). "Clients, consumers or collaborators? Parents and their roles in school reform." Madison, WI: Consortium for Policy Research in Education, August.

Gormley, W. (Ed.). (1991). *Privatization and Its Alternatives*. Madison: University of Wisconsin Press.

Herrnstein R., and C. Murray. (1994). *The Bell Curve: Intelligence and Class Structure in American Life*. New York: Free Press.

Hess, G. A. (1999). "Community participation or control? From New York to Chicago." *Theory into Practice, 38*(4), 217–224.

Horton, M., and P. Frèire. (1990). *We Make the Road by Walking.* Philadelphia: Temple University Press.

James, D. W., S. Jurich, and S. Estes. (2001). *Raising Minority Academic Achievement.* Washington, D.C.: American Youth Policy Forum.

Jencks, C. (1972). *Inequality.* New York: HarperCollins.

Jencks, C., & Phillips, M. (1998). "The Black-White test score gap: An introduction." In C. Jencks and M. Phillips (Eds.), *The Black-White Test Score Gap* (pp. 1–51). Washington, DC: Brookings Institution.

Katznelson, I., and M. Weir. (1994). *Schooling for All.* Berkeley: University of California Press.

Kozol, J. (1991). *Savage Inequalities.* New York: Crown Books.

Lareau, A. (1987). "Social class differences in family-school relationships: The importance of cultural capital." *Sociology of Education, 60,* 73–85.

Lareau, A. (1989). *Home Advantage: Social Class and Parental Intervention in Elementary Education.* New York: Falmer Press.

Lareau, A. (1996). "Assessing parent-involvement in schooling." In A. Booth and J. F. Dunn (Eds.), *Family-School Links: How Do They Affect Educational Outcomes* (pp. 57–64). Mahwah, NJ: Erlbaum.

Linn, R. (2000). "Assessments and accountability." *Educational Researcher, 29,* 4.

Maeroff, G. (1989). "Withered hopes and stillborn dreams: The dismal panorama of inner-city schools." *Phi Delta Kappan, 69,* 632–638.

Massey, D., and N. Denton. (1993). *American Apartheid.* Cambridge, MA: Harvard University Press.

McWhorter, J. (2000). *Losing the Race.* New York: New Press.

Miller, S. L. (1995). *An American Imperative*. New Haven, CT: Yale University Press.

Noguera, P. (1996). "Confronting the urban in urban school reform." *Urban Review*, 28(1), 1–19.

Noguera, P., and A. Akom. (2000). "Disparities demystified." *Nation*, June 5.

Noguera, P., and M. Bliss. (2001). *A Four Year Evaluation Study of Youth Together*. Oakland, CA: Arts, Resources and Curriculum.

Office of Economic Development. (1994). *Creating a Community Vision: Community Goal Statements and Proposal Implementation Strategies*. Oakland, CA: City of Oakland.

Orfield, G., and Eaton, S. E. (1996). *Dismantling Desegregation: The Quiet Reversal of Brown v. Board of Education*. New York: The New Press.

Perry, T., and L. Delpitt. (1997). The real Ebonics debate. *Rethinking Schools*, 12(1).

Portes, A., and R. Rumbaut. (2001). *Legacies: The Story of the Immigrant Second Generation*. Berkeley: University of California Press.

Putnam, R. (1995). "Bowling alone: America's declining social capital." *Journal of Democracy*, 6(1), 65–78.

Rouce, C. (1999). *Rhetoric Versus Reality*. Washington, DC: Rand Corporation.

Saegert, S., P. Thompson, and M. Warren. (2001). *Social Capital in Low-Income Communities*. New York: Russell Sage Foundation.

Sampson, R. (1998). "What community supplies." In R. Ferguson and W. Dickens (Eds.), *Urban Problems and Community Development*. Washington, D.C.: Brookings Institute.

Steele, S. (1996). *The Content of Our Character*. New York: St. Martin's Press.

Stone, C. (2001). *Building Civic Capacity*. Lawrence: University of Kansas Press.

Thompson, C. (2001). "Class struggle." *East Bay Express, 23*(27).

Wacquant, L. (1998). "Negative social capital: State breakdown and social destitution in America's urban core." *Netherlands Journal of Housing and the Built Environment, 13*(1).

Wilgoren, J. (1997). "Young Blacks turn to school vouchers as civil rights issue." *New York Times,* April 27.

Woolcock, M. (1998). "Social capital and economic development: Toward a theoretical synthesis and policy framework." *Theory and Society, 27,* 151–208.

Chapter Twelve: Transforming Urban Schools Through Investments in Social Capital

Notes

1. Through an analysis of the social and economic transformations that have occurred in urban areas in the United States since World War II, Wilson (1998) demonstrates how such a devaluation of Black labor has occurred and resulted in the formation of an urban underclass.

2. Several commentators have debated whether a "crisis" actually exists in education. In part, this is because the term *crisis* implies that there were "good old days" when conditions were better. In a discussion of the "dropout" debate, Meier (1992) argues that the good old days really weren't so good. It could also be argued that conditions in schools are very uneven and that the public is largely satisfied with schools that serve middle- and upper-class students (Tyack and Cuban 1995), while those that serve the poor are doing an admirable job given the resources at their disposal.

3. In Richmond, California, the coach of the Richmond High School basketball team received considerable media attention and a visit from the newly elected governor because he forced the entire team to forfeit a regularly scheduled game due to poor academic performance of the players. (The team had been undefeated prior to the forfeit.)

4. Although the assailants in the Jonesboro shootings were young white males, the older boy was said to have been a member of the Cripps—a Los Angeles gang most commonly associated with African American youth. The fact that his parents were divorced was also cited as a factor contributing to his delinquency.

5. This finding is supported by a poll conducted in 1994 by Public Agenda on behalf of the American Federation of Teachers ("What Americans Expect from the Public Schools," *American Educator*, Winter 1994–1995) and in California by a poll conducted by Policy Analysis for California Education in March 1996.

6. Medi-Cal is a public health insurance program for low-income individuals and families.

7. Interview with the executive director, October 1996.

8. The viability of vouchers is further limited by the fact that the amount of the subsidy generally falls well below the cost of tuition at most elite private schools. Vouchers may cover the cost of working-class parochial schools, but even these schools have selective admissions criteria and limited space.

9. The dollar amount allocated under most voucher plans is insufficient to cover the cost of tuition at the more elite private schools. Even if the amount of the voucher is sufficient to cover the cost of working-class parochial schools, such schools typically have admissions requirements that are used to screen out less desirable students, as well as greater flexibility in removing students who are disruptive or difficult to serve.

10. Text taken from the Economic Opportunity Act, 1964, cited in Fantini et al. (1970, p. 10).

11. Moynihan, D. P. (1969). *Maximum Feasible Misunderstanding: Community Action in the War on Poverty*. New York: Free Press.

12. Reconstitution is a strategy that was made available to SFUSD as a result of the consent decree on school desegregation. The policy allows the district to reconstitute a school—remove all or part of the personnel from a school deemed low performing—as a way to

improve achievement for minority students. Since 1993, fourteen schools in SFUSD have been completely or partially reconstituted.

13. My consulting work with the SFUSD has focused on an evaluation of the impact of the new admissions policy at Lowell High School on students admitted under the plan.

14. Proposition 187 was approved by voters in 1996 and was intended to restrict undocumented aliens and their children from having access to public services. Proposition 209 was approved by voters in 1997 and eliminated the use of race and gender as factors that could be considered in admissions for higher education, employment, and contracting in publicly funded organizations. Proposition 227 was approved by voters in 1998 and banned the use of bilingual education in public schools.

15. I have attended parent education workshops, honor roll marches, and issue-oriented events sponsored by all three centers. Each event drew a significant number of parents from constituencies not typically involved in school activities.

References

Alsop, J. (1968). "Ghetto Education." *Teachers College Record*, 69(6), 517–528.

Anyon, J. (1996). *Ghetto Schooling: A Political Economy of Urban Educational Reform.* New York: Teachers College Press.

Apple, M. (1982). *Education and Power.* Boston: ARK Publications.

Barrett, P. (1999). *The Good Black.* New York: Dutton.

Berkeley Alliance. (1999). Comprehensive Report on Student Achievement. Unpublished manuscript.

Bourdieu, P. (1985). "Social Space and the Genesis of Social Groups." *Theory and Society*, 14(6).

Bourdieu, P. (1986). "The Forms of Capital." In J. Richardson and P. Bourdieu (eds.), *Handbook of Theory and Research for the Sociology of Education* (pp. 241–258). Westport, CT: Greenwood Press.

Bourdieu, P. (1988). *Outline of a Theory of Practice*. Cambridge: Cambridge University Press.

Bourdieu P., and L. Wacquant. (1992). *An Invitation to Reflexive Sociology*. Chicago: University of Chicago Press.

Bowles, S., and H. Gintis. (1976). *Schooling in Capitalist America*. New York: Basic Books.

Brookover, W., (1992) and E. Erickson. (1969). *Society, Schools and Learning*. East Lansing: Michigan State University Press.

Carnoy, M., and H. Levin. (1985). *Schooling and Work in a Democratic State*. Stanford, CA: Stanford University Press.

Chubb, J. E., and Moe, T. M. (1988, Dec.). "Politics, Markets, and the Organization of Schools." *The American Political Science Review, 82*(4), 1065–1087.

Cobb, C. W. (1992). *Responsive Schools, Renewed Communities*. San Francisco: Institute for Contemporary Studies Press.

Coleman, J. (1988). "Social Capital in the Creation of Human Capital." *American Journal of Sociology, 94*, S95–S120.

Coleman, J., E. Campbell, C. Hobson, J. McPartland, A. Mood, F. Weinfeld, and R. Yonk. (1966). *Equality of Educational Opportunity*. Washington, DC: U.S. Department of Health, Education and Welfare, Office of Education.

Comer, J. (1981). "New Haven's School-Community Connection." *Educational Leadership*, March, pp. 42–48.

Cose, E. (1993). *The Rage of a Privileged Class*. New York: HarperCollins.

Cose, E. (1995). *A Man's World: How Real Is Male Privilege—And How High Is Its Price?* New York: HarperCollins.

Cremin, L. (1988). *American Education*. New York: HarperCollins.

Delpitt, L. (1988). "The Silenced Dialogue: Power and Pedagogy in Educating Other People's Children." *Harvard Educational Review*, 58(3), 280–298.

Dillard, J. (1972). *Black English*. New York: Vintage Books.

Eckert, P. (1989). *Jocks and Burnouts*. New York: Teachers College Press.

Epstein, J. (1991). "School and Family Connections: Theory, Research, and Implications for Integrating Societies of Education and Family." In D. G. Unger and M. B. Sussman (eds.), *Families in Community Settings: Interdisciplinary Perspectives*. New York: Haworth Press.

Fantini, M., M. Gittell, and R. Magat. (1970). *Community Control and the Urban School*. New York: Praeger.

Ferguson, A. (1995). "Boys Will Be Boys: Defiant Acts and the Social Construction of Black Masculinity." Unpublished doctoral dissertation, University of California, Berkeley.

Fine, M. (1993). "(Ap)parent Involvement: Reflections on Parents, Power, and Urban Schools." *Teachers College Record*, 94(4).

Fine, M., L. Weis, L. Powell, and L. Mun Wong. (1997). *Off White: Readings in Race, Power, and Society*. New York: Routledge.

Fischer, C., M. Hout, M. S. Jankowski, S. Lucas, A. Swidler, and K. Voss. (1996). *Inequality by Design: Cracking the Bell Curve Myth*. Princeton, NJ: Princeton University Press.

Foster, M. (1997). "Ebonics and All That Jazz: Cutting Through the Politics of Linguistics, Education and Race." *Quarterly of the National Writing Project*, 19(1).

Frazier, E. F. (1957). *Black Bourgeoisie*. New York: Free Press.

Fordham, S. (1996). *Blacked Out: Dilemmas of Race, Identity, and Success at Capital High*. Chicago: The University of Chicago Press.

Fredrickson, G. (1981). *White Supremacy: A Comparative Study of American and South African History*. New York: Oxford University Press.

Fuller, F., and Elmore, R. (Eds.). (1996). *Who Chooses? Who Loses? Culture, Institutions and the Unequal Effects of School Choice*. New York: Teachers College Press.

Gargiulo, M., and Benassi, M. (Mar.–Apr., 2000). "Trapped in Your Own Net? Network Cohesion, Structural Holes, and the Adaptation of Social Capital." *Organization Science, 11*(2), 183–196.

Giroux, H. (1988). *Teachers as Intellectuals: Toward a Critical Pedagogy of Learning*. New York: Bergin and Garvey.

Greenberg, M., and D. Schneider. (1994). "Violence in American Cities: Young Black Males Is the Answer, But What Was the Question?" *Social Sciences and Medicine, 39*, 179–187.

Hacker, A. (1992). *Two Nations: Black and White: Separate, Hostile, Unequal*. New York: Ballantine Books.

Hall, S. (1992). "What Is This 'Black' in Black Popular Culture." In G. Dent (ed.), *Black Popular Culture*. Seattle, WA: Bay Press.

Harris, C. (1993). "Whiteness as Property." *Harvard Law Review, 106*, 1709–1791.

Haymes, S. (1995). "White Culture and the Politics of Racial Difference: Implications for Multiculturalism." In C. Sleeter and P. McLaren (eds.), *Multicultural Education, Critical Pedagogy, and the Politics of Difference* (pp. 105–128). Albany: SUNY Press.

Ignatiev, N. (1995). *How the Irish Became White*. New York: Routledge.

Katznelson, I., and M. Weir. (1985). *Schooling for All*. Berkeley: University of California Press.

Kirp, D. (1982). *Just Schools*. Berkeley: University of California Press.

Kochman, T. (1969). "Rapping in the Black Ghetto." *Trans-Action, 6*, 26–34.

Kochman, T. (1973). *Rapping and Stylin' Out: Communication in Urban Black America*. Urbana: University of Illinois Press.

Kozol, J. (1991). *Savage Inequalities*. New York: Crown Books.

Ladson-Billings, B. (1992). "Reading Between the Lines and Beyond the Pages: A Culturally Relevant Approach to Literacy Teaching." *Theory into Practice*, *31*(4), 312–320.

Lareau, A. (1990). "Social Class Differences in Family-School Relationships: The Importance of Cultural Capital." *Sociology of Education*, 60, 73–85.

MacLeod, J. (1987). *Ain't No Makin' It*. Boulder, CO: Westview.

Maeroff, G. (1988). "Withered Hopes, Stillborn Dreams: The Dismal Panorama of Urban Schools." *Phi Delta Kappan*, 69, 632–638.

Massey, D., and N. Denton. (1993). *American Apartheid: Segregation and the Making of the Underclass*. Cambridge, MA: Harvard University Press.

Meier, D. (1992, Sept. 21). "Myths, Lies and Public Schools." *The Nation*, 255, 271.

National Research Council. (1989). *A Common Destiny: Blacks and American Society*. Washington, DC: National Academy Press.

Nocera, J. (1990). "How the Middle Class Helped Ruin the Public Schools." *Utne Reader*, September–October.

Noguera, P. (1995). "Ties That Bind, Forces That Divide: Berkeley High School and the Challenge of Integration." *University of San Francisco Law Review*, 29(3).

Noguera, P. (1996). "Confronting the Urban in Urban School Reform." *Urban Review*, 28(1).

Ogbu, J. (1978). *Minority Education and Caste: The American System in Cross-Cultural Perspective*. Orlando, FL: Academic Press.

Ogbu, J. (1987). "Variability in Minority Student Performance: A Problem in Search of an Explanation." *Anthropology and Education Quarterly*, 18, 312–334.

Olsen, L. (1997). *Made in America: Immigrant Students in Our Public Schools*. New York: New Press.

Omi, M., and H. Winant. (1986). *Racial Formation in the United States*. New York: Routledge.

Orfield, G., and S. Eaton. (1996). *Dismantling Desegregation*. New York: New Press.

Payne, C. (1986). *Getting What We Ask For*. Westport, CN: Greenwood Press.

Perlstein, M. (1992, Nov. 6). "Guns Are Protection, Teens Explain." [New Orleans] *Times-Picayune*, p. A1.

Pinkney, A. (1984). *The Myth of Black Progress*. Cambridge: Cambridge University Press.

Putnam, R. (1995). "Making Democracy Work: Bowling Alone: America's Declining Social Capital." *Journal of Democracy*, 6(1), 65–78.

Rist, R. (1973). *The Urban School: A Factory for Failure*. Cambridge, MA: MIT Press.

Roediger, D. (1991). *The Wages of Whiteness*. New York: Verso Press.

Schrag, P. (1967). *Village School Downtown*. Boston: Beacon Press.

Skolnick, J. K., and Currie, E. (1994). *Crisis in American Institutions* (9th ed.). New York: HarperCollins.

Solomon, R. P. (1992). *Black Resistance in High School: Forging a Separatist Culture*. Albany: State University of New York.

Spindler, G., and Spindler, L. (Eds.) (1987). *Interpretive Ethnography of Education: At Home and Abroad* (pp. 333–359). Hillsdale, NJ: Lawrence Erlbaum.

Steele, C. (1997). "A Threat in the Air: How Stereotypes Shape Intellectual Identity and Performance." *American Psychologist*, June.

Tierny, W. (1996). "Affirmative Action in California: Looking Back, Looking Forward in Public Academe." *Journal of Negro Education*, 65(2).

Tyack, D. (1980). *The One Best System*. Cambridge, MA: Harvard University Press.

Tyack, D., and L. Cuban (1995). *Tinkering Toward Utopia*. Cambridge, MA: Harvard University Press.

Valencia, R. (1991). *Chicano School Failure and Success*. London: Falmer Press.

Wacquant, L. (1998). "Negative Social Capital: State Breakdown and Social Destitution in America's Urban Core." *Netherlands Journal of Housing and the Built Environment, 13*(1).

Wells, A. S., and Crain, R. L. (1992). "Do Parents Choose School Quality or School Status?" In P. W. Cookson (ed.), *The Choice Controversy* (pp. 65–82). Thousand Oaks, CA: Corwin Press .

Wilson, W. J. (1981). "The Black Community in the 1980s: Questions of Race, Class, and Public Policy." *The ANNALS of the American Academy of Political and Social Science, 454*(1), 26–41.

Wilson, W. (1996). *When Work Disappears*. New York: Knopf.

Wolters, R. (1984). *The Burden of Brown: Thirty Years of School Desegregation*. Knoxville: University of Tennessee Press.

Woodson, C. G. (1933). *The Mis-Education of the Negro*. Washington, DC: Associated Publishers.

Woolcock, M. (1998). "Social Capital and Economic Development: Toward a Theoretical Synthesis and Policy Framework." *Theory and Society, 27*, 151–208.

Epilogue
Joaquin's Dilemma Revisited

My son Joaquin has never quite forgiven me for using his experience to make a point about racial identity and the academic performance of middle-class children of color. For one thing, I didn't ask his permission. I wrote about his experience in school because it served as a useful anecdote for addressing a larger array of similar cases, and it allowed me to make it clear that as a parent, I too had struggled with finding ways to support my own son, despite how much I understand about young people, education, and the school system. He pointed out to me that when he searches for his name on the Web, the article is the first thing to come up, and on more than one occasion, strangers have approached him to ask if he is the Joaquin I wrote about. Joaquin likes to point out that perhaps even more important than my invasion of his privacy, what bothered him the most about the essay was that I didn't get the whole story right. He likes to remind me that part of the reason that he struggled in school was the unfair expectations his teachers placed on him because he is my son. As the former president of the Berkeley School Board and a professor at the University of California, Berkeley, I was well known by most of his teachers, and many of them unfairly assumed that because he was my son, he would excel academically. When he struggled in certain classes, he felt he didn't receive the support he needed because his teachers assumed that like other middle-class parents, I would hire a private tutor to support him. What his teachers did not understand was that although I was clearly middle class, I hadn't been raised that way. I was raised by working-class, immigrant parents who didn't help me with my academic work because of their limited education and because they believed hard work was the remedy for any challenge. My own upbringing prevented me from intervening to support Joaquin effectively because I thought that he would find a way to overcome the challenges he faced on his own as I had.

Fortunately, things turned out fine for Joaquin. Not only did he go on to excel in college, but today he is a middle school social studies teacher. His experience as a student who struggled academically has proven to be a tremendous asset to him as he reaches out to his own students who don't grasp new ideas and skills quickly. Moreover, because he spent time hanging out with young people who were drawn to street life and all the perils that accompany life in the inner city, he has no trouble relating to his students who come from poor New York City neighborhoods and have a greater affinity for the streets than the classroom.

Sadly, too few teachers in urban schools have backgrounds like Joaquin's. Too many of our nation's teachers come from privileged backgrounds, and many of them experience difficulty in crossing boundaries related to race, class, and culture. Although such differences need not be insurmountable obstacles to effective teaching, in too many cases they are. Too often middle-class White teachers have difficulty relating to students of color. In many cases, lack of rapport limits their ability to teach effectively and contributes to their inability to maintain order in the classroom. It also limits their ability to create a positive learning environment in which students believe that their teachers are invested in their success.

Hence, the real lesson of Joaquin's dilemma is not merely what it reveals about racial identity and achievement, but what it suggests about why so many students with tremendous intellectual potential end up falling through the cracks of the educational system. Fortunately, Joaquin had parents who supported him through the travails of adolescence and made sure that he got through a difficult phase without becoming too estranged or hurting himself. Far too many students lack such systems of support at home. To prevent a greater number from becoming casualties of impersonal schools, we need more teachers like Joaquin.

Index